Analyzing Marx

Morality, Power and History

RICHARD W. MILLER

Princeton University Press

D0208484

ANALYZING MARX

To Peggy

Contents

HISTORY

A Note on References

THE WORKS by Marx to which I most frequently refer will be cited in the following editions:

Marx, *Economic and Philosophical Manuscripts* (1844), in T. B. Bottomore, ed., *Early Writings* (New York, 1964).

Marx and Engels, *The German Ideology* (1846), ed. C. J. Arthur (New York, 1980).

Marx and Engels, *Manifesto of the Communist Party* (1848), in Marx and Engels, *The Marx-Engels Reader*, ed. Robert C. Tucker, 1st ed. (New York, 1972).

Marx, *Wage-Labor and Capital* (1849), in *Marx-Engels Reader*.

Marx, *The Eighteenth Brumaire of Louis Bonaparte* (1852), in *Marx-Engels Reader*.

Marx, *Grundrisse* (1857–58), trans. M. Nicolaus (New York, 1973).

Marx, Preface to *A Contribution to the Critique of Political Economy* (1859), in Marx and Engels, *Selected Works in Three Volumes* (Moscow, 1973), vol. I.

Marx, *Wages, Price and Profit* (1865), in *Selected Works*, vol. II.

Marx, *Capital* (1867, etc.), (Moscow, n.d.)

Marx, *The Civil War in France* (1871), in *Marx-Engels Reader*.

Marx, *Critique of the Gotha Program* (1875), in *Marx-Engels Reader*.

Marx and Engels, *Selected Correspondence* (Moscow, n.d.)

ACKNOWLEDGMENTS

Some of my work on this book was done during a sabbatical year which was partly supported by a Rockefeller Foundation Humanities Fellowship. Parts of Chapters One, Two and Five appear in the following essays of mine, and are used here with permission of the publishers:

"Marx and Morality" in *Marxism: Nomos* XXVI, ed. J. Roland Pennock and John W. Chapman. Copyright 1983 by New York University.

"Productive Forces and the Forces of Change" in the *Philosophical Review*, 90 (1981).

"Producing Change" in Terence Ball and James Farr, ed., *After Marx*, Cambridge University Press.

ANALYZING MARX

Introduction

THIS BOOK has two goals. One is to show that Marx should be a central figure in non-Marxist philosophy. He serves important needs that all philosophers share. The other is to develop a more political interpretation of Marx, in which power-relations, rather then technology, and struggles for power, pursued outside of the workplace, typically play a primary role. Readers now have to choose between economic determinist approaches that underrate political structures and conflicts, and eclectic interpretations that ignore Marx's obvious, pervasive and distinctive emphasis on economic processes. I will be developing a third kind of alternative.

These goals are closely related. Despite the grand metaphysical sound of some economic determinist statements, the more political version of Marx makes him more philosophically useful. On the other hand, the style and skills of contemporary philosophy, which have created clearer and more flexible readings of philosophers from Plato to Kant, are just what is needed to develop interpretations of Marx that are neither narrowly economic nor piecemeal. The interdependence and urgency of these goals will, I hope become clearer as I discuss them more, in turn.

USES FOR MARX, USES FOR PHILOSOPHY

If the arguments of this book are right, Marx should play a central role in any style of philosophy. However, my case for Marx is most explicitly addressed to one way of doing philosophy, "analytic philosophy," as it is called by its practitioners and, even more commonly, by its enemies. This is the dominant way of doing philosophy in English-speaking countries. It is also the hardest case for the view that Marx should be central to philosophy, since it is the most important approach in which Marx is treated as a marginal figure.

This philosophical subculture (in which I largely function) is held together not by common doctrines but by common standards of successful practice. Above all, there is a heavy emphasis on clear statements of what one wants people to believe and clear arguments as to why they should believe it, based on premises that would be plausible to many, if not all. Historically, substantive philosophical assumptions, first derived from British empiricism and reinforced by logical positivism, have played an important role when philosophy is done in this style. But now those assumptions are often questioned, in the analytic way. This book is meant to contribute to that questioning, by showing that Marx is best read and best used when the style of analytic philosophy is divorced from positivist substance.

When analytic philosophers look at the history of philosophy, they discern certain classical figures, usually the same as everyone else's. Hume on virtually every topic and Mill in ethics are two uncontroversial examples. To be a classic, here, is not to be recognized as having been right, or even as having been most correct among the alternatives that were available. Rather, the classics represent standard options that a philosopher should consult, supporting, amending, interpreting or attacking them, as he or she does philosophy. It is in this sense that Marx should be a classic for modern philosophy, including analytic philosophy.

To the contrary, in English-speaking countries, the relation between Marx and philosophy has been almost wholly antagonistic, at least until very recently. Almost all analytic philosophers, if they did not ignore Marx's writings, tried to show that Marx fell so far short of proper standards of clarity, plausibility, scientific justification or explanatory adequacy that it would be a waste of time to investigate his theories empirically or to derive their philosophical implications. "Metaphysics" was one of the nicer charges.

This antagonism should be replaced by cooperation, of at least three important kinds. First, some of Marx's ideas shed light on leading problems of philosophy, issues that are important not just for Marxists (or anti-Marxists), but for everyone. For example, in the first two chapters I shall try to show that Marx's criticism and replacement of justice, equality and the moral point of view, as bases for judging social arrangements, ought to be a standard position in ethics. His arguments are as central as the question, "How should institutions be judged?" In Chapter Seven, I will use Marx's theory of history as a model of the kind of legitimate theory that positivist philosophy of science excludes, and base a sketch of post-positivist but nonrelativist philosophy of science on the logical structure of this theory.

In the second place, philosophers can use Marx's writings to make a positive contribution to the social sciences. Social and political philosophers and philosophers of science are now separated from social scientists by frustrating departmental divides. Lacking appropriate training, information or professional rewards, philosophers today, quite unlike their most eminent predecessors, find it hard to contribute to actual debates over the nature of social reality. Yet many social scientists suspect that distinctive possibilities of analysis and explanation are being missed as a result of the easy assumptions and the confusions that philosophical reflection should challenge. As the most powerful explanatory framework outside the mainstream, Marx's social theories often yield such alternatives, if reconstructed with the clarity and conceptual resourcefulness of contemporary analytic philosophy. In Chapters Three and Four, I use Marx's writings in this spirit, to show that assessments of political power are incomplete, unless Marx's distinctive concept of power is used as one yardstick. Similar analyses of Marx's ideas might have a liberating effect elsewhere—for example, in breaking the deadlock between "formalism" and "substantivism" in economic anthropology, or in determining the scope and limits of economic theory, in a world where equilibrium arguments are increasingly vacuous and the impact of international politics on economic processes is increasingly pervasive.

Finally, the tradition of detailed, abstract and imaginative analysis in English-speaking philosophy has an enormous contribution to make to Marxist social theory. Interpreters of Marx are confronted by two very different kinds of passages: general formulations that are highly condensed, fragmentary or metaphorical, often all three, and discussions of particular phenomena that are richly detailed, often quite plausible and utterly contrary to natural readings of the general formulations. There are two corresponding temptations, and most interpreters succumb to one or the other. One can derive the underlying theories from the general statements, taken in isolation. Or, appreciating the diversity and plausibility of many of the specific discussions, one can dilute Marx into mere common sense. These temptations are especially powerful in the three areas I will examine, morality, political theory and history. Either Marx has one grand general argument to offer against morality, say, that moral ideas are shaped by social interests and hence are ideological. Or he was simply claiming that contemporary moralities placed too great an emphasis on property rights or social harmony. Either he regards politics as a passive reflection of economic necessities. Or he merely warns us to be sensitive to the influence of economic interest groups on political decision making. Either he takes the desire to produce more efficiently as the driving force of history. Or he regards the economic factor as an important and often underrated aspect of large-scale change. The neglect of Marx has partly resulted from a situation in which such choices dominate sympathetic Marx interpretation. Most people, reflecting on the realities of social change, find the grand statements implausible, the modest ones truistic.

The frustrating state of Marx's texts is understandable in light of his enterprise. In part, it reflects the diverse political interests that often moved him to write. In part, it reflects the nature of social reality, since statements about general kinds of social processes must be vague to be true and must be applied

6

to particular events with unpredictable provisos, specifications and hedges. Still, we can learn much more from Marx if we do not accept this obscurity or elevate it to the status of a special logic. We can extract plausible but distinctive theories from these texts. Analytic philosophy offers a promising style of interpretation, here, since it demands clarity, tolerates abstraction and complexity, and responds to the impact of contexts on what people mean. I hope to show that the most accurate and interesting interpretations of Marx's account of morality (and his replacement for the moral point of view in politics), his theory of the state and his theory of history can be constructed in this style.

There is an irony here. Positivist conceptions of explanatory adequacy and of confirmation that dominated analytic philosophy until very recently had a major distorting influence on Marx interpretation. As I shall argue in Chapter Seven, sympathetic interpreters were led to make Marx's social theories a form of technological determinism because they supposed that no other reading could give his theories explanatory power and make them subject to experimental test. It is poetic justice if post-positivist analytic philosophy clarifies what positivism obscured.

The Marx who emerges from these interpretations will have controversial views, to put it mildly. But the philosophical uses for Marx that I will describe, the first two kinds of "cooperation," do *not* depend on his more controversial factual claims. Surprisingly, Marx's arguments for the inappropriateness of the moral point of view in politics depend on assessments of social conflict and historical diversity that many, perhaps most, non-Marxists share. His theory of the state provides a distinctive tool for measuring the distribution of political power, useful even for those who do not come up with Marx's own measurements. The antagonism between philosophy and Marx has not just obscured the implications of the facts as Marxists see them. It has made most non-Marxists less aware of the bearing on philosophy and social methodology of their own views of the world.

INTRODUCTION

Two Versions of Marx

The second broad goal of this book is to replace one conception of Marx with another. According to a common conception, probably the dominant academic one in the United States, Marx, in his later years, was, in a special but important sense, anti-political. He took people's pursuit of individual economic self-interest to be what changes and shapes society. It is as if Adam Smith's "invisible hand" was at work, but sometimes at work to produce large-scale change, rather than equilibrium. By contrast, politics, that is, the quest for power outside the productive unit, is given a subordinate role. In some versions of this outlook, the economic conditions that make change possible make an organized violent attack on the old economic structure superfluous.[1] In others, people's deliberations over whether to subordinate individual self-interest to large-scale loyalties are supposed to have no systematic effect.[2] In others, power-relations are said to adapt to the demands of efficient material production.[3]

The idea that Marx in his later writings is an economic determinist is true in important respects. It is also basically false. Marx does have the following view of history, which might be called "economic determinist", though very misleadingly. The most important features of a society are ultimately determined by its mode of production, that is, the relations of control, the

---

[1] For example, Shlomo Avineri claims, "For Marx the wielding of power as a distinct political means admits that circumstances (and consciousness is one of their components) are yet unripe for change. . . . One can summarize Marx's position by saying that for Marx physical power will either fail or prove to be superfluous" (*The Social and Political Thought of Karl Marx*, [Cambridge, 1970] p. 218.) In Chapter Three, I will discuss Avineri's views in detail, together with the similar interpretations of George Lichtheim and Stanley Moore. Allen Wood is often inclined toward this view in "The Marxian Critique of Justice," *Philosophy and Public Affairs* 1 (1972) and in *Karl Marx* (London, 1981), an inclination that will turn out to be crucial to his interpretation of Marx on morality.

[2] See, for example, Allen Buchanan, "Revolutionary Motivation and Morality," *Philosophy and Public Affairs* 9 (1979).

[3] Most prominently argued in recent years, in Gerald Cohen, *Karl Marx's Theory of History: A Defense* (Princeton, 1980). See also William Shaw, *Marx's Theory of History* (Stanford, 1978) and John McMurtry, *The Structure of Marx's World-View* (Princeton, 1978).

8

modes of cooperation and the technology that govern material production. More specifically, while a society is stable, the system of political and ideological institutions and the climate of respectable ideas are such as to serve the function of maintaining the dominance of the economically dominant social group, the group who mainly extract the surplus from those directly engaged in material production. If radical change comes about through processes internal to a society, it is due to self-destructive tendencies of the mode of production. Because of the nature of the mode of production, processes that initially maintained the old relations of control eventually give a nondominant group the ability and the motivation to destroy the old system of relations and dominate a new one. In the ensuing struggles, the crucial alliances are determined by people's class situations, their locations in that network of relations of control.

Since the mode of material production is primary, this outlook might be called "economic determinist". But if the economic is contrasted with the political, the label is utterly misleading. The mode of production is partly defined by relations of control over aspects of production, including land, labor-power and people. A specific relation of control may, in turn, be partially defined with reference to distinctive means and consequences of control. The self-destructive processes may include tendencies toward conflict internal to this system of power-relations, for example, the tendency of feudal relations of production to give rise to civil war among the overlords. Surely, systems of control and the conflicts to which they give rise are, in a broad sense, political as well as economic. The "subordination" of the political is simply this: the main features of separate political institutions are explained as due to the need of the economically dominant group to maintain their dominance; alliances in revolutionary periods are primarily explained on the basis of class situations.

I will be arguing that Marx is not an economic determinist *in any other respect*. He does not believe that the pursuit of immediate economic self-interest spontaneously produces radical social changes, that political organization with large-scale

9

social goals is unimportant, that economic developments make political revolution superfluous, that deliberations over one's larger loyalties are unimportant in the typical case, or that the pursuit of more efficient production is the basic mechanism for change. I will discuss the last, technological determinist interpretation in detail, in Chapter Five. On the whole, I will criticize economic determinist interpretations as they become obstacles to an appreciation of Marx's insights in moral philosophy and political theory.

The subjects of the three sections of this book are, as such, relatively independent: Marx's criticism of the moral point of view as a basis for social choice and his replacement for it; his concept of the ruling class and the usefulness of that concept in clarifying the nature of political power; the content and the scientific status of his general theory of social change. But because an overemphasis of his economic determinism has been pervasive, one section will often reinforce another, sometimes depend on another. The criticisms of morality as a basis for social choice in Chapter One will depend on a relatively high estimate of the depth and acuteness of conflicting needs. The attribution of this assessment to Marx will be strengthened in Chapter Three, where his hypothesis that there is a ruling class is so interpreted that it entails that assessment. Similarly, I will argue in Chapter Two that the nature of Marx's criticism of morality cannot be appreciated if Marx is supposed to have subordinated conscious political deliberations to the pursuit of immediate economic interests; and the latter assumption loses its force if Marx did not regard the pursuit of material efficiency as the engine of change, the anti-technological view I defend in Chapter Five. The notion of a ruling class that I extract from Marx in Chapter Two will be the basis for my later interpretation of his general theory of history. While I sketch the methods by which ruling-class hypotheses might be tested in the middle section of the book, the larger methodological issues will be considered in most detail in the last chapter. For it is above all in the interpretation of the materialist conception of history that prejudices about the nature of scientific testing have distorted the understanding of both sympathetic and unsympathetic readers. In short, though the three sections are intelligible when read apart from one another, it is as a whole, not just as a sum, that they make the strongest case for setting strict limits on economic determinism in the reading of Marx. The more political Marx is more accurate as exegesis, more useful as social science, and more illuminating as a resource for philosophy.

Outside of ethics, political theory, history, and the philosophy of science, this alternative perspective on Marx suggests other interpretations and uses of his writings, which I will not be developing systematically. For example, Marx's economics is, I think, less economic determinist than usually supposed. Sympathetic readers often take *Capital* to be an argument for the primacy of spontaneous economic processes over broadly political processes of large-scale, long-range and deliberate collective action. But the theory of surplus-value would be simply a grand bookkeeping device if it were not an argument that the dynamics of capitalism are shaped by class struggle, often collective and organized, together with technological change. And as between these causal processes, the first has a certain primacy, since increased needs for labor discipline have a dramatic impact on the relevant trends in technology.[4] Thus, Marx is not digressing in the hundreds of pages of *Capital*, volume one, where he discusses the reciprocal impact of power struggles and market mechanisms: the history of the struggle over the working day, the descriptions of uses of mechanization to increase labor discipline, the account of the rise of capitalism in Britain, and the discussions of the forms and economic meanings of colonialism. In general, if the perspective of this book is extended elsewhere, Marx's writings become more of a piece. The alternative is either Marx the eclectic or Marx the economic theorist who is constantly distracted by the temptations of journalism, political history or philosophy.

I hope that this book will be ready by people working in philosophy, in the social sciences, and in the interpretation of

[4] See *Capital* (Moscow, n.d.), vol. I, chap. 15, secs. 3–5.

Marx's writings, and by those concerned with the sources and significance of social conflict and social change. This audience may include everyone. I hope that readers will be tolerant of one consequence, occasional quick summaries of positions and controversies quite familiar to those in the relevant field.

Morality

CHAPTER ONE

Against Morality

IN A VERY broad sense, Marx is a moralist, and sometimes a stern one: he offers a rationale for conduct that sometimes requires self-sacrifice in the interests of others. That the conduct he calls for will sometimes involve "self-sacrificing heroism" is epitomized in his praise of the "heaven storming" men and women who defended the Paris Commune.[1] His concern that conduct be reasonable and well-informed is clear when he distinguishes the scientific basis for present-day workers' struggles from the "fantastic," even "reactionary" misconceptions supporting workers' struggles in the past.[2]

At the same time, Marx often explicitly attacks morality and fundamental moral notions. He accepts the charge that "Communism . . . abolishes . . . all morality, instead of constituting [it] on a new basis."[3] The materialist theory of ideology is supposed to have "shattered the basis of all morality, whether the morality of asceticism or of enjoyment."[4] Talk of "equal right" and "fair distribution" is, he says, "a crime," forcing "on our Party . . . obsolete verbal rubbish . . . ideological nonsense about right and other trash so common among the democrats and French Socialists."[5]

Evidently, the very broad usage in which Marx might be called a moralist is artificially broad and misleading in his own view. In the abstract, this is no paradox. Though philosophers commonly ignore it, there is a vast territory in between narrow self-interest and what would naturally be called morality. For example, Max Weber sometimes asserts his commitment to

---

[1] *The Civil War in France*, in Robert C. Tucker, ed., *The Marx-Engels Reader*, 1st ed., (New York, 1972), p. 568; Marx to Kugelmann, April 12, 1871, Marx and Engels, *Selected Correspondence* (Moscow, n.d.), p. 247.

[2] *Communist Manifesto*, in Tucker, *The Marx-Engels Reader*, pp. 359f.

[3] Ibid., p. 351.

[4] *The German Ideology*, ed. C. J. Arthur (New York, 1980), p. 115.

[5] *Critique of the Gotha Program*, in Tucker, *The Marx-Engels Reader*, p. 388.

world power for his nation, a commitment requiring self-sacrifice and supported in part by rational reflection on courses of action and their consequences. He accepts that his nationalism does not give equal weight to the interests of everyone, for example, to his own, to French nationalists' and to the interests of those Germans who would prefer the situation of "a 'little' people" to that of "a people organized into a Great Power."[6] When he speaks of his nationalist commitment as political, not moral, and capable of overriding moral commitments in his hierarchy of concerns, we understand him, even if we are repelled. Similarly, Nietzsche's outlook is amoral but not at all self-centered, since the elite are committed to the hard-fought defense of their common excellence. In everyday life, loyalty to family or friends that exceeds moral requirements is also located in between self-centeredness and morality.

It is not clear, however, in just what ways Marx's outlook differs from morality. Nor is it clear for just what reasons people are to make his move away from morality. In pursuing these questions, I will try to be fair to the texts. But my main interest is to present plausible arguments for a radical departure from the moral point of view, at least as philosophers have conceived it. When its foundations are brought to light, Marx's rejection of morality as the basis for social and political choice turns out to be complex, well-argued, and humane, though, in an important sense, anti-humanitarian. Moreover, it is based on aspects of Marx's social theory that many non-Marxists would accept. Whether or not his views are ultimately valid, they should have a status that they lack at present: a standard alternative that must be addressed in thoughtful discussions of morality.

The Distinctness of Morality

As a basis for resolving political questions, that is, for choosing among social arrangements and strategies for attaining

---

[6] Max Weber, "Zwischen Zwei Gesetze," in *Politische Schriften*, ed. J. Winckelmann (Tuebingen, 1971), p. 143.

them, morality, in the narrower sense, is distinct from self-interest, class interest, national interest or purely aesthetic concerns. The bases for political decision that we most comfortably classify as moral tend to display three features:

1. *Equality*. People are to be shown equal concern or respect or afforded equal status. In the manner appropriate to choices of institutions and political strategies, everyone is to be treated as an equal. Of course, there are big disagreements as to what the appropriate form of equality is. But some standard of equality is to be the ultimate basis for resolving conflicts among different people's interests.

2. *General norms*. The right resolution of any major political issue would result from applying valid general norms to the specific facts of the case at hand. These rules are valid in all societies in which there is a point to resolving political disputes by moral appeal, roughly, all societies in which cooperation benefits almost everyone but scarcity is liable to give rise to conflicts (Hume's and Rawls' "circumstances of justice").

3. *Universality*. Anyone who rationally reflects on relevant facts and arguments will accept these rules, if he or she has the normal range of emotions.

In portraying Marx as a critic of the moral point of view in politics, I mean that he argues against all three principles as inappropriate to choosing what basic institutions to pursue. As I have mentioned, there is still a broad sense in which he does describe a moral point of view. He makes arguments for strategies that might require self-sacrifice. Distinctions between decency and indecency, what ought to be done and what ought not have a role in his outlook. His arguments, primarily directed at choices among political and economic systems, may leave standing most ordinary morality concerning actions toward individuals. But it is also natural to adopt the narrower usage, and to see Marx as advancing a non-morality. The three principles, after all, capture the important ways in which a basis for choice might be seen as neutral and as displaying a concern for all. The first requires neutrality among different people's interests. The second requires impartial reference to

17

the social circumstances of all historical societies concerned with morality. The third requires arguments which impartially appeal to everyone's rational capacities. It is the neutrality of the moral point of view that we emphasize in distinguishing obviously moral outlooks from obviously non-moral ones.

Admittedly, some philosophers whom we take to offer a morality reject some of the three principles, at least on a rigid interpretation of them. Aristotle, for example, has no ultimate premise of equality (or so I have argued elsewhere).[7] Dewey, and Rawls in his recent writings, defend their outlooks on political morality as appropriate to the discourse of a quite particular kind of society. But when we encounter someone who rejects all three principles, Weber, for example, in his discussions of international relations, most of us naturally take him or her to have departed from the moral point of view.

Despite these considerations, some people might be disinclined to follow Marx in associating the moral point of view as such with commitment to at least some of the three premises. After all, the premises are highly abstract, while "morality" is an everyday term, not a product of philosophical reflection. Beyond a point, the disagreement is purely verbal. What is important is that Marx attacks pervasive philosophical assumptions about morality, that his attack separates him much further from typical moral philosophers than they are separated one from another, and that his consequent outlook on basic social choices is unexpectedly close to outlooks that we would all be inclined to call non-moral. Granted, the content of this outlook, as I shall interpret it, would lead most people to regard it as decent and humane in its values. In this way, it differs from Nietzsche's or Weber's. That is, in itself, an interesting result. If Marx is right, motivations that initially attract us to the three premises should lead most of us to reject them when we reflect on their consequences for political decision.

[7] Richard W. Miller, "Marx and Aristotle: A Kind of Consequentialism," in K. Nielsen, ed., *Marx and Morality, Canadian Journal of Philosophy*, Supp. vol. 7 (1981).

EQUALITY

Most of the anti-moral arguments suggested by Marx's writings attack the first premise, the premise of equality. Before developing them, however, I need to sketch the grains of truth that Marx discerns in the demand for equality. Otherwise, my interpretation will seem perverse.

Marx advocates social arrangements that would, in his view, make people much more equal in power and enjoyment than they are at present. Initially, at least, these arrangements would embody standards that Marx explicitly characterizes as standards of equal right, for example, "To each according to his or her labor."[8] Marx's case for these arrangements and standards is that they would enhance people's lives, not that they would conform to some ultimate standard of equality. Yet, among the dimensions of life that Marx emphasizes, two are especially connected with equality. Under socialism and communism, most people are less dominated, more in possession of their lives, since they are better able to develop their capacities in light of their own assessments of their needs. Moreover, people's interactions will be governed to a greater extent than now by mutual well-wishing and concern. In Marx's view, these goods of freedom and reciprocity are what most people have really desired, when they have made "Equality" their battle cry. In sum, an ultimate standard of equality, though a mistake for most people, is a mistake that often leads people in the right direction. It is often a one-sided or confused expression of rational desires really satisfied by communist society.[9]

Ultimate demands for equality are of four kinds: distributive ones, requiring that all possess an equal bundle of goods, resources or opportunities; rights-based ones, requiring con-

---

[8] *Critique of the Gotha Program*, pp. 386–88.

[9] See Engels to Bebel, March 18–28, 1875, *Selected Correspondence*, p. 276; and Engels, *Anti-Duehring*, ed. R. Palme-Dutt (New York, 1966), p. 118. I give a more detailed account of the role of equality and fairness as means that often produce important goods for Marx in "Marx and Aristotle: A Kind of Consequentialism," and in "Rights or Consequences," *Midwest Studies in Philosophy* 7 (1982): *Social and Political Philosophy*.

formity to certain rights possessed equally by all; attitudinal ones, requiring that equal concern or respect be shown to all; and standards of impartiality, requiring that the general welfare be promoted, without bias toward the good of some. All of these prove inadequate as ultimate bases for decision in the face of inescapable conflicts in class-divided societies. In certain cases, institutions should treat people equally in certain specific ways. But they should not do so to satisfy a standard of equality. Rather, a good form of equality is a good tool for producing certain effects, assessed without applying such a standard.

EQUAL DISTRIBUTION

Distributive ideals are especially important to Marx because of their influence on the workers' movement through proposals of Proudhon's and Bakunin's. He argues that a distributive standard is inappropriate for basic social choices if it is a general demand for equal goods and powers, while it is utopian if it takes the form of Proudhon's and Bakunin's more specific criteria of equality.

The general demand that all have an equal bundle of goods, resources and opportunities is inappropriate as the main standard for judging social arrangements, because people's main concern is with social relations and well-being, not with equal distribution as such. Equality could, in principle, be achieved by dragging everyone down to a common, low level. Marx labels the outlook that would then be satisfied "crude communism." He points out that it would corrupt interactions, because it is motivated by envy. Moreover, it is self-destructive because unconcerned with the growth of people's satisfactions and powers.[10]

A parallel argument is suggested by Marx's emphasis on exploitation, as against unequal distribution. Exploitation produces inequalities no greater than those in many nonexploitive situations, such as the inequalities produced by the differing fertility of independent family homesteads. Yet the existence

[10] See *Economic and Philosophical Manuscripts*, in T. B. Bottomore, ed. *Early Writings* (New York, 1964), pp. 152–55, and *Communist Manifesto*, p. 359.

of exploitation provides a much more urgent rationale for change. In sum, the most basic social choices should be guided by mutual concern and respect, the pursuit of material and cultural well-being, and the avoidance of exploitation, not by distributive equality as such.

While these criticisms are relevant to utterly general demands for distributive equality, they may not do justice to the demand for equal distribution that Proudhon and Bakunin had in mind. Equality for them probably meant sufficient equality of resources and opportunities to guarantee full and equal independence for all. This full and equal independence is distinguished both from the economic subordination of those who must work for others in order to live and from the political subordination of those subject to state interference. This ideal of equal independence leads Proudhon and Bakunin to pursue a politically decentralized society of independent producers, sufficiently equal in resources that no one economically dominates others. In Marx's view, this ideal is utopian. Sufficient equality of productive resources is ephemeral, at best, in a modern setting of physically interdependent production. The network of production, if carried out by independent units, must be regulated by market mechanisms. Even if the distribution of productive resources is initially equal, luck, if nothing else, will soon create some inequalities. Market mechanisms will magnify the first inequalities, as the rich get richer through economies of scale, thicker cushions against calamity, greater access to credit, and greater capacity to innovate. The eventual result is financial ruin and dispossession for the many and their subordination to the few who come to control the means of production. "[E]xchange value . . . is in fact the system of equality and freedom, and . . . the disturbances which they encounter in the further development of the system are disturbances inherent in it, are merely the realization of equality and freedom, which prove to be inequality and unfreedom."[11]

[11] *Grundrisse*, trans. M. Nicolaus (New York, 1973), pp. 248f.

EQUAL RIGHTS

These problems with distributive equality make rights-based standards all the more attractive. For a society may respect rights when goods are partitioned in a variety of changing patterns. But rights-based equality encounters its own distinctive problem. There are too many rights. The conflicting interests of different groups set equally basic rights in conflict. These conflicts are properly resolved by treating rights as means for enhancing people's lives, not as ultimate standards.

The first stage of socialism would, for example, fulfill the right of each to an income according to his or her labor. But, just by that token, it violates the communist standard, to each according to his or her needs, since the frail worker with children to bring up gets no more than the strong, childless worker. "This equal right is an unequal right for unequal labor. . . . It is, therefore, a right of inequality in its content, like every right."[12] By comparison with capitalism, too, the first stage of socialism violates rights which should claim the attention of a rights-based moralist. The factories of Horatio Alger types, acquired through hard work and honest bargains, are confiscated, just as robber-barons' are. People are kept from investing hard-won resources in private factories and farms. In short, the right to reward in proportion to labor is preserved by violating the right to the results of nonaggressive labor and honest bargains.

One can say that the socialist right is a higher right, the communist standard a right in a very broad sense, which is higher still. But on what scale have these rights been weighed? In the final analysis the weighing cannot be done on the scale of a further, super-right. Any right is "a right of inequality," conflicting with others in ways that demand resolution.[13] These conflicts are to be resolved by treating rights as means to life enhancement, choosing those that would most enhance well-being if embodied in society at the time in question.

[12] *Critique of the Gotha Program*, p. 387.
[13] Ibid.

Marx's most detailed discussion of conflicts among rights, in the *Critique of the Gotha Program*, concerns rights to income. But a similar conflict among political rights also emerges from his writings. The equal right of all to be left alone by government and the equal right of all to effective participation in government are independent and important aspects of rights-based political equality. In a class-divided society, they inevitably conflict. Without collective ownership dominated by a workers' state (with the interference that entails), economic power becomes concentrated in the hands of a few, who dominate effective participation in government as a result. Yet the demand for noninterference is not in general misguided or purely ideological. Individuality and independence are real needs.[14]

As with all the conflicts among rights which Marx describes, analogous conflicts arise for most people who accept interference with laissez-faire capitalism, even if they reject Marx's socialism. The right to participation must be balanced against the right to noninterference. For most of us, attracted both to nonsubordination and to noninterference, the only reasonable way to secure both rights is to treat both as instruments, and find institutions and strategies that most enhance people's lives in society as a whole.

Most of these conflicts reflect a more general split among rights-based standards of equality. On the one hand, people have a right to an equal distribution of the benefits, powers and burdens of the basic social arrangements that dominate their lives and that can only be avoided at great cost, if at all. In economics, this demand for equal terms for cooperation leads to the socialist or the communist standard—in politics, to the demand for equal influence on the political process. On the other hand, people have an independent right peacefully to pursue their interests without interference. This implies a right to invest, retain and bequeath in the economic realm and a right to freedom from state interference in politics. In modern systems of interdependent production, these two dimensions

[14] See, for example, *Economic and Philosophical Manuscripts*, pp. 122f.; *Communist Manifesto*, p. 347; *Grundrisse*, p. 488.

of rights inevitably conflict. Yet most of us, so far as we base social choice on rights, regard neither dimension as intrinsically superior. (Marx's arguments are not meant to convince someone who approves of rights to noninterference no matter what the consequences.) The existence of this conflict between noninterference and fair terms for cooperation is the general, though nonconclusive, reason for supposing that rights-based equality generates conflicts that only a non-rights basis for choice can resolve. Marx's specific and explicit arguments continue the case for saying that every right is a right of inequality. They are meant to show that no right which his contemporaries had advanced was preeminent enough to resolve conflicts without encountering a contrary, equally basic right. That the general problem had not been resolved even approximately, despite centuries of trying, made it a good bet, by Marx's time, that it was insoluble.

A modern assessment of Marx's attack on morality would have to be anachronistic and consider twentieth-century attempts to solve the general problem. I will just mention one aspect of this further assessment. Rawls' theory of justice is, in part, an effort to reveal the one overriding version of equality appropriate to the choice of basic institutions. But, if I have posed the problem about rights correctly, Rawls' theory seems too biased toward one dimension of rights to solve the problem without begging the question.

In Rawls' view, we have an ultimate, equal right to be governed by principles that we would choose in fair deliberations over rules for assessing basic institutions. For such deliberations to be fair, the bargainers must not use knowledge of their actual situation in society. If actual resources are known, the outcome might reflect the coercive capacities of some. It would even be unfair for deliberants to be aware of their talents, for this might affect the choice of rules for basic institutions, while basic institutions will determine what capacities are talents, that is, are valuable. Appropriate deliberations turn out to be those that take place behind a "veil of ignorance," as one pursues self-interest in ignorance of one's particular advantages or life-plans. To prefer a standard of right that conflicts with the outcome of such reasoning is to choose principles in an unfair way. Someone concerned that justice be done and the rights of all be given their due weight should, rationally, reject the conflicting standard. Also, adopting this "original position" as the favored perspective for choice reflects a desire for autonomy, that is, a desire that one's choices among ways of life not be constrained by biases built into the fabric of basic institutions, and a desire to make one's most basic moral choices unconstrained by inclinations that are shaped by contingent circumstances.[15]

In fact, institutions governed by principles emerging from the original position might violate independently valid standards of equal right, creating conflicts that Rawls' choice procedure cannot resolve in a non-question-begging way. This is so, even if the original position is, indeed, a uniquely fair basis for deliberation over institutions. Suppose, as most people accept, that Rawlsian economic principles would have a stronger bias toward distributive equality than the Lockean principle, "To each the results of his or her honest toil and exchanges." (If this is not the case, the right to be governed by the original position will instead conflict with some relatively egalitarian principle, such as, "To each according to the amount of his or her labor-time." Analogous problems will result.) Honest, non-violent people with capitalist inclinations, potential Horatio Algers, will be denied the opportunity to use all the fruits of their self-sacrifice to set up and develop factories and farms. When they complain that their equal right to the results of honest toil is violated, it is no answer to tell them that they would have accepted the relevant restrictions in fair deliberations. Of course, they did not actually consent to these restrictions. The Rawlsian contract is purely hypothetical. Moreover, it is not the case that the honest-toil principle derives whatever moral force it has from the hypothetical fair deliberations. By way of thought experiment, we can even imagine that principles which are fairly chosen would produce so many

[15] See, in particular, John Rawls, *A Theory of Justice* (Cambridge, Mass., 1971), secs. 1, 3, 13, 40, and "The Basic Structure as Subject," *American Philosophical Quarterly* 14 (1977), pp. 159–66.

reasonable charges of unfairness, through violating the honest-toil principle, that it would be immoral to institute them. Suppose some form of socialism is dictated by the fairly chosen principles. But most people want to set up as petty capitalists, only to be thwarted by the situation they would choose in deliberations where they cannot rely on knowledge of their skills, fortunes, or particular inclinations. Here, the injury might be so widespread that the fairly chosen arrangement is pervasively unfair.

A relevant response to the complaints of unfair restriction is: the right to be governed by rules that would emerge from fair deliberations has more moral weight than the right to the results of honest toil, at least as those principles affect people's lives in the real world. But on what scale have those rights been weighed? No further standard of equal right seems fit to serve as the balance. No doubt, preference for the results of fair deliberation is more in accord with the judgment that people have a right to cooperate on fair terms when cooperation is inevitable and the stakes are high. But this judgment is no more obvious or basic than the judgment that people have a right to be left alone in their initiatives if they do not interfere with others. And that moral inclination favors the right to the results of honest toil. When the original position is used to answer basic questions about competing rights, parallel questions are begged, it seems, at a higher level. As for the appeal to autonomy, while the original position may best satisfy the goals of autonomy Rawls describes, there are other such goals. One kind of autonomy is the freedom to pursue whatever desires one has without interference. Surely, this dimension of autonomy has independent value. And the honest-toil principle is best suited to it.[16]

---

[16] Of course, an effective criticism of Rawls' theory must be much more detailed. I develop this sketch further in "Rights Or Consequences" and present other criticisms in "Rights and Reality," *Philosophical Review* 90 (1981), a study of the main present-day attempts to resolve conflicts of interest on the basis of respect for rights.

A MISTAKE ABOUT MARX AND RIGHTS

Despite his explicit attack on appeals to rights of equality in the *Critique of the Gotha Program*, many readers, as different as Benedetto Croce and Robert Nozick, have taken Marx in his economics to condemn capitalism on just these grounds. For capitalism to endure, the typical working day must have an "unpaid" portion, in the sense that the wage earner continues to work after creating goods of the same value as the goods he can buy with his wage. But, Marx's alleged argument infers, this means that capitalism violates an overriding principle of equality in exchanges. Commodities that are exchanged should be of equal value. Or, in any case, people whose lives are dominated by exchange should not bargain in a framework where their one significant commodity must typically be exchanged below its value. And this is necessarily so for proletarians, who live by selling their labor-power.

Marx discusses this argument in many passages, since it played an important role among those for whom "A fair day's wage for a fair day's work" was the central demand of the labor movement. He always rejects the argument. No valid principle of equality need be violated in the typical wage bargain. A full survey of these texts would duplicate the conclusive textual case which Allen Wood has made in an influential series of writings.[17] I will concentrate on a few texts that show clearly not just what Marx believed but why. The denial that typical wage bargains are unfair is not simply a belief Marx happened to have, or an expression of his antipathy to certain political trends. He offers compelling arguments based on common sense and important aspects of his economic theory. Ironically, in the next chapter, an understanding of Marx's rationale will turn out to undermine Wood's use of these passages in his own interpretation of Marx on morality.

[17] His article, "Marx on Right and Justice" (originally in *Philosophy and Public Affairs* 8 [1979]), in M. Cohen et al., *Marx, Justice, and History* (Princeton, 1980), is especially concise and compelling.

One reason why Marx regards surplus-value creation as no injustice is that it is not unjust according to the very principles that the partisans of equality implicitly use in judging whether exchanges are too unequal to be just.

The product is the property of the capitalist and not that of the labourer, its immediate producer. Suppose that a capitalist pays for a day's labour-power at its value; then the right to use that power for a day belongs to him, just as much as the right to use any other commodity, such as a horse that he has hired for the day. To the purchaser of a commodity belongs its use, and the seller of labour-power, by giving his labour, does no more, in reality, than part with the use-value that he has sold. From the instant he steps into the workshop, the use-value of his labour-power, and therefore also its use, which is labour, belongs to the capitalist. By the purchase of labor-power, the capitalist incorporates labour, as a living ferment, with the lifeless constituents of the product. . . . The product of this process belongs, therefore, to him, just as much as does the wine which is the product of a process of fermentation completed in his cellar. . . . The circumstance, that on the one hand the daily sustenance of labour-power costs only half a day's labour, while on the other hand the very same labour-power can work during a whole day, that consequently the value which its use during one day creates, is double what he pays for that use, this circumstance is, without doubt, a piece of good luck for the buyer, but by no means an injury to the seller.[18]

This is an excellent and effective piece of ordinary-language philosophy. No one says that the renter of a horse's labor-power has unjustly profited if the resulting gain to the harvest is worth more than the cost of the horse's labor-power. The surplus simply shows that the purchaser of labor-power was not stupid or unlucky. So why should the production of a surplus as a result of a wage bargain show that the purchaser has violated a right to equality?

Marx's other argument depends on part of his economic theory to which he was clearly and deeply committed, for good or ill, his labor theory of value. According to the measure of value that can claim validity for purposes of economic science,

[18] *Capital* I, pp. 180, 188.

commodities of equal value *are* exchanged in the typical, surplus-producing wage bargain.

We must now examine more closely this peculiar commodity, labour-power. Like all others it has a value. How is that value determined?

The value of labour-power is determined, as in the case of every other commodity, by the labour-time necessary for the production, and consequently also the reproduction, of this special article. . . . Therefore the labour-time requisite for the production of labour-power reduces itself to that necessary for the production of those means of subsistence; in other words, the value of labour-power is the value of the means of subsistence necessary for the maintenance of the labourer.[19]

In *Wages, Price and Profit*, Marx makes the same point more vividly, again using the illustration of horsepower.

The value of the labouring power is determined by the quantity of labour necessary to maintain or reproduce it, but the *use* of that labouring power is only limited by the active energies and physical strength of the labourer. The daily or weekly value of the labouring power is quite distinct from the daily or weekly exercise of that power, the same as the food a horse wants and the time it can carry the horseman are quite distinct. The quantity of labour by which the value of the workman's labouring power is limited forms by no means a limit to the quantity of labor which his labouring power is apt to perform.[20]

In sum, a wage bargain is an equal exchange if the wage embodies or commands the social labor needed to maintain the worker for the period in question. And Marx takes pains to show that this amount of labor will typically be less than the labor expended under the wage bargain.

Marx certainly thought that any system in which production depends on wage bargains resulting in surplus value would eventually generate widespread servitude and suffering. Such were his reasons for being against all economic systems of this

---

[19] Ibid., p. 167.

[20] *Wages, Price and Profit*, in Marx and Engels, *Selected Works in Three Volumes* (Moscow, 1973.), vol. II, p. 212.

kind. This is a very different indictment from the charge that systems depending on surplus value should be condemned because surplus value violates a right to equal exchange.

EQUAL CONCERN

It might seem that the failures of distributive and rights-based equality are due to their rigid reliance on abstract rules, rather than concrete emotions. Equality and morality ultimately rest on a humanitarian feeling of equal concern and respect for all.

Marx criticizes this heartfelt equality by opposing it to the attitudes required for effective change in a class-divided society. "[T]rue socialism [i.e., the movement of that name in Germany in the 1840s] concerned no longer with real human beings but with 'Man,' has lost all revolutionary enthusiasm and proclaims instead the universal love of mankind."[21] Given Marx's view of social reality, this contrast is psychological common sense. For example, the militant strikes that can improve the status of the working class harm the vital interests of factory owners and may drive some into bankruptcy. Yet, as Marx often emphasizes, many of these factory owners are personally decent. So are many of the police whom militant strikers must often fight off, sometimes quite violently. And a militant strike is among the mildest of the confrontations that are crucial levers of change for Marx. To give sharp confrontations a crucial role and require that they be based on a feeling of equal concern for all would be either hypocritical or self-defeating. That is so, in any case, unless reference to equal concern is reference to respect for principles of distribution, rights or impartiality. But then we are back in the troubled realm of rigid and abstract rules of equality.

This general criticism of the humanitarian outlook crucially depends on the specific strategies of change that Marx recommends. Voting for the distinctive institutions of socialism and communism or arguing that they are superior to capitalist

[21] *German Ideology*, p. 130.

institutions is an activity that humanitarian emotions would sustain. If humanitarian equality is inadequate, that is because morality should be a guide to actions capable of realizing its ideals. As we will see in more detail, in Chapter Three, Marx argues that strategies entirely concerned with voting and persuasion lack this effectiveness for the ideals he recommends. Here, as elsewhere, Marx's abstract theoretical claims must be understood in the context of his practical political commitments.

UTILITARIANISM

Everything said so far might, in principle, be said by a utilitarian. In utilitarianism, only one kind of equality is fundamental. The general welfare is to be determined without bias toward some people's well-being. For Marx, this unbiased determination of the general welfare is impossible.

If the general welfare is identified with some homogeneous happiness-stuff, valuable in proportion to intensity and extent, we commit "the apparent stupidity of merging all the manifold relationships of people in the one relation of usefulness."[22] A society of frenetically self-aggrandizing shopkeepers, each feeling intense pleasure at routine triumphs in getting the best of others but not crestfallen by routine defeats, is less desirable, all else being equal, than a society of people who wish each other well and enjoy acting on their mutual concern. Yet in the two societies, people might, in principle, "use" their relations to produce equal amounts of pleasure. Some relations, activities and experiences are more to be promoted than others whose enjoyment is just as intense and pervasive. By the same token, to adopt the intensity-and-pervasiveness standard is not really to embrace a neutral standard. Only to care about the intensity and pervasiveness of enjoyment is, at best, to adopt a quite definite and idiosyncratic conception of welfare. This conception is rejected by most people (perhaps all) when they refuse to merge all relationships into the one relation of using

[22] Ibid., p. 110.

31

others for one's pleasure, and rationally reflect on the different relationships that one might enjoy.

A generally acceptable standard must distinguish between different bases for equally intense enjoyment. However, we cannot make the necessary discriminations without social bias. No ranking of all important goods, including, say, leisure as against material income, the enjoyment of competitive striving as against the enjoyment of cooperation, and the chance to occupy the top of hierarchies as against the guarantee of a secure, moderately comfortable life, is faithful to the needs or the reflective desires of all—industrial workers, farmers, investment bankers, housewives, shopkeepers and professors alike. If we seek a ranking that all would accept if they had relevant data, we are pursuing what does not exist. If we adopt the ranking of those who have actually tasted all kinds of pleasure, we show bias toward the upper strata who are able to practice such connoisseurship. In short, Mill's proposal to weigh different kinds of experience impartially, by relying on the expertise of those who have experienced all the kinds in question, is either biased or ineffective.

These troubling connections between social location and psychological structure are the basis for an important and neglected attack on utilitarianism in *The German Ideology*:

The philosophy of enjoyment was never anything but the ingenious language of certain social circles who had the privilege of enjoyment. Apart from the fact that the manner and content of their enjoyment was always determined by the whole structure of the rest of society and suffered from all its contradictions, this philosophy became a mere *phrase*, as soon as it began to lay claim to a universal character and proclaimed itself the outlook on life of society as a whole. . . .[I]t was given a generalized character by the bourgeoisie and applied to every individual without distinction, thus it was divorced from the conditions of life of these individuals. . . . The connection of the enjoyment of the individuals at any particular time with the class relations in which they live, and the conditions of production and intercourse that give rise to these relations, the narrowness of the hitherto existing forms of enjoyment which are outside the actual content of the life of people and in contradiction to it, the connection of every philosophy of enjoyment with the enjoyment actually present and the hypocrisy of such a philosophy when applied to all individuals without distinction—all this, of course, could only be discovered when it became possible to criticize the conditions of production and intercourse in the hitherto existing world. . . . That shattered the basis of all morality, whether the morality of asceticism or of enjoyment.[23]

Later on, in *Capital*, the charge that utilitarianism neglects the impact of social processes on basic human wants reemerges in a savage paragraph on Bentham. Marx says, in part:

. . . To know what is useful for a dog, one must study dog-nature. This nature itself is not to be deduced from the principle of utility. Applying this to man, he that would criticise all human acts, movements, relations, etc., by the principle of utility, must first deal with human nature in general, and then with human nature as modified in each historical epoch. Bentham makes short work of it. With the driest naivete he takes the modern shopkeeper, especially the English shopkeeper, as the normal man. Whatever is useful to this queer normal man, and to his world, is absolutely useful. . . .[24]

Finally, at the end of his life, Marx reaffirms the social relativity of human needs in his notes on Adolf Wagner's *Lehrbuch der politischen Oekonomie*:

[If 'Man'] means Man, as a category, he has . . . no . . . needs at all. If it means man confronting nature by himself, one has in mind a non-social animal. If it means a man who is already to be found in some form of society . . . one must begin by presenting the particular character of this social man, i.e., the particular character of the community in which he lives, since here production, and thus *the means by which he maintains his existence* already have a social character.[25]

Again, a development since Marx's time is relevant to the larger argument. Modern economics has produced conceptions of the general welfare that rely on functions ranging over in-

[23] Ibid., pp. 114f.
[24] *Capital* I, p. 571.
[25] Marx's emphasis. See Marx and Engels, *Werke* (Berlin, 1958), vol. 19, p. 362. Some other passages asserting the social relativity of needs are *Capital* I, p. 168; *Wages, Price and Profit*, p. 225; and *Wage-Labor and Capital*, in Tucker, *The Marx-Engels Reader*, p. 180.

dividual preferences. In effect, the summing of experiences in classical utilitarianism is replaced by ideal voting schemes. The economists' utilitarianism seems, however, to be much less appropriate to choices of basic institutions than Bentham's or Mill's. Interpersonal comparisons of intensity play no role, even though the intensity of someone's total deprivation might reasonably affect our assessment of unequal social arrangements in which he lives. Preference sets are not subject to criticism as making for more or less happiness, even though basic institutions themselves play an important role in determining preferences. Finally, in light of Arrow's famous theorem, preference utilitarianism turns out to lack the virtues of precision and generality that make it attractive in the first place, as against the traditional alternatives.

The conflicting rankings of goods that cannot be reconciled by effective and impartial methods are extremely important in the choice of basic institutions. A socialist state, for example, cannot offer everyone whatever education or occupation he or she wants. Under capitalism, such choices are often constrained by finances or family background. Most people, if they accept Marx's factual claims about capitalist constraints and socialist possibilities, would prefer to work out these problems of choice in a socialist framework. But not every sane person would. Some care too deeply, for their own and for others' sake, that striving for personal betterment, free from direct interference, be allowed, even if lack of resources often makes the prospects dim. Similarly, the institutions of Marx's classless society allow little scope for purely self-interested competition. For some, this activity is an important positive good. Surely, Marx does not expect everyone to postpone the transition to this society until no one has this individualist attitude. If he did, this veto power would be the opposite of utilitarian concern with the greatest happiness of the greatest number. Again, there must be a trade-off between different conceptions of happiness.

If the different rankings of goods are different enough, there is no feasible compromise, since feasible economic systems violate either one conception of the good or the other. That the

34

majority would have their preferences served by Marx's favored arrangement is not sufficient, since acute deprivation in a minority can, in principle, override the satisfaction of the majority. We must weigh different conceptions of happiness to rank the rivals. And here, for reasons that Marx sketches in the quoted passages, no standard of equality seems to be available. Bentham's standard is one-sided and, for most of us, unreasonable. Mill's procedure cannot do justice to "the connection of the enjoyment of the individuals at any given time with the class relations in which they live." (Here, as elsewhere, almost all of those who reject Marx's specific social goals will find that their own outlooks are affected by similar conflicts in analogous ways, when they chose between laissez-faire capitalism and somewhat more collective arrangements.)

As usual, Marx's theoretical criticisms gain in importance when we consider the practical context, the pursuit of means to change society. In his view, the struggles that eventually lead to socialism are often dangerous and uncertain. They sometimes fail, even make matters worse. To sign on to this movement, one ought rationally to believe that it may make the world a lot better if it succeeds. Thus, even if different conceptions of the good were not different enough to affect a preference for socialism when all facts are known with certainty, they might affect a rational decision to take part in the struggle for socialism, in an uncertain and dangerous world.

A Utilitarian Marx

In recent years, Derek Allen has been the most vigorous and erudite exponent of the view that Marx was implicitly a utilitarian, despite the explicitly anti-utilitarian passages. ". . . The arguments which support their [i.e., Marx's and Engels'] moral judgments are," he writes, "utilitarian in all but name."[26] This utilitarianism consists of preferring alternatives solely because of their effectiveness in satisfying people's interests, that is, the desires they would have if adequately informed.

[26] Derek Allen, "The Utilitarianism of Marx and Engels," *American Philosophical Quarterly* 10 (1973), p. 189.

Allen's case for the utilitarian Marx rests on two major claims. The first is right, I think, though not for Allen's reasons. Marx, he claims, "regards any interest, no matter whose, as prima facie worthy of satisfaction."[27] His evidence consists of cases in which Marx supports policies that favor bourgeois as well as proletarian interests, for example, the repeal of high British tariffs on grain. But this seems beside the central utilitarian point, that one should take the fact that someone's interest is served as, intrinsically, a reason for choosing an alternative. A nonutilitarian might care nothing for capitalists' satisfaction, but choose policies that do satisfy them, just because workers' interests are served. After all, farmers do not show intrinsic concern for sheep's interests when they serve them nutritious food to make more meat on the hoof.

Still, a plausible case might be made that Marx did give some prima facie weight to the satisfaction of anyone's interests, regardless of the class he or she happened to be in. In his writings on India, he condemns harms to nonproletarian colonial subjects as "monstrous," "brutal," "profound hypocrisy and inherent barbarism."[28] He counts it as an advantage of socialism that it serves the interests of more people than capitalism does:

All previous historical movements were movements of minorities, or in the interests of minorities. The proletarian movement is the self-conscious, independent movement of the immense majority, in the interests of the immense majority.[29]

In his relations with his best friend, Engels the textile manufacturer, Marx gave the well-being of a capitalist considerable weight. It is a reasonable inference from these facts that in his view the thwarting of anyone's interests, itself and prima facie, makes the world worse.

All this, however, is still very far from utilitarianism. Utilitarians are committed to a version of the premise of equality, namely, "Give everyone's interests equal weight," not just to

[27] Ibid.
[28] Marx and Engels, *On Colonialism* (New York, 1972), pp. 36, 40, 86.
[29] *Communist Manifesto*, p. 344.

the relatively weak principle that everyone's satisfaction be given some prima facie weight. More precisely, they want to weigh the satisfaction of desires without ultimate bias toward desires of certain people or desires with a certain internal content. That is why Mill is so troubled by the challenge to account for the greater weight of certain "qualities of pleasure," and why he tries to justify his weighing procedure as the only intellectually respectable one, quite apart from prior value commitments: ". . . [B]etter to be Socrates dissatisfied than a fool satisfied. And if the fool, or the pig, are of a different opinion, that is because they only know their side of the question. The other party to the comparison knows both sides."[30] Again, the example of Weber's nationalism makes the role of equality vivid by contrast. Weber did take the thwarting of French and Russian people's satisfaction as a prima facie reason against a policy. But in his personal system of values, the satisfaction of German desires to be citizens of a world power is more important than the satisfaction of incompatible French desires, no less deeply felt and no more harmful to people's desires around the world. Surely, this is not a utilitarian outlook.

The other main part of Allen's case is essential, then, as he is certainly aware. He claims that when Marx gives more weight to some kinds of needs and ways of life than others, "over-all Marx appears to reason" in a utilitarian way, ranking something as higher just because people would prefer it, if adequately informed. Any problem, here, is one "he shares . . . with utilitarians," not a basis for his rejecting utilitarianism.[31] This is what I have denied.

Allen gives no example of Marx's justifying a ranking of a kind of desire in the Millian manner he describes. Certainly, Marx never says anything remotely like this, Allen's epitome of such reasoning: "[I]f in fact people prefer idleness to education, then idleness is the 'higher' activity."[32] Far from en-

[30] John Stuart Mill, *Utilitarianism*, S. Gorovitz, ed., (Indianapolis, 1971), p. 20.
[31] Allen, "The Utilitarianism of Marx and Engels," p. 199.
[32] Ibid.

dorsing this utilitarian method for weighing satisfactions, Marx emphasizes the diversity and social determination of needs and, in two long passages quoted in part before, condemns utilitarians for ignoring such facts.[33] The condemnation is strong. The passage from *Capital* ends by calling Jeremy Bentham "a genius in the way of bourgeois stupidity." Note that the issue is not whether Marx would regard it as a good thing for someone to be coercively "reeducated" to adopt higher goals, or would count it as intrinsically good for someone to be forced to lead a higher way of life than he would chose.[34] Marx's strong emphasis on free development precludes this.[35] But Marx can point to conflicting needs of different people, at least some of which must be neglected in favor of others by all feasible social arrangements. Our preference among social arrangements must be a preference among needs, and the bias cannot be removed in the Millian style. This is the reasonable reconstruction of these passages.

Allen needs to find deep-seated, contrary aspects of Marx's social theory, if he is to show that Marx does not really mean it when he seems to identify neglect of the diversity of needs as a lethal problem for utilitarianism. Allen's writings contain one such claim, an important departure from the view of Marx I have offered: "But, it may be further objected, the majority . . . is . . . not everybody. . . . Mill and Bentham advocated the greatest happiness of the greatest number, not just of the majority. But this objection will not do either. . . . Marx insists that 'universal human emancipation'—the emancipation of the bourgeoisie no less than of proletarians—is at stake in the abolition of private property."[36] If everyone would indeed be helped by socialism or communism, I was wrong to ascribe to Marx the view that we need to discriminate among different conceptions of happiness to decide among basic social alternatives. Marx is concerned to satisfy human interests as such,

[33] *Capital* I, p. 571; *German Ideology*, p. 115.
[34] Cf. "The Utilitarianism of Marx and Engels," p. 198.
[35] See, for example, *Economic and Political Manuscripts*, in Bottomore, *Early Writings*, pp. 122f.; *Communist Manifesto*, p. 353; *Grundrisse*, pp. 307f.
[36] "The Utilitarianism of Marx and Engels," p. 194.

bases his case on the thwarting of interests by capitalism and their satisfaction by socialism, and regards it as unnecessary to favor some kinds of satisfactions over others in actual social choices. For everyone will be made happier by socialism, or would be if everyone's preferences were based on adequate reflection and information. Seeing morality as a means to guide action in the real world, this Marx might well have opted for utilitarianism.

The two passages that Allen cites will not bear this weight. The remark about "universal human emancipation" is from the 1844 manuscripts and is immediately glossed by Marx as follows: "For all human servitude is involved in the relation of the worker to production, and all types of servitude are only modifications or consequences of this relation."[37] So Marx is not claiming that the most greedy and power-hungry Manchester mill owner will be happier in communist society, if fully informed. He is claiming that the proletarian's situation epitomizes all servitude, and that communist society makes it possible to end servitude and domination, including the domination that the mill owner may thoroughly enjoy, even need. The other text, from *Capital*, simply says that "objects . . . rule the producers instead of being ruled by them." No doubt, the mill owner wishes he could control market forces and the like. This does not mean he would be happier, on balance, under socialism or communism.

What texts are there on the other side, suggesting that deep-rooted and urgent needs of some will be offended when social change takes place according to the strategies which Marx supports? In addition to the general reflections on psychology and utilitarianism that I have cited, the crucial ones are statements about the political basis for change. The clash of interests is so deep that revolution will generally be necessary to bring about socialism. "In depicting the most general phases of the development of the proletariat, we traced the more or less veiled civil war, raging within existing society, up to the point at which the war breaks out into open revolution, and where

[37] *Economic and Philosophical Manuscripts*, p. 132.

39

the violent overthrow of the bourgeoisie lays the foundation for the sway of the proletariat."[38] This is not the statement of someone who believes that all resistance to socialism rests on misinformation. Apart from the revolutionary conception of change, the emphasis on ultimate conflict emerges in the claim that the state in transition from capitalist to classless society "can be nothing but the *revolutionary dictatorship of proletariat.*"[39] In his letters, Marx singles out this thesis as one of his three distinctive contributions to social theory[40] and speaks of such a state's necessary concern with "intimidating the mass of the bourgeoisie."[41] Just what forms of coercion support the talk of class dictatorship is left quite unclear by Marx. When subsequent Marxists have added specifics, the results have sometimes been tragic. But the general, unspecific statements are important for our purposes. Surely, they would not be made by someone who thought no one's interests would be offended, deeply and on balance, by socialism. In his central political ideas, Marx was not a believer in universal emancipation of the kind Allen's argument requires.

I have just connected one controversy with others, not with settled issues in Marx scholarship. Despite the cited statements, many interpreters argue that Marx, or Marx in his maturity, did not really believe in the general and normal necessity of revolution, and that the talk of proletarian class dictatorship is pure hyperbole. I will discuss the nonrevolutionary interpretation in detail in Chapter Three. For now, I hope to have shown that the politics of change as Marx conceived of it—that traditional subject of strategic disagreements among Marxists—has an important bearing on what seems utterly abstract, Marx's assessment of the moral point of view. If Allen did not claim that the bourgeoisie is helped by socialism, he would have no basis for explaining away Marx's attacks on utilitarianism. But to portray Marx's goals as universal, in this very strong sense, means explaining away the

---

[38] *Communist Manifesto*, pp. 344f.
[39] *Critique of the Gotha Program*, p. 395; Marx's emphasis.
[40] Marx to J. Weydemeyer, March 5, 1852, *Selected Correspondence*, p. 64.
[41] Marx to F. Domela-Nieuwenhuis, February 22, 1881, ibid., p. 318.

passages in which Marx asserts the general necessity of revolution. I hasten to add that Marx might well have doubted that socialism would benefit everyone, even if he were not a revolutionary. Most nonrevolutionaries doubt this, especially if they share Marx's sensitivity to the social determination of needs.

GENERALITY

The second typical feature of moralities, after the equality they require, is the generality of the norms on which they rely. We can assess any social arrangement by applying to the particular facts at hand norms that are valid whenever moral appeals have a point. Or at any rate, the major questions about stable features of societies can be settled in this way, whatever dilemmas arise in emergencies.

The basic reason why Marx denies that general norms rate all societies when applied to relevant facts is that the goods now to be pursued have typically been in deep and irreconcilable conflict in past societies. Marx's paradigm of this conflict is classical Athens. The Greeks, he says, "excused the slavery of one on the ground that it was a means to the full development of another."[42] Behind this excuse was a reality. The technological capacities of ancient Greece made cultural development dependent on leisure for some based on enforced drudgery for others. The competing goods, here, are so important and different that there is no basis for determining whether Greek institutions were desirable. Not moral reasoning, but the course of history produced a solution to this dilemma, the dependence of the development of human powers on subordination, monotony, and violence. "In proportion as labor develops socially, and becomes thereby a source of wealth and culture, poverty and destitution develop among the workers, and wealth and culture among the non-workers. . . . This is the law of all history hitherto. . . . [I]n present capitalist society, conditions have at last been created which enable and

---

[42] *Capital* I, p. 385.

compel the workers to lift this social curse."[43] The enhancement of life in society as a whole, governed by Marx's conception of the good, is not meant to be a standard by means
of which past societies can be rated. Marx never suggests that
there is a fact of the matter as to whether classical Athens was
better as a slave society rich in cultural goods than it would
have been had it remained a cluster of villages based on subsistence farming. The norms that ought to guide us now and
in the future are not suited for judgments of the past. But
Marx's non-morality claims no more than guidance for the
present and the future.

Because of the absence of general norms, Marx's outlook on
politics and institutions has a different logical structure from
moral theories, at least as philosophers usually conceive them.
Moral theories offer norms that yield a ranking of alternative
institutions when applied in light of the facts. The validity of
those norms does not depend on highly controversial empirical
claims. In contrast, actual recommendations about institutions
may be tentative or missing in a moral theory. For they depend
on empirically controversial commitments about the facts.
Thus, whatever maximizes the general welfare is best, for the
utilitarian. But he or she may claim to know little about what
would actually maximize welfare. Factual questions about institutions and strategies largely, if not entirely, belong somewhere outside moral theory—in politics, social theory, or social engineering.

In place of general norms, Marx offers a motley array of
goods to be pursued. They are not guaranteed to yield a ranking of major alternatives. Indeed, they do not for many of the
alternatives. That pursuit of the recommended goods is a coherent goal in the present day is a matter of empirical controversy. There is no basis, here, for distinguishing between the
justification of basic principles and the justification of a political program. For the arguments that the goods provide a coherent and applicable standard of choice (at present) *are* the

[43] *Critique of the Gotha Program*, p. 384. "Wealth", here, clearly refers to
really beneficial resources.

42

empirical arguments that justify the pursuit of certain institutional arrangements as the best way to promote these goods.

These logical differences from traditional moral theories are, at the same time, resemblances to scientific theories, as viewed in post-positivist philosophy of science. A scientific theory is chosen for its success along a number of diverse dimensions, for example, good fit with the data, the absence of explanatory loose ends, broad scope and fruitfulness. This motley of goals is not intrinsically determinate. A theory might be superior on some dimensions, inferior on others. There seems to be no dominant goal of science in terms of which the others can be weighted, so that we can always say whether a theory is best, given the theory, its rivals, and the data. Rather, the argument that a theory can now be confirmed or disconfirmed is an empirical argument appealing to the actual shape of the data, past debates, and present background theories. In contrast, traditional moral theories are like traditional logics of induction, which try to justify, on general and a priori grounds, norms that assign at least a rough degree of confirmation to every hypothesis, given any body of data.

UNIVERSAL RATIONALITY

The third feature of typical moralities is a kind of epistemological equality. Moral norms are supposed to be accepted by anyone who rationally reflects on appropriate arguments, accepts relevant factual claims, and possesses the normal range of emotions.

I have already mentioned one reason why Marx rejects this claim to universality. Different people attach different importance to rival goods, as important for themselves and for others—say, competitive striving as against cooperation, material income as against leisure. Institutions cannot be neutral in all these rivalries. Everyone cannot be brought to agree by rational persuasion.[44]

---

[44] Compare Rawls' estimate of the power of persuasion to settle such differences in "Fairness to Goodness," *Philosophical Review* 84 (1975.)

Beyond this, Marx must have been impressed by facts of historical diversity. In ancient Greece and Rome, he emphasizes, everyone accepted slaves as appropriate to the functioning of a normal household. In medieval Europe, everyone gave customary restrictions and obligations of kinship great moral weight, much more so than in the present day. It simply is not true that all intelligent normal modern people, aware of relevant facts and arguments, accept the earlier rules as morally valid in their respective settings. Nor is it true that ignorance or unreason were the basis for the older views. That Aristotle would have changed his mind about slavery if he had appreciated some fact or argument does not fit what we know about Aristotle and his contemporaries.[45]

Marx, as I have interpreted him, is an implicit noncognitivist, that is, various central issues of social choice cannot be resolved, in his view, by the use of reason and evidence. But it is an open question just how far the limits of reason extend, just how many judgments are affected by this noncognitivism. The above arguments against the universal rationality of some important judgments are not based on any alleged general distinction between moral discourse and statements of facts. Presumably, there are many needs and reflective desires which all rational people capable of the normal range of emotions do share. The corresponding goods and the ordering among them will dictate certain social choices, perhaps the rejection of slavery in a modern productive setting. To what extent they do so depends on a variety of facts concerning which alternatives are feasible, what are the consequences of feasible alternatives, and what ratings of needs and desires are shared, on adequate reflection. In this last category, for example, the 1844 Manuscripts persuade many readers that a high rating for diverse work chosen for its own sake is dictated by urgent, generally shared needs.

At some point, however, Marx requires that commitments be nonrational. If he did not, his attacks on morality would

[45] See M. I. Finley, "Was Greek Civilization Based on Slave Labor?" in *Economy and Society in Ancient Greece* (New York, 1982; originally published 1959).

be utterly unfair. For his arguments against utilitarianism depend on the denial that relevant disagreements over goals can always be resolved by rational means.

Marx's noncognitivism does not preclude his constantly making arguments to justify political choices. Rather, it means that his arguments are not addressed to a universal audience, though they are addressed to a very large one. In effect, Marx relies on an expectation that his intended readers will share enough in the way of initial outlooks and reflective desires to be persuaded by the facts he advances. Those who find this a tenuous basis for a life devoted to public argument might ask themselves whether they rely on more in actual political discussions. In practice, we have to assume a vast background of shared beliefs and attitudes in order to pursue political (or scientific) discussions in the time we have. We know that this background is not shared by everyone. Sometimes we are dramatically surprised. (In a discussion of war, someone once told me, with apparent sincerity, that he thought there was nothing bad about the death in battle of innocent people.) Still, the surprises are rare or peripheral enough to make our expectations a reasonable basis for arguing. Marx is simply saying that such expectations are indispensable in principle as a basis for rational persuasion—not merely indispensable in practice, as everyone allows.

IDEOLOGY

Marx sometimes summarizes his rejection of morality in the statement that morality, like religion, is ideological.[46] An ideology, for Marx, is a system of beliefs and attitudes that distort reality and that result from social forces, characteristic of class societies, having no tendency to bring ideas in line with reality.

Granted that Marx analyzes the origins of moral ideas in this way, it is not clear what, if anything, the analysis adds to his criticism of morality. For one thing, the label of "ideology" presupposes the arguments already investigated, in which mo-

[46] See, for example, *Communist Manifesto*, p. 351; *Critique of the Gotha Program*, p. 388.

45

rality is criticized as intellectually defective. Ideology is *false* consciousness. In Marx's meta-ethics, just as much as in his economics, the case that a system of ideas is ideological must include arguments that it is invalid. So far, these arguments have been independent of historical examinations of social origins.

In defining ideology, for Marx, as a product of *truth-distorting* social forces, I have just made a very controversial claim. Its defense merits at least a short digression. That ideology distorts reality is more or less explicit in Engels' later writings.[47] But it is not explicit in Marx's discussions. Still, the conception of ideology that I have described best accounts for some pervasive features of Marx's usage. Marx often traces ideas and outlooks to their social origins. Sometimes he regards them as distortions, sometimes as valid. For example, the explanations, in the *Manifesto* and *Capital*, of how proletarians come to perceive their common interests are in the latter category. Yet Marx only uses the term "ideology" in connection with ideas and outlooks that he takes to be distortions, and he often combines the usage with obviously pejorative language. Moreover, by making the label highly tendentious, we can explain Marx's tendency to shuttle between different emphases in his general statements about ideology. Sometimes he emphasizes its socially stabilizing role, sometimes the fact that people with ideologies do not know where their ideas come from, sometimes the specific tendency for ideologies to attribute to ideas an excessively independent role in history. Just within the first sections of *The German Ideology*, he shuttles between these emphases on pages 64f., 37 and 66f., respectively. These shifts are to be expected if, as I would propose, the concept of ideology is a theoretical device used to answer a pressing historical question, "why have so many socially important ideas distorted reality when available data, reasonable inference and the state of science dictated no corresponding mistake?" Each emphasis highlights one side of the tendency of class domination to produce such false ideas.

[47] See, for example, the letters to Schmidt and to Mehring, *Selected Correspondence*, pp. 400f., 434.

If the charge that morality is ideology has the force that I have described, then the question is whether it adds anything to the criticism of morality that is not contained in the more internal arguments just presented. Note than an even more pressing version of this question is raised by interpretations that make no intrinsic connection with the distortion of truth: Does the claim that morality is ideological have any connection at all with the criticism of morality as an invalid standpoint for social choice?

Apart from these issues of their relevance to his attack on morality, Marx's actual historical discussions of the social origins of moral ideas are themselves very fragmentary. The scattered remarks are intriguing. In his view, the modern ideas about equality, freedom, justice and the general welfare that he criticizes are in part a cultural inheritance from the bourgeoisie's triumph over feudal restrictions.[48] In part, they are the result of a kind of wishful thinking to which a middle-class background gives rise, a false hope that the burdens of big-business domination can be overcome within a system of individual competition.[49] In part, they result from the tendency of bourgeois media to limit and stultify discontent, say, by presenting fair treatment by employers as the only proper goal of workers' activism, or by limiting the proper role of government to the satisfaction of people's equal rights. Consider, for example, traditional conservative efforts to limit social demands by confining them to the fulfillment of rights, as in David Stockman's recent remark, "What people don't realize is that there are plenty of things they want that they don't have a right to." For Marx, such a comment simply reveals that rights are less important than many suppose. For a rights-based liberal or socialist, Stockman's remark imposes a real burden of argument.[50] These speculations about social origins are as

[48] *German Ideology*, p. 84; *Grundrisse*, p. 245.
[49] *Communist Manifesto*, pp. 354f.; *Grundrisse*, pp. 248f.
[50] In *Wages, Price and Profit*, Marx emphasizes that demands for fairness tend to presuppose basic social relations, while calling for their readjustment: "Instead of the *conservative* motto, 'A fair days' wage for a fair day's work,' they [i.e., the working class] ought to inscribe on their banner the *revolutionary* watchword, 'Abolition of the wages system'" (p. 75; Marx's emphasis).

convincing as any current hypothesis about the origins of modern moral ideas. But they are fragmentary speculations, nonetheless.

With its limited role and speculative status, does the distinctive, causal aspect of Marx's thesis that morality is ideology make any contribution to his case against morality? I think it does. By offering an alternative interpretation of our feelings of attraction toward the moral point of view in politics, the thesis of ideology undermines the use of those feelings as evidence.

Many people who are intellectually attracted to the antimoral arguments previously sketched still feel reluctant to embrace the conclusions. I feel this way, myself. Such feelings are not irrelevant to the decision whether to accept Marx's antimoralism. One might, after all, find it so obvious that social choices should be made on the basis of equal concern for all that Marx's arguments merely convince one that a sufficiently abstract and flexible basis for equal concern has not yet been described. Nonetheless, one may feel, some such standard must exist. However, feelings of obviousness and implausibility, attraction and repulsion, need to be interpreted before they can be given evidential weight, and interpretation, here, includes causal explanation. Suppose crucial feelings that the interests of all must be treated equally are due to a cultural background ultimately shaped by bourgeois needs to tame discontent, and to a lack of personal exposure to hard social realities. Interpreted in this way, they should not lead one to resist the force of Marx's case against morality. And the Marxist explanation is at least as well-grounded as any claim that these feelings are based on an accurate moral sense. By analyzing their origins, Marx makes appeals to moral feelings less compelling in much the same way as Freud undermines reliance on religious feelings by offering an alternative interpretation of their origins in terms of the dependency and fears of childhood and the unity of self and world felt in early infancy.

The argument from origins to the assessment of validity is supposed to be a fallacy, so monstrous that it has a name, "the genetic fallacy." What would be fallacious is the assumption that ideas are debunked simply by tracing their origins to social interests. This assumption is especially implausible for moral ideas. For example, a strong duty to be hospitable to strangers is accepted by traditional Eskimoes because of a common interest in such hospitality in a semi-nomadic society where any family may be struck down in the constant battle with Nature. This explanation does not debunk. If anything, it justifies. Still, some causes are so inappropriate to some beliefs that the belief should be abandoned if we find it, in the final analysis, to be due to such a cause. Historic bourgeois interests in domination, together with a protected middle-class upbringing, are not appropriate as ultimate causal bases for a belief that all should be treated equally. Similar arguments about inappropriate causes are, after all, a normal aspect of scientific criticism. If contamination from the lab-technician's hands caused the streptococcus colony in the petri dish and the consequent belief that the patient had strep throat, that is a ground for withdrawing the belief. Perhaps the patient does have a strep throat. Still it is no fallacy to deny that we are in a position to make this claim, since the causes of our belief would be inappropriate.

In all these cases, the line between appropriate and inappropriate causes of evidence is drawn in roughly the following way: the claim that a phenomenon is evidence for a hypothesis is supported by a causal explanation making it unlikely that the phenomenon would have occurred if the hypothesis had not been valid. By the same token, the evidential claim is undermined by a causal account making it likely that the phenomenon would have occurred regardless of the validity of the hypothesis. Thus, if the technician's dirty hands caused the strep colony, there would have been a strep colony regardless of whether there was a rampant strep infection in the patient's throat. Accepting that one's attraction to the moral point of view in social choice is due to bourgeois domination and a protected upbringing makes it unreasonable, for almost everyone, to give that attraction evidential weight. For almost no one believes that those causal factors have an inherent tendency to promote an accurate appreciation of how to make choices.

49

To the extent that the causal account is valid, one would have had the same feelings regardless of the validity of the moral point of view. On the other hand, the explanation in terms of Eskimo needs for hospitality is not undermining. For believers in the code of hospitality are quite prepared to assert that feelings emerging from the need for reciprocity have a tendency to reveal how one should behave.

In sum, if a feeling of commitment to the moral point of view has the ultimate sources that Marx describes, it is bad evidence for the validity of that commitment. If his is as good a causal analysis as anyone has developed, the feeling is no basis for supposing that a defensible version of the moral point of view can somehow be constructed, capable of withstanding his other criticisms. Instead, one should set about replacing morality.

CHAPTER TWO

Replacing Morality

IF MARX did not believe that there were norms which dictated the right political choices for every historical situation, he certainly wanted political choices in his time to be guided by large-scale and long-term norms, not by caprice or short-term interests. "The Communists fight for the attainment of the immediate aims . . . of the working class; but in the movement of the present they also represent and take care of the future of that movement."[1] If he does not address his arguments for guiding principles to the needs and the basic desires of all, he is certainly concerned to address those arguments to the working class as a whole, along with as many as share in the interests of the working class on account of social situation or personal commitment. It is important to Marx that this intended audience is enormous. In a number of writings, he takes it to be an attraction of communism that it reduces the barriers to rational social choice by appealing to interests that most really share, and by constructing a society in which basic choices will eventually be guided by the interests of all as outlooks become increasingly harmonious.[2] In short, with respect to a very large audience, Marx advocates principles that are supposed to guide present-day social and political choice in the same way as a political morality.

I want to sketch the outlines of this set of principles, connecting them, at the very least, with familiar claims and arguments in Marx. My sketch will often be tentative and speculative, sometimes a construction of what Marx should have said if asked to clarify or defend what he did say. However,

---

[1] *Communist Manifesto*, p. 361.
[2] See, for example, *German Ideology*, pp. 55f., 66; *Communist Manifesto*, pp. 344, 353.

we need to investigate the system of norms implicit in Marx's writings in order to assess his actual attack on the moral point of view as a basis for social choice. Before abandoning that point of view, people ought to have a good idea of what is to replace it. After all, Marx's general style for choosing among institutions, strategies, and actions may have distinctive problems of its own, more severe than those for which he criticizes the moral point of view in politics.

In broadest outline, Marx's non-morality has the following shape. Marx's arguments for certain social arrangements are partly based on an appeal to a diverse assortment of goods: freedom, reciprocity, self-expression, the avoidance of pain and premature death and other relatively familiar goods which are obviously a part of Marx's case for socialism. However, the catalog of general goods does not entirely determine that socialism be chosen, when combined with the social facts as Marx sees them. Trade-offs between different aspects of these goods must be resolved by further specification and ranking. The specific scale of values entailing the choice of socialism cannot be defined or justified in a non-question-begging way. Marx's outlook is decent, since constrained by the catalog of goods. But it does not justify all urgent trade-offs by applying the catalog. *Basic social choices help to constitute the outlook, are not just its consequence.*

The adoption of socialist goals does not complete Marx's premises for social choice. His outlook is more articulated than that. His political strategy for achieving socialism, while partly recommended as a means, is independently supported by its intrinsic value, assessed through similarly complex connections with general human goods. Finally, the basic question of whether and how to participate in the movement is determined by a further, partly independent standard, a conception of what character traits are to be admired and cultivated. I will fill in this outline of a highly articulated outlook through a series of contrasts with simpler bases of choice, which are often ascribed to Marx.

GENERAL GOODS AND SOCIETAL GOALS

The foundations for the choice of social arrangements in Marx are usually assumed to resemble utilitarianism in form, if not in content. Social arrangements are to be judged by their capacity to maximize along some favored dimension or dimensions. On some accounts, this dimension is material productivity. The best social arrangement is the one that contributes the most to the development of material productive powers, either in the circumstances in question or in the long run. Alternatively, the standard of choice is supposed to be the capacity to maximize certain aspects of human experience: pleasure or happiness, if Marx is taken to be a utilitarian, or a plurality of independent goods, including reciprocity, self-expression and freedom.

In fact, basic societal choices in Marx are not determined by any logically prior maximizing standard. Consider, first, the productivity standard. As a description of a relation between successively evolving social forms, this standard is faithful to Marx's general statements about historical change. But as a standard of evaluation, it conflicts with several aspects of his writings. For one thing, if he had a productivity standard, his response to the violence, pain and drudgery imposed by past social arrangements would be to excuse them, as necessary to the heightening of productivity. The proper outcome would be a justification of Athenian slavery, rather than Marx's actual nonjudgment. In the second place, Marx, both early and late, attacks the one-sidedness and monotony of work characteristic of industrial capitalism, while acknowledging the contribution of industrial capitalism to the growth of productive powers.[3] Moreover, he portrays it as an advantage of socialism that people will be able to choose leisure over material production when this suits their preference.[4] It would be arbitrary for someone who acknowledges the importance of goods conflicting with

---

[3] *Economic and Philosophical Manuscripts*, p. 124; *Capital* I, pp. 340f, 604; *Critique of the Gotha Program*, p. 388.
[4] *Capital* III, p. 820.

material production to rate material productivity the sole measure of a social system's worth. Finally, the one-sidedness of a productivity standard does not even have the advantage of rendering people's political choices more determinate. Those who resist processes of productive change, for example, English workers opposed to the regimentation of industrial work, certain early utopian socialists, and Sepoy mutineers, make a positive contribution to history as Marx sees it, at least as much as those who develop the productive forces. Through resistance to productive change, workers may acquire the knowledge and the unity to make successful revolutions and to control a post-revolutionary society. Working-class unity is a result of processes increasing productivity. But it is based, in part, on resistance to the necessary costs of such progress.[5] Thus, a productivity standard would not tell most people what they ought to do in basic political choices.

I have already discussed certain distinctive problems of portraying Marx as a utilitarian. But Marx might still be taken to seek the maximization of each of a plurality of independent goods. This pluralist maximizing standard may not be effective for all societies, or justifiable to everyone. However, apart from this relativism, Marx's outlook would be an example of "ideal utilitarianism", like G.E. Moore's in *Principia Ethica*.

The problem with this interpretation is that it gives a commitment to general goals, not specified in terms of institutional arrangements, an absolute priority that it does not receive in Marx's writings. Certainly, Marx never presents his arguments in this ideal utilitarian style. More important, a criticism of this attempt to keep ultimate general goals separate and all determining is implicit in Marx's actual arguments: stated in general terms, the goals are too vague fully to determine basic social choices; there is no way to make them appropriately determinate, except by redefining them in terms of social choices that are partially independent of the general goals.

Consider, for example, the goal of freedom. A concern for freedom is certainly one of the reasons why people should take

---

[5] See *Communist Manifesto*, pp. 342f.; *Capital* I, chap. 15, sec. 5.

seriously Marx's descriptions of how capitalism works, and his comparisons of capitalism with socialist possibilities. A concern for freedom gives that sociology a bearing on choice. But someone might accept those social descriptions and reject socialism, if he or she puts enough weight on noninterference as an aspect of freedom, as against the possession of resources that make desires effective.

There is no reasonable way of specifying the emphasis on resource-freedom that a choice of socialism requires, without defining it as "sufficient emphasis to support the choice of socialism, given Marx's view of the facts." It will not do to say that Marx's standard of choice rates resource-freedom as always and intrinsically more important than noninterference-freedom. There are imaginable situations in which the interference required to maintain resource-freedom for most people is so pervasive and repellent to so many that Marx himself and his intended audience would opt for noninterference. Imagine that most workers were so deeply committed to capitalist success that a socialist state must constantly intervene to prevent them from trying to set up independent factories and farms. Even in the real world as Marx sees it, the case for socialism does not depend on a rigid, lexical priority for resource-freedom. To some people, it is a crucial aspect of the case for socialism that capitalism is apt to generate the direct and brutal forms of repression which Marx labeled "Caesarism" and "imperialism," later Marxists "fascism". They are deeply concerned with noninterference and need a specific empirical argument as a basis for the decision that capitalism does not have overriding advantages on this dimension. People for whom choice would be indeterminate apart from this factor surely are not excluded from Marx's intended audience.

An absolute priority among aspects of freedom would be too rigid. But there seems to be no other, more flexible rating that is general, that determines basic social choices in the present day, and that accurately expresses standards that people bring to those choices. In particular, quantitative ratings that are specific enough to render choice determinate are overspecific to the point of absurdity. Is resource-freedom supposed to trade for noninterference at a rate of six-to-one at the margin?

Marx's social choices are supposed to be justified among those concerned with freedom, reciprocity, the avoidance of suffering and other goods, *if* the emphases they place on different aspects of these goods are sufficient to support the choice of socialism. This circularity is not to be removed by a more careful definition of the required emphases. It corresponds to the logic of justification, here. People concerned in general with freedom, reciprocity, the avoidance of suffering, and other familiar goals are presented with an empirical argument about the inevitable consequences of capitalism and the possibilities for change under socialism. If they accept those arguments and respond with a basic social choice, it is usually a choice of socialism. That choice further defines their underlying goals. In an epistemological turn characteristic of both Marx and Hegel, rational people move from the general (the abstract goals) to the particular (the grasp of actual social consequences) and back to a revision of the general (the further specification of goals.) Similarly, the determination of goals by choices in Marx corresponds to the account of moral insight in Hegel's *Philosophy of Right*: the will transforms itself and renders itself determinate by reflective choice among increasingly concrete alternatives (see especially the Introduction.)

To a significant extent, the goods that socialism uniquely promotes must be specified and chosen as part of the choice of socialism itself. Thus, it was potentially misleading of me to say that Marx recommends social arrangements according to their tendency to enhance people's lives. There are diverse standards of enhancement, leading to different choices of social arrangements, possessed by actual rational people. None is uniquely reasonable, just as none is uniquely fair.

Conflicts among different aspects of freedom are especially important in present-day philosophical controversies over Marx and morality. For in his thoughtful and erudite contributions to these debates, George Brenkert has portrayed Marx as committed to a moral theory that is neither rights-based nor utilitarian: instead, Marx's standard is the promotion of freedom. ". . . Marx's analysis of capitalist private property is . . . a critique on behalf of freedom. . . . [I]f by 'moral theory' one will allow that we refer to a view which relates to some fundamental good for all humans and which is also of overriding importance, then there is no difficulty in saying that Marx had a moral theory and that freedom played a crucial role in it."[6]

Very likely, every aspect of freedom is *an* intrinsic good for all humans, or at least all sane ones. But one reason why social change is so hard is that different people rank these aspects differently, and arrangements favoring the rankings of some violate those of others. Very likely, everyone regards it as good for people to have the resources to pursue their goals, and good for people's self-interests to harmonize.[7] But people also care about noninterference and the zest of competition. Some care about the latter aspects enormously, so much so that their goal of freedom may be violated when the goal of others is fulfilled. If the moral point of view is to be a perspective from which such differences can be judged, there must be a neutral way of deciding among these rankings. I have argued, and Brenkert does not argue to the contrary, that this neutral method does not exist, for Marx.

These conflicts do not play a role in Brenkert's writings partly because of the heavy emphasis on Marx's vision of an ultimate communist society. "What is also required for genuine freedom is an end to the separation and conflict of interests which have characterized pre-communist societies."[8] No doubt, the conflicts that I have described would disappear at some point, if not at first, in the higher stage of socialism that Marx calls "communist society". But by itself this tells us nothing about what to do and what to change in our very precommunist world. Perhaps everyone would be happier if we were all brought up speaking Esperanto. This does not mean that I

[6] George Brenkert, "Freedom and Private Property in Marx" (originally in *Philosophy and Public Affairs* 8 [1979]), in M. Cohen, et al. *Marx, Justice, and History* (Princeton, 1980), pp. 86, 104.

[7] The latter is an aspect of freedom for Brenkert. See ibid., p. 99; and George Brenkert, "Marx and Utilitarianism," *Canadian Journal of Philosophy* 5 (1975), p. 430.

[8] "Freedom and Private Property in Marx," p. 99.

should learn Esperanto, or raise my children to speak it, or even that the costs of bringing about world Esperantic conversion are worth the gains. While ultimate goals are certainly important for Marx, to confine principled reflection on choice to the discernment of the best future society is to be the sort of utopian Marx condemns as writing recipes for the kitchens of the future.[9] Nor is it especially humane to judge present action solely by its effectiveness in bringing about the society in which the free development of each is a condition for the free development of all. At least if arguments of the next chapter are valid, Marx thought that conflict and coercion were necessary aspects of such change. All coercion that speeds the change is not thereby justified. The humane course is to deal humanely with these facts of conflict, not to ignore them, judging strategies solely by their tendency to produce ultimate harmony. While Brenkert dissociates his version of Marx from Kantian morality,[10] it is just this turning away from contemporary conflict that is the essence of Marx's dismissal of Kant: "Kant was satisfied with 'good will' alone, even if it remained entirely without result, and he transferred the *realization* of this good will, the harmony between it and the needs and impulses of the individual, to *the world beyond*. Kant's good will fully corresponds to the impotence, depression and wretchedness of the German burghers, whose petty interests were never capable of developing into the common, national interests of a class . . ."[11]

I have emphasized the goal of freedom partly because of its role in important interpretations of Marx, partly because of the relative familiarity of the ambiguities of freedom. But other general goals have similar indeterminacies, requiring revision through the investigation of specific social arrangements. For example, reciprocity cannot be promoted in every way whenever socialism is instituted. In many countries that are not technologically advanced, socialism would almost certainly require some official discrimination in favor of working-class

[9] *Capital* I, p. 26.
[10] "Freedom and Private Property in Marx," p. 104.
[11] *German Ideology*, p. 97; Marx's and Engels' emphases.

58

families and against formerly bourgeois families in the provision of higher education. It would be hypocritical, here, to claim that the child of a formerly wealthy family is being treated on a basis of reciprocity. Also, the desire of the formerly wealthy for expensive goods will not be given any special weight, even if it is so urgent and entrenched as to constitute a real need and even if special needs are elsewhere accorded special treatment. Neglect of, even scorn for bourgeois sensitivities is hardly a basis for reciprocity. While neither example is found in Marx, he would hardly have described the beginning of socialism as a "dictatorship of the proletariat" if he expected complete reciprocity to be the rule. (Cf. the description of a higher stage of socialism in the *Manifesto*: "an association in which the free development of each is the condition for the free development of all.")[12] Most people, if they accept Marxist accounts of the disruptions, social divisions and restrictions of life under capitalism would accept that the socialist alternative is preferable as a means of increasing reciprocity in society as a whole. But surely there is no calculus of reciprocity, based on a prior general standard, which justifies this choice.

This movement from the general to the specific and back to the revision of the general is not familiar in political philosophy and economics. It is utterly foreign to the academic theory of choice and decision. But it is ubiquitous in real-life choices. Consider a banal example of multidimensional choice along dimensions with no natural numerical measure, the choice of a car. Handling, acceleration, fuel economy, looks and comfort are all relevant. Given his or her expectations as to what alternatives will be encountered, a prospective buyer can often sketch in a rough way his or her priorities among these dimensions. But an unexpected car may be encountered which handles so well, let us say, that it is worth the loss in fuel economy, even though that had seemed more important. It is bad psychology to claim that in every such case the prospective buyer has shifted from one set of goals to another. Rather, they

[12] *Communist Manifesto*, p. 353.

have become clarified in light of the facts. It is myth making, rather than science, to suppose that the clarified goals can always be expressed without reference to particular car models. Given the complexities of the choice, such a standard would have to take the form, "At this level of handling, a loss of a unit of handling will begin to be acceptable if the following gains are made along other dimensions: three units of comfort, . . ." But any number assigned to the degree of fulfillment of a dimension of choice, here, is arbitrary, a numerical mask over the real facts of preferences among *particular* models. In effect, the neoclassical economist's paradigm of preferences among different baskets of commodities, each kind available in certain numbers of identical units, is being pressed into service where it does not belong. In the real world of choice, the decision, say, for a certain Renault over a certain Fiat may be supported by the willingness to sacrifice the greater fuel economy of the one particular model for the superior handling of the other, a preference not accurately specifiable in more general terms. Similarly, in social choice the essential trade-offs are guided by a willingness to make sacrifices for gains specifiable only in terms of particular available alternatives.

THE PROCESS OF CHANGE

If my reconstruction of Marx's logic is valid, commitment to a catalog of general goods, together with acceptance of his empirical arguments, would not make one answer to the question, "What social arrangements are best at present?" rationally compelling for all. In this way, a commitment to socialism is part of the foundations of Marx's outlook. Are there other, independent commitments, similarly foundational, and necessary for a resolution of equally basic questions? Or, once the societal goals are chosen, are the other basic choices rationally determined? In particular, is the effective achievement of socialism now the only, or at least the overriding consideration in the choice of strategies and actions? If so, Marx is, once again, fairly close to utilitarianism in the form of his basic standard. The ultimate standard is the efficiency with which a good is pursued—in this case, the speed with which socialism is reached.

Marx never explicitly answers these questions. But the purely instrumental standard is implausible, given extremely common attitudes that Marx can be assumed to share. And it is unnecessary, given Marx's beliefs about the means to socialism. In the best reconstruction of his arguments, Marx is recommending his conception of the workers' movement both as something that effectively creates socialism, and as something with positive value in the context of capitalism. Both features play an important, independent role.

On the purely instrumental standard, where only the goal is important, the secure establishment of socialism is to be pursued if it requires, say, five generations of enormous, avoidable suffering, with widespread intentional brutality and self-brutalization. The losses in the intermediate future are outweighed by the long-term gains. Few people are willing to accept such an extreme instrumentalism. In his writings, including his private correspondence, Marx, though he sometimes justifies workers' violence that the press condemns, never appeals to the consideration that everything is excused if it contributes to socialism. He seems to have shared in the general rejection of extreme instrumentalism.

More important, in Marx's nonutilitarian framework, there is no motivation for this instrumentalism. Utilitarians can base their instrumentalism on an argument about rational choice: people's experiences are all that a rational person cares about in the final analysis; so the rational choice of an alternative solely depends on how it affects experiences; thus, a means is no more or less desirable than the experiential results of adopting it. This argument may be wrong, but it is worth taking seriously. It extrapolates from a plausible model for rational self-interested choice. A theory that makes self-interested rationality continuous with socially responsible rationality is certainly attractive, especially in light of the distinctive problems of rights-based morality. However, an instrumentalism basing everything on the promotion of a specific social arrangement has no such appeal. It is not at all plausible that the institutional end results of political processes are all that a rational person cares about. No doubt, effects on long-term outcomes are important constraints on choices of courses of action. But reflection on feasible means of reaching a social goal might lead to a new choice of social goals. No argument from a model for self-interested choice makes such reflections look unreasonable. Indeed, at analogous levels of specificity, self-interested choosers often revise their goals after reflection on feasible means.

Admittedly, on a pessimistic assessment Marx might have adopted an extreme instrumentalism as his way out of a dilemma: the concerns that attract us to socialism make any feasible means of attaining this goal repellent. This is not Marx's view, however. Communists, he emphasizes, lead important fights for reforms, even while they connect them with long-term goals.[13] Were it not for these reform struggles, the economic pressures of capitalism, even apart from its pressures toward war, would cause most people "to be degraded to one level mass of broken wretches past salvation."[14] Moreover, aside from reforms that are won, the workers' movement that Marx supports is said to be a humanizing movement on account of the cooperation, internationalism, rationality and initiative that it prompts. "The working class . . . know that in order to work out their own emancipation . . . they will have to pass through long struggles, through a series of historical processes, transforming circumstances and men."[15]

As Marx conceives of revolution, it involves disruption, violence and "necessary measures for intimidating the mass of the bourgeoisie."[16] At the same time, the process enhances the lives of participants on balance, because of the way in which solidarity and self-respect are heightened and broadened. This overall assessment is not dictated by some general ranking of goods and evils. It is a response to the actual complexities of

[13] *Communist Manifesto*, p. 361.
[14] *Wages, Price and Profit*, p. 75.
[15] *Civil War in France*, p. 558.
[16] Marx to Domela-Nieuwenhuis, February 22, 1881, *Selected Correspondence*, p. 318.

62

the case, like the choice of socialism as I have described it. In short, the workers' movement is to be promoted not just because of the society or the general goods it produces, but on accout of its internal and specific value.

A MODEL OF CHARACTER

Before, I argued that Marx's general goals could not dictate the choice of a social arrangement when supplemented by arguments that would be rationally compelling to every normal person who possesses appropriate evidence. The goals must be further specified in response to the facts revealed by empirical argument. Then, I argued that a preference for socialism did not determine the choice among political means to that goal. Conforming to Marx's style of reasoning, someone might reasonably be concerned with the intrinsic character of a movement, besides the speed with which it moved toward socialism. Now, I want to argue that the repertoire of standards for choice is still incomplete. The basic questions of social and political life still cannot be answered by adopting the above standards and adding arguments that are rationally compelling to all who are committed to the standards. For the question of whether to take part in the movement, in ways that are required for its success, is not yet settled.

Suppose that socialism would improve the life of every worker. Still, it is true of every worker that socialism might triumph, to his or her benefit, even if he or she does not take an active part in the struggle. If the risks of participation were not severe, one might regard the free rider as not really accepting the standards previously introduced, the desirability of socialism and of the workers' movement that Marx describes. But the achievement of socialism requires substantial risks on the part of many people. So people can say without hypocrisy, "I think that the goal and movement are for the best, but I will stand aside." For example, in his writings on the Commune, Marx presents "the heroic self-sacrifice"[17] of the Com-

---

[17] *Civil War in France*, p. 568.

munards as a necessary episode in the struggle for socialism, scolding his friend Kugelmann for philistine neglect of this aspect of the struggle.[18] Immediate self-interest and approval of the workers' movement are too narrow a motivation for the success of that movement. Admittedly, if it were true that workers have nothing to lose but their chains, no special outlook would be needed to justify the risky choices, given the alleged advantages of socialism. But, as Marx must have known when he wrote the *Manifesto*, workers have other things to lose in the revolutionary process. They may lose their jobs, be imprisoned, or be killed, not to mention the torture of revolutionaries and their families, which was much rarer in Marx's gentler era. Perhaps, when he wrote the line about having nothing to lose, Marx was influenced by the theory of wages he held at the time, according to which actual wages were bound to decline to the level of bare physical survival, often dropping below it.[19] In that case, a new standard of motivation is at least required by the later Marx, since he had rejected this "iron law of wages" by 1865 at the latest.[20]

Marx's general program cannot succeed unless many people accept risks that are not adequately motivated by a sincere desire that his goals and strategy be accomplished. His politics require further basic commitments, not dictated by the others, further commitments implicit in a certain model of character. This is the character that Marx associated with the hero Prometheus and saw embodied in generations of class-conscious workers, including Chartists, the participants in the Silesian weavers' uprising, the workers of Paris, Berlin and Vienna in 1848–49, and the men and women of the Paris Commune. The development of this character is central to the capsule history of the modern working class in the *Manifesto*.[21] As portrayed there, and in Marx's historical vignettes, it unites hatred of oppressors with concern for the oppressed, truculence where

[18] April 12, 1871 in *Selected Correspondence*, p. 247. See also *Civil War in France*, pp. 569, 574.

[19] See *Communist Manifesto*, p. 345.

[20] See *Wages, Price and Profit*, pp. 71f., 75; *Capital* I, p. 168; *Critique of the Gotha Program*, pp. 391f.

[21] *Communist Manifesto*, pp. 340–45.

interests are basically opposed with a positive desire to co-operate elsewhere, discipline with creativity and tolerance for risks. There is no question that Marx admired this combination of traits and sought to encourage it. The logic of Marx's argument gives this admiration and encouragement an independent role in his outlook.

Some of the most important questions about Marx's replacement for morality concern this model of character. For one thing, how can he expect and recommend widespread subordination of immediate self-interest, while criticizing the philanthropic attitude of the "True Socialists"? In a widely read article, Allen Buchanan has argued that Marx fails to answer this question. In Buchanan's view, Marx has no detailed and plausible account of revolutionary motivation that can solve the problem of proletarian "free riders." "Marx's claim to a non-moral, strictly scientific analysis of capitalism would seem to be in harmony with his account of revolutionary motivation. [H]owever, . . . Marx's account of revolutionary motivation is extremely weak and . . . remedying its defects may require significant revisions in his social theory."[22] If an adequate account of revolutionary motivation can be given in the general framework of Marx's theories and social goals (Buchanan has doubts about this possibility), the first step is "conceding a significant role to moral principles" as a basis for socialist arguments.[23]

Buchanan's objection is not that class-centered interests have in fact been rendered ineffective by divisions that Marx saw as ideological, for example, racial and ethnic antagonisms. Nor is he appealing to the actual resilience of capitalism since Marx's time, either to alleged ameliorative trends or to the failure of revolution in advanced capitalist countries.[24] Rather, he claims that Marx has no account of workers' psychology that could make the necessary risk taking rational, even assuming that his

---

[22] Allen Buchanan, "Revolutionary Motivation and Rationality" (originally in *Philosophy and Public Affairs* 9 [1979]), in Cohen, *Marx, Justice, and History*, p. 264.

[23] Ibid., p. 286.

[24] See ibid., p. 267.

views are otherwise correct.[25] Because it cuts so deep, Buchanan's challenge is squarely addressed to the concerns of this
chapter, and to the larger project of providing an acceptable
framework for replacing the moral point of view as a basis for
social choice.

If Marx's replacement for morality as a source of motivations
is inconsistent with his arguments against morality and compatible, plausible psychological claims, that is a serious objection to his attempt to undermine the moral point of view in
politics. Indeed, such a gap would cast doubt on the whole
enterprise of criticizing the moral point of view, not just his
own effort in that direction. In general, such efforts arouse the
suspicion that a radical departure from the moral point of view
will avoid brutality or callousness only at the cost of inconsistency, relying on the moral considerations it officially criticizes or tacitly assuming a community of interests that it officially denies. As the most humane and detailed departure
from the moral point of view, Marx'x political outlook is a
useful test case. If it is not coherent, in the indicated ways,
the general suspicion that brutality or callousness will be
avoided at the cost of incoherence is strongly confirmed. If it
is coherent, it may provide a useful model for other non-mor-
alities, based on somewhat different assessments of the social
facts. For, as we shall see, the factural assumptions of Marx's
case against morality (in contrast to his specific alternative to
it) are relatively uncontroversial.

Marx certainly wants to have it both ways, locating a motivation for revolution that is neither personal self-interest nor
altruistic equal concern for all. The point is made explicitly in
The German Ideology: "[T]he communists do not put egoism
against self-sacrifice or self-sacrifice against egoism, nor do
they express this contradiction theoretically either in its sen-
timental or in its highflown ideological form. . . . The communists do not preach *morality* at all, such as Stirner preaches
so extensively. They do not put to people the moral demand:
love one another, do not be egoists, etc.: on the contrary, they

[25] Ibid., p. 268.

are very well aware that egoism, just as much as self-sacrifice, is in definite circumstances a necessary form of the self-assertion of individuals."[26]

There is no logical contradiction in accepting self-sacrifice as a rational form of self-assertion while rejecting morality. People can make sacrifices not out of equal concern for the interests of all mankind, but out of a commitment to upholding working-class interests or the interests of the vast majority of mankind whose interest is the triumph of the working class. After all, when parents make sacrifices for their children, they need not be motivated by morality. Still, though there is no logical contradiction, there is now, as Buchanan insists, an urgent need for a rationale. Why should Marx suppose that class interest is an effective basis for change, as opposed to moral concerns, when class interest requires so much sacrifice?

In part, Marx is relying on the plausibility of the following idea. As a basis for self-sacrifice to bring about social change, morality is less effective, for most people, than concern for a group with whom one shares common enemies and with whom one frequently cooperates on the basis of real and growing reciprocity. In part, he seeks to make this idea more compelling, as it applies to contemporary societies, by pointing out its good fit with contemporary events, above all, the revolutions of 1848–49. In his accounts of those revolutions (and, later, the Paris Commune), he constantly contrasts the heroism of those taking part in relatively class-conscious worker-led uprisings with the timidity of their liberal bourgeois compatriots, whose moral concern was engaged but whose class interest was ambiguous.

However, he also needs something more general than the piecemeal historical accounts and more empirical than the plausibility argument. He needs a theoretical account of modern workers' history describing mechanisms specially apt to produce class-centered concerns that are specially apt to support socialist revolution. This he does most explicitly in the account of the development of workers' solidarity which dominates Part

[26] *German Ideology*, pp. 104f.

67

I of the *Communist Manifesto*. As capitalism develops, it creates and strengthens solidarity among workers and related lower-middle-class groups. Within the working class, capitalism breaks down barriers of locale and status, unites people in far-flung interdependent production that encourages interdependent resistance, and concentrates and coordinates the capitalist power that workers resist. Here are a few details from this long and complex account of how "the bourgeoisie . . . produces . . . its own grave diggers:"[27]

"Modern industry has converted the little workshop of the patriarchal master into the great factory of the industrial capitalist. Masses of laborers, crowded into the factory, are organized like soldiers. . . . The more openly this despotism proclaims gain to be its aim, the more hateful and the more embittering it is. . . . The proletariat goes through various stages of development. . . . At first the contest is carried on by individual laborers, then by the workpeople of a factory, then by the operatives of one trade in one locality against the individual capitalist who exploits them. . . . At this stage the laborers still form an incoherent mass scattered over the whole country, and broken up by their mutual competition. . . . But with the development of industry, the proletariat not only increases in number; it becomes concentrated in greater masses, its strength grows, and it feels that strength more. The various interests and conditions of life within the ranks of the proletariat are more and more equalized, in proportion as machinery obliterates all distinctions of labor, and nearly everywhere reduces wages to the same low level. . . . Thereupon the workers begin to form combinations (Trades Unions) against the bourgeoisie . . . Now and then the workers are victorious, but only for a time. The real fruit of their battle lies, not in the immediate result, but in the ever-expanding union of the workers. This union is helped on by the improved means of communication. . . . The advance of industry, whose involuntary promoter is the bourgeoisie, replaces the isolation of the workers, due to competition, by their revolutionary combination, due to association."[28]

This is not a story of how self-interest in coordinated resistance finally emerged where none existed before. Nation-

[27] *Communist Manifesto*, p. 345.
[28] Ibid., 341, 342, 343, 345.

wide strikes for better conditions would certainly have been in the interests of the earliest victims of the Industrial Revolution. Though there is a brief reference to improved means of communication, this is not primarily the story of new technical means of coordination. Rather, industrial development is said to create new forms of interaction ("association") among workers leading to broader and more determined cooperation in resistance, ultimately "revolutionary combination." The psychological mechanisms seem to be the following. From the first, workers resist capitalist efforts to cut wages, speed up work, and the like, but they first do so through individual protests, the defense of special privileges, and the withholding of special skills. As those special skills and privileges become largely obsolete through industrialization, cooperation becomes a much more effective resource. Some workers ask others to help them in resistance, at least by not accepting strikebreaking work. They expect and often receive a positive response from those who can expect to benefit from reciprocal help later. As different factories become more interdependent, as control becomes concentrated in larger firms and as communication improves, the opportunities for such reciprocity spread. Meanwhile, cooperation in resistance makes an increasingly powerful impact, on account of its growing scope and the economy-wide effects of industrial conflict in crucial industries. The growing cooperation and a growing awareness of the similar situation of other proletarians contribute to a heightened willingness to take risks for others in order to advance common interests. Ultimately, they lead to "revolutionary combination." This is a story of the growth of self-sacrificing concern for others, but not of the growth of moral commitment. For the others are allies in conflicts that split society, not the objects of equal concern for all members of society.

In *Capital*, this process is illustrated in detail and at great length. The economic struggles of preindustrial proletarians rely on the withholding of special individual skills. They are ultimately defeated through the introduction of industrial equipment.[29] The immediate result is more intense, longer, and more monotonous labor. But the breakdown of divisions within the workplace and the concentration of control over production in fewer and fewer hands give rise to the solidarity expressed in the fight for the ten-hour day and the subsequent growth of trades unionism. As Marx tells the story in *Capital*, the Industrial Revolution compels and facilitates working-class cooperation at the same time as it increases the oppressiveness of work. "[T]he general conversion of numerous isolated small industries into a few combined industries carried on upon a large scale . . . the concentration of capital and the exclusive predominance of the factory system . . . [the destruction of] both the ancient and the transitional forms behind which the dominion of capital is in part concealed . . . the combination on a social scale of the processes of production" all provide "along with the elements for the formation of a new society, the forces for exploding the old one."[30]

The special power of commitments based on the historically developing ties is crucial for changing society. For such change, Marx believes, requires risky actions, involving boldness and initiative on the part of many people acting at the same time against a better-armed, well-coordinated enemy. Humanitarian sympathy for everyone does not supply a strong enough motive, and no historical process sufficiently strengthens it. Indeed, if such humanitarianism is too pervasive, it weakens the bases of necessary actions. Thus, communism, as against

---

[29] See *Capital* I, chaps. 14–15. Marx cites Andrew Ure as a shrewd judge of this process. "Ure says of a machine used in calico printing: 'At length the capitalists sought deliverance from this intolerable bondage' [namely, the, in their eyes, burdensome terms of their contracts with the workmen] 'in the resources of sciences, and were speedily reinstated in their legitimate rule, that of the head over the inferior members.' Speaking of an invention for dressing warps: 'Then the combined malcontents, who fancied themselves impregnably intrenched behind the old lines of division of labor, found their flanks turned and their defenses rendered useless by the new mechanical tactics, and were obliged to surrender at discretion" (p. 411).

[30] *Capital* I, p. 472. The immediate context is an analysis of the effects of the extension of factory legislation to all trades. However, Marx is clearly describing general tendencies in the growth of industrial capitalism that are somewhat hastened by the factory laws through their destructive impact on small and marginal employers.

70

similar prescriptions based on morality, is not "an ideal to which reality will have to adjust itself", but "the real movement which abolishes the present state of things."[31] Socialism and communism require further changes in the bases of solidarity, corresponding to new forms and levels of cooperation produced by further struggles.[32]

Speaking of "the goods of community, fraternity and solidarity which they experience in the common struggle," Buchanan says, "Marx nowhere suggests that such derivative goods of association, rather than the proletariat's interest in the overthrow of the system, are a major factor in the revolutionary motivation of the proletariat. . . . Marx fails to develop an account of how the competitive, egoistic barriers to these goods . . . can ultimately be overcome. Nor does he attempt to assign a significant role to them. . . ."[33] In fact, the growth of solidarity among workers is a major subject of Marx's two most famous works, and, in both, a major factor in revolutionary motivation. Probably Marx would not say (in any case, he should not) that people take risks in revolutions because the *experience* of solidarity rates so high as compared with goods they jeopardize. That is not how solidarity works, in social classes, in families, or, for that matter, in happy academic departments. People who help one another, perhaps in nonself-sacrificing ways, may come to care about one another enough to motivate substantial sacrifices. The caring is the main motivation, not the desired experience of a good. Here, in another and different way, the commercial model of rationality in academic decision theory makes Marx's point implausible or obscure. As for the barriers of competition, Marx thinks that rank-and-file trade unionists have been right to believe that success in collective economic struggle is more likely to affect a worker's economic well-being than individual competitive striving. Solidarity is essential for such success. Without even limited success in ·collective economic struggles, workers "would be degraded to one level mass of broken wretches past

[31] *German Ideology*, p. 57.
[32] Ibid., p. 57; *Civil War in France*, p. 558.
[33] Buchanan, "Revolutionary Motivation and Rationality," p. 276.

71

salvation."[34] Marx may be wrong in this denial of the reign of market forces. But this is the most substantial difference between Marxist and neoclassical economics, not the gap in Marx's theories that Buchanan discerns.

Put in very general terms, Marx's analogue to moral psychology involves three main tendencies:

1. If a large social group is faced with a common enemy and cooperation in resistance is a necessary means to reduce much subordination and suffering for the group, some members will inaugurate that resistance, hoping for reciprocity from others.
2. If people in that group have benefited from such initiatives and are appealed to for cooperation, most would find their self-esteem reduced, if they stood aside as free riders. As a result, some will reciprocate, when there is a reasonable prospect that the group will benefit from their actions.
3. The broader past cooperation has been within the group, the more important its benefits for the group have been and the more likely are gains from expanded cooperation, the greater the subsequent increase in cooperation will be.

Of course, there are countervailing psychological tendencies, as well, competitiveness, for example, or patriotism uniting groups whose interests really are antagonistic. Marx thinks that the three tendencies toward solidarity will actually lead to "revolutionary combination" among workers, given the persuasion and leadership of modern socialists and the resources for effective cooperation produced by modern industrial capitalism. That this is so is his inference from the history of workers' resistance and rebellion, a highly specific complement to the general psychology.

Marx does not explain why people have the general tendencies. But then, no one denies their existence. It *would* be a charge against Marx if he appealed to cooperative tendencies that would make moral concerns an effective basis for change. But to make the jump from class solidarity to morality is to forget that *equal* concern for *all* is part of specifically moral

[34] *Wages, Price and Profit*, p. 228.

motivations. Marx's account of class solidarity faces empirical problems and his prediction of revolution may prove wrong. Still, the theory of solidarity is a useful model for any outlook that avoids the moral point of view while calling for changes requiring self-sacrifice.

Marx has a distinguished predecessor in his theory of motivation. Ironically, he is Hume on the sources of respect for rules of property. "I observe, that it will be in my interest to leave another in the possession of his goods, *provided* he will act in the same manner with regard to me. He is sensible of a like interest in the regulation of his conduct. When this common sense of interest is mutually expressed, and is known to both, it produces a suitable resolution and behavior. . . . [T]he actions of each of us have reference to those of the other and are performed upon the supposition that something is to be performed on the other part."[35] The sentiments which spontaneously arise from such cooperation incline us to respect property in particular cases in which our private interest is thereby infringed, even in cases where secrecy will prevent ramifications.[36] The content of the coordinating rules to one side, the main difference with Marx is that Hume's kind of cooperation is said to benefit all, and, when we contemplate it, we are supposed to be moved to approval by impartial sympathy for all affected; that is why the approval is moral.[37] If Marx's theory of history is Hegel's set on its feet, his psychology, here, is Hume's in the discussion of property, removed from the terrain of morality and stability and applied to cooperation in attacking the status quo.

The answer to the first question about Marx's moral outlook, "How can it work without lapsing into the moral outlook?" makes another especially urgent: Do Marx's model revolutionaries have respect and concern for strangers who are not allied with the proletariat? I argued before, in partial defense of Derek Allen, that everyone, for Marx, is prima facie a proper

[35] David Hume, *A Treatise of Human Nature*, ed. L. Selby-Bigge (Oxford, 1973), III.2.ii.490. See also p. 498.
[36] Ibid., III.2.i.480f.
[37] Ibid., p. 500.

object of some concern. But this in itself might seem to conflict with Marx's emphasis on class solidarity. Even more worrisome is the problem of how much conern is appropriate. Certainly, general, precise but nonegalitarian rules, "100 units of concern for proletarians, 60 for small farmers, 5 for nonvicious capitalists," seem both callous and silly.

Probably, the balance between humanitarianism and narrowness is best understood in a causal way, in terms of a model of character formation. The character that Marx recommends is the product of certain experiences and interactions: love and reciprocity sufficient to create a willingness to make sacrifices for others even outside of one's personal acquaintance, the hatred of oppression and angry contempt for oppressors, and, finally, the mutual well-wishing that arises from cooperation against oppression. The attitudes to which such a personal history gives rise, when informed by awareness of relevant facts, determine the levels of concern of which Marx approves.

In logical form, this model is similar to ideal-observer theories of morality. The right decision is the one that would be made by those appropriately qualified in cognitive and motivational makeup, when they are fully informed. However, the choice of qualifications, here, is not justifiable to all or justifiable from unbiased perspectives. Nonetheless, despite the element of bias in defining this outlook, the concerns of people from other classes would surely be given some weight by those who have this outlook.

Of course, this model is a speculation, an attempt to describe one basis for Marx's various specific statements of approval and disapproval. It is not a theory that Marx himself asserts. What is important is that Marx does not have to abandon his ideal of the proletarian revolutionary when he shows concern for those who make no contribution to proletarian struggles.

For many, the absence of fundamental rules dictating the measure of appropriate concern is the most troubling aspect of Marx's non-morality. There is no equivalent to the injunction to treat everyone as an end, not a means, or to maximize the happiness of all, with equal sympathy for each, or to adopt the standpoint of the original position. Unless people consult

74

such general rules as ultimate constraints, it might seem that excesses of revenge and envy are bound to be encouraged.

This worry depends, I think, on a moral psychology that Marx attacks and that few accept today. According to this psychology, our tendency to accept constraints of conscience has a source that is different in kind from the history of love and hatred, cooperation and conflict that otherwise produces our adult character. Moral self-restraint is based on a special inborn source of motivations, such as respect for moral law in Kant. In fact, reflection on social and historical diversity makes this hypothesis implausible. The most productive research in the psychology and anthropology of morals has depended on abandoning it.

Suppose that our tendency to conform to moral principles, in deeds and emotions, has the same origins as other character traits, grumpiness, say, or a cheerful disposition, fearfulness, diffidence, or extraversion. Then the actual power of morality to constrain revenge and vicious envy need not be greater than the mixture of love and hate, cooperation and conflict that goes into the making of Marx's revolutionaries. Indeed, it is surprising, on reflection, that people have believed that moral constraints have irreplaceable powers. Certain deep aversions concerning defecation or eating, together with non-moral ties between parents and children are, after all, among the most deeply inhibiting constraints, even though they do not depend on moral conscientiousness and may have little to do with rules.

While respect for general rules of appropriate concern has no ultimate role for Marx, derivative rules might be adopted. We may want to impose rules on ourselves to prevent the violation of our basic commitments in the heat of the moment, to regularize social expectations, or to reduce conflict through standard cooperative procedures. These instrumental rationales are as available to Marx's revolutionaries as to others. Of course, they will be adopted as the facts of the case warrant. It may be that certain decisions, say, are better made heatedly than by consulting general rules.

In sum, we should accept Marx's model character type as complex and stable, at least as complex and stable as Aristotle's great-hearted man or Rousseau's Emile. This is not to say that Marx's model revolutionaries are just like liberal humanitarians except for different goals and different strategies. They are less upset at beating up police in strikes and uprisings. They are less disturbed at the real excesses that inevitably accompany revolutions. But they are, on the whole, at least as warm and kind as other people and quite concerned with the welfare of most nonproletarian strangers.

THE STRUCTURE OF A NON-MORALITY

My description of Marx's positive outlook is now complete. It can be seen as a hierarchy of independent but related recommendations, passing from a catalog of general human goods to a description of social arrangements to be pursued, to a description of the workers' movement that achieves them, to a sketch of the character traits that motivate individual choices. A lower-level standard is partly, but not wholly determined by the next highest. Most, but not all, rational people who are committed to the higher-level choice will be led to make the lower-level choice if they accept Marx's evidence and social theories. Similarly, the higher, more general standards eliminate some, but not all, rivals to the lower, more specific ones. Someone committed to the general catalog will not choose the elitist goals of a Nietzsche, but might, in principle, opt for a form of capitalist democracy. Someone who regards a Marxist workers' movement as desirable could not coherently lead the life of a Christian evangelist. But he or she might stay on the sidelines, wishing the movement well without taking part.

This is not the structure of Bentham's or Mill's outlook or, for that matter, Moore's in the ideal utilitarianism of *Principia Ethica*. Too little is determined by the general catalog of goods, combined with the injunction that they be promoted. But Marx's outlook does resemble, in form, that of the philosopher he seems most to have admired, Aristotle.[38] Aristotle recom-

---

[38] For other parallels, see Richard W. Miller, "Marx and Aristotle: A Kind of Consequentialism," in K. Nielsen, ed., *Marx and Morality, Canadian Journal of Philosophy*, supp. vol. 7 (1981).

mends an array of goods to be pursued, the active exercise of various human capacities that are, in the final analysis, ranked in a rigid order. But despite this ranking, the catalog of goods does not dictate the choices among rival constitutions in the *Politics*. It does not dictate the choice between arrangements promoting a life of excellence for some at the cost of a degraded existence for most, on the one hand, and arrangements affording most a life of moderate virtue, on the other hand. In particular, Aristotle's list of human goods does not justify his preference for a slave-owners' aristocracy over a farmers' democracy.[39] In fact, reflection on the consequences of the various arrangements leads him to single out the aristocratic arrangement as best. Similarly, though the catalog of goods and the political recommendations put important constraints on ratings of character traits, they hardly support the more detailed ideals, expressed with almost novelistic precision, in Book IV of the *Nichomachean Ethics*. The general ranking of faculties does exclude approval of those who prefer eating to creative initiatives. But it hardly dictates the combination of generosity and aloofness, risk taking and rational deliberation embodied in Aristotle's great-hearted man.

In his moral epistemology Aristotle's outlook is much closer than Marx's to the paradigmatic moral point of view. For his standards are presented as rationally compelling for all and determinate for all social situations in which rational people can establish a constitution. But in their internal structure, his recommendations depart both from rights-based morality and from utilitarianism in ways that parallel Marx's outlook.

Probably, Marx's outlook also has the same structure as the political thinking of most people, Marxist or anti-Marxist, as against the simpler standards that philosophers have pursued. This helps to explain the fact that Marx, quite apart from his attacks on morality, sometimes attacks philosophy as such,

---

[39] Aristotle *Politics* 1318b6–1319a19; VII: 9. The argument for Aristotle's aristocratic ideal cannot just be that the slaves are to be those congenital retardates whom he takes to be slaves by nature. The ideal aristocratic society includes degraded, noncitizen, but nonslave artisans and tradesmen, in addition to the slaves who do the brute work of farming. And no one is an artisan or tradesman by nature. (See *Pol.* 1260b1f., 1289b32f., 1328b33–40.)

most colorfully in the quip, "Philosophy stands to the investigation of reality as masturbation to sexual love."[40]

ALLEN WOOD'S ALTERNATIVE

Among English-speaking philosophers, the current revival of interest in Marx's moral views stems, in large part, from Allen Wood's thoughtful and provocative article, "The Marxian Critique of Justice." Among sympathetic interpretations of Marx' views of morality, his is now the most influential one that takes seriously Marx's anti-moral theme. Admittedly, Wood's primary concern is with justice and allied notions of equality, rights and fairness, not with morality as a whole. Still, his interpretation of Marx on justice contrasts with the one suggested by the interpretation of Marx on morality that I have defended. In any case, in a reply to his critics, "Marx on Right and Justice," and in his book, *Karl Marx*, Wood has further developed his account of Marx's critique of morality as such.[41] In discussing Wood's views, I will emphasize my differences, hoping that the large areas of agreement are sufficiently clear. Those differences will illuminate a surprising connection between the dispute over Marx's criticism of morality and justice and the other leading interpretative debate at present, the dispute as to the ways in which Marx was or was not an economic determinist. My alternative view of Marx on justice and morality depends on ascribing a more independent role to political struggles than Wood's interpretation can allow.

According to Wood's interpretation, "the standards of right and justice appropriate to a given society are those which in fact fulfill a function in social production."[42] They "correspond" to it, and "harmonize" with it.[43] Wood's remarks on

[40] *German Ideology*, p. 103.
[41] See Allen Wood "The Marxian Critique of Justice" (originally in *Philosophy and Public Affairs* 1 [1972]) and "Marx on Right and Justice" (originally in *Philosophy and Public Affairs* 9[1979]), in Cohen, *Marx, Justice, and History*; and *Karl Marx* (London, 1981).
[42] "Right and Justice," p. 107.
[43] Ibid. see also "Critique," pp. 15–19.

the role of justice support the following conception of this functional fit: something is just in virtue of its conformity to standards of justice the propagation and enforcement of which best serve to stabilize and defend the current mode of production. As he says in his book, "The laws and moral precepts which arise out of the existing order are charged with the function of protecting that order. . . ."[44] Thus, if the justice of institutions in a capitalist society is in question, the appropriate standards include freedom of contract and formal equality before the law. But they do not include equality of economic resources or the equal right to work of all able-bodied people, since the latter standards are economically incompatible with the structure of capitalist production. Wood concludes that Marx regarded the characteristic institutions of capitalism as just. Of course, Marx did not approve of them. His taking them to be just reflects his view that justice is an aspect of social regulation, not a standard of judgment.

In effect, the previous discussion of Marx on rights-based morality was an argument against taking the notion of justice as a tool for reasonable and informed moral criticism of basic institutions. To this extent, I have been extracting Marx's rationale for claims that Wood locates in his writings. (I will soon be challenging the rationale Wood offers.) What I have not said, and now want to dispute, is that Marx regarded justice and allied notions as corresponding to something real, though unconnected with rational approval. Strictly and literally, such terms as "justice" do not refer to any real property of basic institutions, including the stabilizing property of interest to Wood's Marx. If Marx uses such terms, it is to refer to people's moral beliefs or to single out phenomena which those beliefs would force them to approve. But he is no more acknowledging that institutions really are just than, say, Freud acknowledged that demons really had existed when he claimed that demonic possession in the Middle Ages was schizophrenia based on infantile guilt and fear.

[44] *Karl Marx*, p. 141.

The texts in which Marx uses such terms as "justice," "rights," and "equality" do not resolve this disagreement. They are as one would expect on either view. Often, he is attacking people who use these terms as devices for moral criticism. The terms tend to be either flanked with quotation marks, relativized explicitly to a mode of production or moral outlook, or used in passages with a sarcastic edge that at least verges on irony. Some examples are: "Do not the bourgeois assert that the present-day distribution is 'fair'? And is it not, in fact, the only 'fair' distribution on the basis of the present-day mode of production?"[45] "This sphere that we are deserting, within whose boundaries the sale or purchase of labor-power goes on, is in fact a very Eden of the innate rights of man. There alone rule Freedom, Equality, Property and Bentham."[46] Nowhere is there a nonrelativized, unequivocal statement that capitalism is just. This is what one would expect if Marx does not regard justice as a fit category either for political recommendations or for scientific analysis. He would still be eager to connect his own reasoning with more typical discourse, within which notions of justice prominently figure. Occasionally, in arguing against those who condemn capitalism for being unjust, he would speak of institutions and practices as just, when what he literally means is that they are not unjust and would be just if basic presuppositions of justice-talk were valid. His use of "just," here, is like an atheist's use of "God" when he says, "God must be evil, since He is all-powerful and little babies die painful deaths."

The state of the texts also fits Wood's interpretation almost as well. Even if Marx regarded justice as a scientific category, he would be well-aware of its usual normative implications, while finding them inappropriate. The use of quotation marks or an ironic tone would often serve as a warning that the usual implications of reference to justice should not be drawn.

The issue between Wood's sociological interpretation and my no-justice interpretation cannot be resolved just by sifting through the texts in which the key words are used. Rather,

[45] *Critique of the Gotha Program*, p. 322.
[46] *Capital* I, p. 172.

we need to ask which assessment of typical moral discourse is supported by Marx's arguments against the use of justice in moral criticism, in the context of Marx's social theory as a whole.

Marx has arguments, which I sketched before, to the effect that people cannot consistently judge societies using standards of justice, rights or equality, given the actual nature of social conflicts. If these arguments are valid, then justice is not a standard by which institutions are to be judged. A basic presupposition of the use of the term, that justice is worthy of praise, is invalid. The normal function of the term in criticism and justification should rationally be abandoned. To say that justice still exists as a property of basic institutions seems now to be as unreasonable as saying that phlogiston exists while admitting that it plays no causal role in combustion, or that caloric exists but plays no role in heat phenomena.[47]

Admittedly, when we assess old categories in light of new discoveries, we do not always abandon them. If the right parallels are preserved, we adopt a new interpretation of the kind of thing that corresponds to those categories, rather than denying that anything corresponds. Aristotle and his contemporaries would have rejected, on deep theoretical grounds, the modern chemist's hypothesis that what they called "*hudor*" is the union of hydrogen and oxygen molecules. But rather than denying that "*hudor*" refers to anything in the world of modern chemistry, we say that the ancient Greeks referred to *HOH* without knowing it. Similarly, for Dalton, it was important that atoms be irreducible units. From the standpoint of particle physics and quantum-mechanical chemistry, we disagree, while accepting that Dalton was referring to something, protons, electrons and other particles organized at the atomic level.

---

[47] Engels might be taken to intend the same analogy in *The Housing Question*: "The confusion becomes worse if one, like Proudhon, believes in this social phlogiston, 'justice,' or if one, like Muelberger, avers that the phlogiston theory is as correct as the oxygen theory" (Marx and Engels, *Selected Works in Three Volumes*, vol. II, p. 366). But he is probably just criticizing a particular, Proudhonist, ahistorical conception of justice ("eternal justice," he usually calls it). My interpretation probably represents just one of Engels' inclinations in his interesting but ambivalent discussions of morality, here and in *Anti-Duehring*.

The rules for this more charitable assessment of the old usage are, roughly, these. Important signs by which the old category was applied should actually, typically reflect the instantiation of the new one. Thus, the fluidity, transparency and other indicators that guided the ancient Greeks in their application of "*hudor*" were in fact due to the presence of batches of *HOH* molecules. Second, important properties that were held to be essential to the old category should, at least approximately and typically, characterize instances of the new one. For example, the new-style atoms of particle physics typically and approximately behave as units in chemical reactions, as Dalton's atoms had to. Finally, the main motivations for employing the old category should not be undermined entirely by the new theory. The point that the old usage had should be one that use of the new category can fulfill. It is this third constraint that the retention of caloric, phlogiston or demons would violate most dramatically. The whole rationale for caloric theory was to suppose that heat is a fluid, so that the normal dynamics of fluids could be applied to heat phenomena. Phlogiston was postulated to maintain a relatively neat correlation between the material composition of objects and their perceptible properties. The motivation for attributing bizarre behavior to demons was to explain it as due to malevolent forces from outside the person who acts so strangely. That is why it is wrong to say, "Caloric exists, but not as a fluid"; "Phlogiston exists, and is oxygen"; or "Demons exist, and are personality disorders."

The "juridical" nature of justice, much emphasized by Wood, might seem to provide the bridge between the old usage and Marx's new theory. Those who deliberate over questions of social justice, before Marx's lessons are absorbed, might be seen as embarked on an enterprise of determining whether institutions fit the best feasible set of rules that can stabilize social interactions by adjudicating conflicts of interest. They assume that there is more than one feasible set of rules that could serve the stablizing function, and often debate which feasible set is best. On a plausible interpretation of Marx, to which Wood subscribes, he shows that the debate over justice is simpler than usually supposed, because one set of stabilizing rules, at most, is feasible in any epoch. Only one standard is feasible, so that there is no need for moral debate as to which is best. More specifically, at a given point in the development of productive forces, only one set of social relations of production is suited to them. Social stability is only possible if these relations actually govern production. As Wood puts it, "These productive forces . . . correspond to, and are expressed in, determinate relations between men, within which alone these forces, in their historically given form, can be applied to nature. These relations Marx calls production relations. . . . Because men are not free to chose the degree of their mastery over nature at a given stage in history, they are also not free to choose the form these production relations will take."[48] A system of relations of production requires a generally accepted set of standards of justice, for stability. For every system, only one set will do the job.

The juridical function of stabilizing interactions by adjudicating conflicting interests is (according to this argument) at once a basic sign that all accept as relevant to detecting justice, an important essential property of justice, and the sole main motivation for employing justice as a category in political discourse. This function is only served by whatever standards of rights and equality conform to the mode of production. Thus, we should regard justice as corresponding to the latter, sociological category. The other, normative aspects should be rejected as sources of confusion. The result is surprising to most users of the old category, but no more shocking than the modern chemical interpretations would be to Aristotle or Dalton.

What are we to say, however, of those situations in which stability is impossible, because an archaic set of production relations still governs, and fetters, the productive forces? It is not clear what Wood's Marx would say. The original article was basically concerned with situations in which justice could serve its social function. Perhaps, in eras of turmoil, there is no justice. After all, many accept that there is no justice when there can be no peace, even if they believe that other moral

[48] Wood, "Critique," p. 7.

83

constraints, such as avoidance of pointless cruelty, should be respected. Or perhaps, in line with some of Marx's descriptions of the sources of social change, a new mode of production should be regarded as latent in the current production process, in the form of production relations that will further the productive forces when they eventually triumph. Justice might then be identified with the adjudicating rules that would fit these burgeoning, progressive, but not yet triumphant relations. After all, these rules are then the most nearly available means of stabilization. But this is no comfort for traditional moralists. Justice might, then, license the coercion of slavery or the degradation and disruption of nascent capitalism.

It is hard to see what other argument would lead us to assess "justice" as we do "*hudor*," not as we do "phlogiston," in light of Marx's social theories. The argument is present, in outline, in Wood's writings.[49] However, it requires either an overly restrictive account of the motivations for talk of justice or excessive limits to the contexts in which social choice has a point.

Suppose that Marx's theory of history was, as Wood proposes, the story of the adaptation of social relations to technological constraints. I will argue at length against this interpretation in Chapter Five. But it is certainly plausible and well-connected with a variety of texts. Wood's account of justice, though, requires something more than a long-run tendency for basic institutions to adapt to technological change. Thoughtful, sustained deliberations over whether to oppose one's institutions must be seen as playing no important causal role in the process by which basic change is produced.

When people speak of the justice or injustice of important, large-scale institutions, a main motivation, indeed the main one, is an interest in choosing how to act as agents in a political process. The motivating question is whether to defend or oppose one's institutions. The main point of appeals to justice is to provide a rationale for embarking on such conduct in face of the fact that others will be hurt if one's conduct is effective. Some people lose in any important change. In the process of

[49] See especially Wood, *Karl Marx*, p. 132.

changing the most basic institutions, disruption or violence dramatically hurts a great many people. Those who appeal to justice see these as costs requiring a strong justification. They take the rectification of injustice to be a specially appropriate one. For many of us, the classic statement of such a case for change is Locke's justification of revolution as a response to the supreme injustice, the violation of the trusteeship of government. For Marx, the most urgent examples were the efforts of working-class radicals to vindicate socialist revolution as a rectification of economic injustice. For instance, in the drafting of the *General Rules of the International Workingmen's Association*, other members of the subcommittee outvoted Marx and obliged him to insert the words, "the emancipation of the working classes means . . . a struggle . . . for equal rights and duties."[50] Whatever their confusions may have been, these socialist partisans of justice had no illusions that they were seeking a system of standards for adjudicating conflicts of interests within capitalist relations of production. Similarly, Proudhon's numerous followers were, quite explicitly, vindicating a program of revolutionary change by appeal to a standard of justice, "the conception of right of the revolution," as they sometimes called it.[51]

If the main motivation for talk of the justice of institutions is deliberation over whether to accept or oppose them, then such talk loses its main point, when interpreted in Wood's way. In particular, talk of justice in basic institutions would lose its main point in the generations, including Marx's as he saw it, in which political choices are most urgent. In those generations, the material conditions are ripe for radical changes, but political and ideological barriers are temporarily effective. Whether they are overcome depends on the outcome of people's conscious deliberations as to whether to support large-scale change. Depending on the outcome of these deliberations,

---

[50] *Selected Works*, vol. II, p. 19. In a letter to Engels, Marx comments, concerning this passage and a few similar ones in the *Rules*, "I was obliged to insert [them] . . . but these are placed in such a way that they can do no harm" (*Selected Correspondence* p. 139).

[51] See the survey of Proudhonist literature in Engels, *The Housing Question*, *Selected Works*, vol. II, pp. 358ff.

more than one mode of production is feasible in that generation. (Only one may be feasible in the long run, but in the long run the deliberators are dead.) Hence, the reflections on feasibility which are supposed to support Wood's interpretation of "justice" cannot preserve its use in rational political deliberations.

Consider the situation of a worker in Great Britain in 1870, deciding whether to criticize or defend her system. At least in Marx's view, the relations of production are no longer suited to the productive forces. Socialism is economically feasible.[52] But capitalist social interactions are stable, on account of ideological and political processes; mainly, antagonism between English and Irish workers, also patriotism within the working class, and demoralization over the co-optation of trade-union leaders and the erosion of previous working-class gains. Different stable modes of production are possible, depending on whether she or others like her decide to work for destabilization of the present one. Deciding what to do, she wonders whether capitalism is unjust. To respond that it is neither just nor unjust, simply because the bad fit between relations and forces guarantees eventual instability, is to say that justice cannot be a rationale for choice when deliberations over choice are most urgent. To say that socialism, in Marx's view, is now just and that this simply means that it fits the productive forces also separates questions of justice from relevant problems of choice. It is surely rational of the worker not to give this question of productivity unique status when she decides what to criticize, what to attack. To say that capitalism is just because it is currently stable leads to an absurd conservatism, if justice is relevant to her choices. After all, she is choosing whether to play a role in challenging this stability. No matter how Wood's identification of justice is adapted to the times, including Marx's and ours, in which Marx would take change to be economically feasible, it fails to be a rational basis for political choice.

[52] *Capital* I, pp. 17, 20; Marx to Meyer and Vogt, April 9, 1870, *Selected Correspondence*, p. 223.

The anti-moral arguments of the previous chapter would show that this activist's talk of justice in basic institutions corresponds to nothing, like the eighteenth-century chemist's talk of phlogiston as against Aristotle's talk of *"hudor."* If she is convinced by those negative considerations, talk of justice loses its main point. This gap, we have seen, cannot be filled by the sociological interpretation. Nor is it true that her actual usage of the term objectively reflects the presence of stabilizing standards harmonizing social interests, as Aristotle's usage of *"hudor"* was objectively a process by which *HOH* was detected. The measures she supports are apt to be, objectively, destabilizing and unharmonious. Finally, her whole use of the term in political deliberations is dominated by the criterion of evenhandedness in the balancing of interests, and nothing corresponds to this property, if Marx is right. The notion of evenhandedness does not apply as a whole to basic institutions. In every respect, "justice" is like "phlogiston," when she uses it in political deliberations.[53]

If "justice" is still interpreted as referring to Wood's sociological property, this must be on account of the unimportance of the kind of deliberation I have described. It must be too unimportant to provide a main point of talk about justice or a context that otherwise determines its reference or logic. Obviously, the kind of person who deliberates, a worker in a period when radical change is possible, is extremely important

---

[53] Suppose that someone has a much more conservative tendency. When he speaks of an institution as just, this is a reliable sign that it fits a stabilizing juridical standard. Moreover, he gives considerable independent weight to specific moral standards that do uphold the status quo, say, laissez-faire principles of economic justice under capitalism. There might seem to be an argument that "justice" as *he* uses the term fits the sociological interpretation. We would then have a case in which different people use the same term with a different reference, even though they speak the same language. Different interests can certainly produce such splits, as when fishmongers and marine biologists use "fish" in a way that corresponds to somewhat different sets of animals. (At the fish stand, whales are fish, and squid and octopus are borderline cases.) Still, an evenhanded balancing of interests is the basic property of justice as everyone uses the term in deliberations over whether to accept or oppose institutions. And Marx's arguments would show that no coherent notions of evenhandedness is available to be applied to institutions. On balance, "social justice" is like "phlogiston," for everyone.

for Marx. The argument must be that this kind of deliberation, sustained reflection on what political action to choose, has no important impact on the actual social process. The only remaining enterprises using "justice" might, then, presuppose the juridical function. One remaining enterprise is the kind of social engineering in which stable piecemeal reform is pursued within the basic societal framework. Another might be the abstract classification of societies as just or unjust, conducted from a disengaged, God's-eye point of view ("Was Athenian slavery just?" asked two thousand years after the fact).

This denial of the causal relevance of reflective political deliberations is a familiar interpretation of Marx, of which Stanley Moore is a recent, resourceful proponent. On this interpretation, Marx, at least in his mature and nonutopian writings, makes radical social change the result of peaceful economic activity motivated by short-term economic goals within the old society, say, bourgeois commercial activity within feudalism, or workers' cooperatives and peaceful trades unionism under capitalism.[54] Organized political movements engaged in militant activities with large-scale, long-term goals are at best unnecessary, and, at worst, cause pointless, bloody, and brutalizing failures. That Wood is attracted to this emphasis on the spontaneous, economic and apolitical is suggested by the previously quoted denial that we have choices where relations of production are concerned, together with characterizations of the political realm such as the following:

Political action is, therefore, for Marx, one subordinate moment of revolutionary practice. Political institutions do not and cannot create

[54] See, for example, "Marx and Lenin as Historical Materialists" (originally in *Philosophy and Public Affairs* 4 [1975]), in Cohen, *Marx, Justice, and History* pp. 222, 226, 233. Moore distinguishes this scientific view of change from an enduring "utopian" strand in Marx's thinking. In the present chapter, I shall confine myself to the most extreme aspect of this view, the denial that organized political activity with large-scale, long-term goals plays an important role in Marx's mature and scientific theory of change. In Chapter Three, I will discuss a more limited claim, which Moore shares, in essence, with George Lichtheim and Shlomo Avineri, namely, that political revolution, that is, large-scale organized violence directed at control of the state, is not essential to radical change.

a new mode of production, but can only be brought into harmony with a mode of production that men themselves are already bringing to birth.[55]

In fact, throughout his life, Marx regarded deliberation over large-scale alternatives, furthered by militant, organized movements as crucial to radical change, effective in appropriate circumstances, and an independent determinant of the coming of change in any given generation. (Perhaps the occurring, sooner or later, of effective deliberations is determined, in turn, by the growth of productive forces. This is the separate issue I will face in Chapter Five.) My description of the context for an English worker's deliberations in 1870 was drawn directly from Marx's writings, especially his letter to Meyer and Vogt on April 9, 1870. There, he writes:

This antagonism [between English and Irish workers] is artificially kept alive and intensified by the press, the pulpit, the comic papers, in short, by all the means at the disposal of the ruling classes. This antagonism is the secret of the impotence of the English working class, despite its organisation. It is the secret by which the capitalist class maintains its power. And the latter is quite aware of this. . . . England, the metropolis of capital, the power which has up to now ruled the world market, is at present the most important country for the workers' revolution, and moreover the only country in which the material conditions for this revolution have reached a certain degree of maturity. . . . It is the special task of the Central Council in London to make the English workers realise that for them the national emancipation of Ireland is not a question of abstract justice or humanitarian sentiment but the first condition of their own social emancipation.[56]

The idea that a mode of production may or may not be born in a given period, depending on the course of political processes, pervades Marx's writings. It is a recurrent theme in his French political histories. There, the French working class is portrayed as having failed to remake society because ideological obstacles, for example, *l'idée napoleonique* and urban-rural antagonisms, have not been overcome, and because not enough

[55] Wood, "Critique," p. 28.
[56] *Selected Correspondence*, pp. 222f.

89

discoveries have been made about how to make a socialist revolution.[57] In his account of the triumph of capitalism, he gives a crucial role to prolonged episodes of organized violence involving large-scale deliberation and persuasion, in particular, the English Civil War and the French Revolution.[58]

There is a major theorist of history who denied that rational choices of social systems play a significant role in their triumph. That theorist is not Marx, but Hegel. For Hegel, world-historical changes are always a ruse of reason, the unintended consequence of the life style of a people and the self-assertion of a hero. The attempt to bring a better world about intentionally, through rational reflection on available social facts, is always doomed. "The owl of Minerva takes flight only a dusk." This passive attitude toward the future is the part of his Hegel heritage that Marx most strenuously renounced. The Marx who could accept the sociological interpretation of "justice" is a Marx revised to fit the Hegelian background.[59]

My subject so far has been the "justice" of social systems. However, much of Wood's case for his interpretation is concerned, in the first instance, with the justice of individual economic transactions. In particular, Marx is supposed to believe that typical capitalist wage bargains are just, since they suit the standard of just exchange that is functionally appropriate to capitalist society. In turn, this interpretation of "just exchange" as a sociological category is taken to support the view that justice is quite generally a sociological category for Marx.

---

[57] See *The Eighteenth Brumaire of Louis Bonaparte* in Tucker, *The Marx-Engels Reader*, pp. 515–21; *Civil War in France*, pp. 559f.; Marx to Kugelmann, April 12, 1872, *Selected Correspondence*, p. 247.

[58] "The revolutions of 1648 and 1789 were not English and French revolutions, they were revolutions of European significance. . . . In them the bourgeoisie was victorious; but the victory of the bourgeoisie meant at the time the victory of a new social order" (Marx, "The Bourgeoisie and the Counter-Revolution," *Selected Works* vol. I, p. 139). The same point is made in *German Ideology*, p. 77; *Communist Manifesto*, p. 362; and *Capital* I, p. 703 in a paragraph ending, "Force is the midwife of every old society pregnant with the new. It is itself an economic power."

[59] Cf. Wood, "For Marx, as for Hegel, the morally rational is determined by the socially actual" (*Karl Marx*, p. 132).

While Wood's textual case against regarding typical wage bargains as unjust is, I think, conclusive, the case for portraying them as positively just, in Marx's view, is doubtful at best. "Not unjust" does not mean "just" here, anymore than an atheist's argument against divine goodness means that divine evil really exists for him. Moreover, once we see the rationale for Marx's denial that the bargains are unjust, we have compelling reasons to suppose that his views on the justice of social systems cannot be extrapolated from his views on the justice of transactions.

Marx does say, as we have seen, that wage bargains yielding surplus value have three characteristics. First, at least if no fraud or violence is employed within the transaction, the right to the use of the labor-power is transferred, so that the product embodying surplus value belongs to the capitalist. Second, in this transfer, no injustice is done to the seller of labor-power. Finally, in the average case, goods of equal economic value are exchanged. For, by the scientifically preferable standard of economic value, the value of a day's labor-power is the social labor necessary to support a day's life-activity at the material level characteristic of workers in the society in question. And this is, on the average, the value of a day's wage-goods.[60]

Wood takes the passages in question as statements that capitalist wage transactions are, typically and on the average, just.[61] But all Marx literally says is that the relevant transactions transfer property rights, are not unjust, and exchange economic equivalents. In short, they are not to be criticized as instances of cheating or unequal exchange. Certainly, Marx's two kinds of arguments in these passages support nothing more than this negative conclusion. The "no cheating" arguments consist of ordinary-language analysis of homely examples involving the purchase of something for its activity in production, for example, a vintner's buying yeast, a farmer's renting a horse for a day. Marx points out that no one concerned with justice in economic transactions believes that there is an in-

[60] In *Capital* I, see pp. 180, 188, 167 for examples of the three claims about property rights, non-injury, and equality.
[61] See Wood, "Critique," pp. 19–26.

justice if the price of the yeast or the rent of the horse is less than what it adds to the product. He challenges those who think typical wage bargains unfair because they generate a surplus to point to the relevant difference. This is not, in itself, to endorse the view that justice is an objective quality of transfers of property rights in the use of labor-power. The other arguments are to the effect that commodities of equal value are exchanged in the average wage bargain, according to the scientifically sound measure of economic value. But the soundness of the measure is supposed to be established by its independent contribution to the explanation of price, profit, growth and employment. Since the category of justice makes no such contribution, these arguments could be used to show that justice in economic transactions is not a scientific category because its use in moral deliberations conflicts with the scientifically sound measure of economic value.

Marx would have at least one excellent reason not to jump from the denial of injustice, here, to the assertion of justice. If, as many of these passages suggest, justice in capitalist exchange means the exchange of commodities at their labor-values, then in peaks and troughs of the business cycle, abnormal levels of demand for labor make wage bargains pervasively unjust—to capitalists in booms, to workers in busts. Though Marx discusses the departures from "the law of value," he never makes this remarkable claim about cyclical injustice.

The mere "no justice" conclusion is quite enough for Marx's evident purpose. In these passages, he means to show that complaints of unfairness are not rational means of radically challenging capitalism, least of all when the labor theory is employed in the fashion of Hodgskin and other left-wing Ricardians. The desired conclusion is not that wage bargains are usually just, but that "Instead of the *conservative* slogan, 'A fair day's wage for a fair day's work!' . . . [the working class] ought to inscribe on their banner the *revolutionary* watchword, 'Abolition of the wages system!'"[62]

[62] *Wages, Price and Profit*, p. 75.

Even if Marx did believe that capitalist transactions *were* just, typically and on the average, there would be no need to transfer this judgment to the capitalist mode of production or typical capitalist institutions. His ordinary-language arguments appeal to considerations quite specific to individual acts of exchange. His other arguments similarly rely on a notion of equal value quite specific to the analysis of capitalist exchanges and their consequences for price, profit and related phenomena. No corresponding body of everyday assumptions or scientific measures of value supports a rational standard of justice for whole economic systems.

Wood's articles and his book on Marx also present a proposal about morality in general, not simply justice and rights, which deserves at least a brief discussion here. According to Wood's tentative suggestion, Marx judges institutions by their tendency to promote "non-moral goods," which include self-actualization, security and physical health. When Marx attacks morality, he is attacking the judgment of institutions by their tendency to promote "moral goods". Wood explains the distinction as follows.

[In] a narrower and I think more proper sense of 'moral', . . . we distinguish *moral* goods and evils from *nonmoral* ones. We all know the difference between valuing or doing something because conscience of 'the moral law' tells us we 'ought' to, and valuing or doing something because it satisfies our needs, our wants, or our conceptions of what is good for us (or for someone whose welfare we want to promote—desires for nonmoral goods are not necessarily selfish desires).[63]

This characterization of Marx's outlook has the virtue of great simplicity. Unfortunately, it makes Marx's outlook too much like traditional morality in one way, too little in another. We need the more complex structure of the conception of morality with which I began to do justice to Marx's point of view.

The pursuit of non-moral goods, in Wood's technical sense, is too close to traditional morality because it might include the pursuit of justice, if based on a certain kind of psychology that

[63] Wood, *Karl Marx*, p. 126.

sometimes does support this goal. A significant number of people want to be in relations of justice with the other members of their society, conscience and the moral law to one side. They have the thirst for reciprocity on a footing of equality that the more naturalistic theorists of justice, such as Rousseau, Rawls, Piaget and Kohlberg, have tried to describe. If convinced, perhaps by a clever Nietzschean, that a higher law dictated departures from relations of justice, they would still value these relations, though perhaps with guilt. They would be like Huck Finn, deciding that he wanted to view a black person as an equal and accepting that this was a perverse tendency, another sign that he was a worthless nobody. It is hard to say how many people value justice in this way, as a non-moral good. However, they seem to include many of those who support workers' struggles and socialist goals, but do so on the grounds that capitalism is unjust. The exclusion of non-moral goods, in the technical sense, would not exclude standards of justice from their evaluative repertoire. Yet the rejection of justice and allied standards as an irrational basis for socialism is surely the core of whatever Marx has in mind, if he is really attacking morality.

In another way, the "moral/non-moral" distinction exaggerates the distance between Marx's outlook and traditional moral standpoints. If socialism is to be created, people must be led to take on burdens out of a concern for others. These others may not be confined to the circle of family and intimate friends. The Communards who risked their lives had no reason to believe that their families and close friends would benefit. Their kin and intimates were all the more likely to be exiled or to live in poverty, if the Commune was defeated. Indeed, Marx recommends a high degree of concern for people one will never meet in other countries, epitomized by the Manchester textile-workers' support for the Union blockade of the Confederacy, antislavery activity that produced long-term layoffs for them as cotton inventories dwindled. In the process of social change, Marx urges on people a concern for others that motivates the taking up of burdens.

Similarly, in the consolidation of socialism, principled resistance to temptations to pursue immediate self-interest plays a necessary role for Marx. In the first stage of socialism, based on the rule, "To each according to the time he or she works," the fear of being fired no longer exists as a spur to intense effort. Such an economy cannot work if people loaf on the job whenever they can get away with it. Even more obviously, the higher stage, governed by the rule, "From each according to ability, to each according to need," presupposes a commitment not to be a free rider. Of course, Marx believes that people's psychology under socialism will involve an increasingly high level of mutual concern and a tendency for self-esteem to be based on striving for the common good. But he insists that people at the first stage will be influenced by individual and immediate self-interest to some degree.[64] And he does not suggest that temptations to put narrow self-interest first will never even be felt at the higher stage. In sum, conscientious struggle against self-centered impulses plays an important role under socialism. This is not to say, however, that conscientious socialist concern for the common good is universal and equal concern for all humans. The remnants of class conflict in the earlier stages of socialism would preclude this, in Marx's view.

When the temptation of immediate individual gain is resisted out of concern for others, it is natural to say that someone has been moved by a *conscientious* awareness of what he or she *ought* to do. Thus, there is no clear sense in which Marx condemns moral motivations in general, in Wood's technical usage.

In this disagreement, as in the first, the role of spontaneity in social choice is probably the underlying issue. Suppose that agonizing over the trade-off between immediate self-interest and concern for others played no useful role in the revolutionary process. Change comes about through the prudential pursuit of economic self-interest combined, perhaps, with spontaneous and unreflective outbursts. Then, Marx might associate deliberations supporting such trade-offs with attention to what ought to be, and condemn such attention in his

---

[64] *Critique of the Gotha Program*, p. 386.

attacks on morality. Social change would require no agonizing over the tension between private and collective well-being. However, this is not Marx's outlook, but one that he himself condemns as "philistine."[65]

A Tempting Conclusion

How far does one have to go with Marx before one is compelled to accept his criticisms of morality? There are, I think, four basic propositions from which the rejection of morality would follow:

1. Various needs of the vast majority are in such conflict with those of minorities that an ultimate standard of equality would have intolerable costs.
2. Strategies for effective change require obstruction and, sometimes, violence that are incompatible with concrete sentiments of equal concern for all involved.
3. In the course of history, normal people have had deep moral differences that were not due to unreason or ignorance. Similarly, in the present day, there are conflicting conceptions of the good that cannot be resolved through rational persuasion.
4. The conflicts between the long run and the short run, culture and minimal well-being for all, productivity and leisure, have sometimes been so acute that no set of basic institutions was the best. Only historical change has removed this incoherence.

Many non-Marxists would accept, on reflection, that these premises are probably valid. They should, then, conclude that morality is not an appropriate basis for political action and social choice. That is part of the fascination of the anti-moral arguments implicit in Marx's writings. For all the radical sound of the anti-moral conclusion, it is based on some of the less controversial Marxist claims about society. Of course, decent

[65] Marx to Kugelmann, April 12, 1871, *Selected Correspondence*, p. 247.

people do not abandon morality if they believe that the alternative is narrow self-interest, caprice or bloodthirsty *Realpolitik*. Here, too, Marx has a special philosophical contribution. More than other writers, he describes an outlook for politics that is decent without being moral.

Power

CHAPTER THREE

The Concept of a Ruling Class

INTRODUCTION

IN THE PREVIOUS chapters, I tried to use Marx's writings on social conflict to shed light on standard problems in philosophy. However, the relation between philosophy and social science should be one of mutual aid. Analytic philosophy's conceptual resourcefulness, clarity and tolerance for abstraction should reveal possibilities of description and explanation that are neglected in the piecemeal research that dominates empirical social science. This is not to say that political philosophers should forget about social facts when they try to help social scientists. Concepts and explanatory programs designed for all historical societies, much less all possible worlds, are apt to be of little use in examining the realities, say, of advanced industrial societies. Philosophers who try to help social scientists had better know enough to be able to judge what options are sufficiently plausible to be worthy of empirical investigation. They *can* help if they describe or clarify explanatory questions that are worth asking, explanatory strategies that are worth trying.

The classic political philosophers, from Aristotle to Marx, all made enormous contributions at this middle level of theorizing, in between pure conceptual analysis and particular empirical findings. Today the fate of political philosophy, as a distinctive field, largely depends on the revival of this enterprise. Otherwise, "political philosophy" will continue to be a label for a branch of ethics and a minor branch of the history of philosophy.

The next two chapters are an exercise in this middle level of theorizing. I hope to show that the careful philosophical reconstruction of Marx's explanatory framework can provide tools for analysis that many non-Marxist social scientists will want to use, once they recognize them for what they are. In particular, I will try to show that the question, "To what extent is there a ruling class, politically?" is an important, but neglected tool for analyzing societies such as the United States, once Marx's conception of a ruling class is understood.

Since the contribution to political science will be based on a charge of neglect, an utterly compressed statement of the major current orientations should help those outside the field to follow the argument. In many ways, the focus of large-scale but empirical political science is still the "pluralism" that flourished at the beginning of the 1960s. Dahl's study of New Haven government, *Who Governs?*, is the most influential example of this approach. Very roughly (a detailed analysis will come later), pluralists study how the different resources possessed by different people affect their respective chances of a successful outcome from the game of politics. The conclusion is always that resources are significantly dispersed, while success rates are limited for all. These conclusions are reached by applying criteria that are behavioral and that do not require much theory for their application. For example, what percentage of nonunanimous votes went in favor of a certain group on a certain committee is an important criterion for the description of power in New Haven, in Dahl's study. Because of this style of argument, and the methodological warnings attending it, the pluralists often considered themselves leaders of a "Behavioral Revolution" in the study of politics.

In calling pluralism the dominant approach, I do not mean that most present-day political scientists are self-described pluralists. Many are. Many others, we shall see, really are, whatever their self-descriptions. But many are committed critics of pluralism. Pluralism dominates in the sense that other general orientations are most usefully defined by relating them to pluralism. The dissent from pluralism has taken many forms, especially in recent years. The most popular, from the beginning, has been the study of "power structures" epitomized in the work of Floyd Hunter, C. Wright Mills and G. William Domhoff. Indeed, pluralists were originally critics of Hunter's and Mills' ideas. The power-structure theorists believe that political power is best described through a map of networks of influence on government, based on institutions and informal social ties. Also, they accept a much broader range of research techniques than the pluralists. For example, Hunter's study of Atlanta relied not on a tabulation of successful and unsuccessful behavior, but on a survey of people's opinions of other people's influence.

Finally, structural functionalism studies the contribution of the political system and the political aspects of culture to the total array of systems through which a society maintains its coherence and distinctiveness. At the level of grand theory, Parsons' work is paradigmatic. Almond and Verba's *The Civic Culture* is the most influential application of structural functional thinking to a rich body of political data. Though attention to the structural and avoidance of rigid rules of inference from data make structural functionalism, in principle, very different from pluralism, the approaches have peacefully coexisted from the outset. Eventually, I will explore some implications of this harmony for the politics of political science.

Despite this mild dose of jargon, the reader should find that the repertoire of technical approaches corresponds quite closely to different approaches in non-academic argument when such common and important questions are raised as, "Are we really living in the democracy?" or "Is government basically run by a few big interests?" (In the United States, about half answer "yes" to the latter quesion!)[1] Also, the investigation of the mod-

---

[1] More precisely, in 1970, the responses to the question, "Would you say the government is pretty much run by a few big interests or that it is run for the benefit of all the people?" were: Few big interests, 49.7%; all the people, 40.5%; other, 9.6%. See Richard Hamilton and James Wright, *New Directions in Political Sociology* (Indianapolis, 1975), p. 26. The figures are from the annual surveys by the University of Michigan Institute for Social Research. Two other questions posed were: "How many of the people running the government are a little crooked? Hardly any/Not many/Quite a lot." "How much of the time do you think you can trust the government in Washington to do the right thing? Always/Most of the time/Some of the time." ("Never" is often volunteered.) The proportion of those giving the most negative response to all three questions, in 1972, was 24% of whites, 31% of blacks, 34% of industrial operatives, and 40% of service workers. Since only 11% of the better-off respondents, that is, those in professional and technical categories, gave such responses, it seems likely that big business often loomed large among the "few big interests" whom respondents had in mind. See Robert Gilmour and Robert Lamb, *Political Alienation in American* (New York, 1975).

ern scientific conceptions of political power has general importance in another way. With the departmental division of labor in twentieth-century universities, philosophers lack a living tradition of contributing to the work of the social sciences. I hope the tactics that follow, mixing the concrete with the abstract, the empirical with the conceptual, and the structure of fields at present with possibilities from the past, will provide useful models for further contributions.

A CHARGE OF NEGLECT

A central task of political theory has traditionally been to discover where political power lies. This tradition will continue to be reasonable so long as people want to change things (or to prevent change) and so long as what government does affects their success. There are, however, not one, but many questions about a society that might be expressed in the words, "Where does political power lie?" Here, political theorists need not feel inferior to natural scientists, who would not dream of abolishing all but one specification of "energy", "wave" or "information-storage in the brain." The danger, rather, is that investigators will ignore the differences between different versions of the question of political power, and lose track of an intelligible, important question, as a consequence. My purpose is to show that this danger is real.

The questions of political power that dominate the study of politics today are, very roughly: "To what extent do various people get what they want out of government?", "By what mechanisms, institutional or informal, do various social groups influence government?" and "What makes government effective and stable?" The question that is missing is (again, very roughly), "Whose interests does government serve?" I hope to show how utterly different the neglected question is from the questions that are pursued, and to suggest that its neglect depends on overly rigid methodologies and on practical political assumptions that political theory should question, not assume.

The dangerously neglected question about political power and social interests needs to be made more specific, since the

104

mere words, "Whose interests does government serve?" are a label for a cluster of questions, in their turn. At one extreme, one might be inquiring after the truth of a conspiracy theory or some other hypothesis in which government officials consciously dedicate themselves to helping one social group, in spite of any conflict with the interests of others. For most modern societies, including the United States, these hypotheses are sufficiently farfetched that failure to investigate them is not dangerous. At another extreme, the question of interests might be understood as a request for a tabulation of the actual costs and benefits of particular government actions for various social groups, without attention to the causal processes linking what government does to what social groups need. At least in policy studies, this question is not ignored.

The question I advocate lies between these extremes. It is the question of the extent to which the role of government in society fits a certain model. To what extent is there a ruling class, in Marx's sense of the phrase?

WHAT IS A RULING CLASS?

Marx's writings on politics have a peculiar shape. On the one hand, his histories of political events, above all, of the political turmoil in mid-nineteenth-century France, have enormous and obvious power. It is no surprise that Engels called a highly specific text, *The Eighteenth Brumaire*, the epitome of the materialist conception of history.[2] On the other hand, Marx has no systematic explication of the theory of politics at work in these writings. Clearly, a leading idea is that the bourgeoisie is the ruling class in politics, in a modern capitalist society. But we are never told, in a reasonably general, detailed and literal manner, what a ruling class is. Partly as a result, the controversy over this part of Marx's meaning, among sympathetic interpreters, now centers on an increasingly sterile controversy between the so-called "structuralist" and "instrumentalist" interpretations.

[2] Preface to the 1885 edition, *Selected Works*, vol. I, p. 397.

What Marx offers, by way of general statement, is a series of dramatic and highly metaphorical pronouncements. The following are typical:

The bourgeoisie has conquered for itself in the modern representative state exclusive political sway. The executive of the modern state is a committee for managing the common affairs of the whole bourgeoisie.[3]

At the same pace at which the progress of modern industry developed, widened, intensified the class antagonism between capital and labor, the State power assumed more and more the character of the national power of capital over labor, of a public force organized for social enslavement, of an engine of class despotism. . . . [The bourgeoisie] used that State power mercilessly and ostentatiously as the national war-engine of capital against labor.[4]

Taken in isolation, these passages have natural interpretations. Talk of an executive committee embodying exclusive political sway suggests a conspiracy theory in which leading politicians and businesspeople regularly meet to decide the course of politics, with the latter handing down orders to the former, when deliberations are done. Talk of enslavement and war engines suggests that the state unremittingly uses force to increase work to the maximum, and to reduce employers' costs to the minimum. However, neither theory is at all plausible, and neither can be Marx's. Far from insisting that major businesspeople are constantly engaged in political planning, he emphasizes the existence of a social division of labor that typically detaches them from direct involvement. For example, Louis Napoleon's Empire is described as at once "the most prostitute and the ultimate form of the State power" that the bourgeoisie controls *and* a setting in which "bourgeois society, freed from political cares, attained a development unexpected even by itself."[5] In his only discussion of class struggle within a relatively stable political order, the history of the British fight for a shorter workday in *Capital*, he describes a limited but real proletarian success in obtaining state interventions.

[3] *Communist Manifesto*, p. 337.
[4] *Civil War in France*, p. 552.
[5] *Ibid.*, p. 553.

Faced with all this moderation, it is tempting to interpret away Marx's fierce language and turn his theory into a form of pluralism: what government does is strongly affected by the balance of influence among different interest groups; great wealth is a source of great influence; big business is the most important single interest group. This theory certainly avoids implausibility. But it comes close to triviality in the process. It would be hard to find an anti-Marxist social scientist who does not agree that money talks in politics, and says a great deal. Certainly, as exegesis, this banal acknowledgment of the relevance of the economic is only to be tried if all else fails. It would be extremely farfetched for Marx to summarize this interest-group doctrine with statements about exclusive political sway, social enslavement, and the state as war-engine.

What we need is an interpretation faithful both to Marx's general and vivid statements, and to his concrete practice as political historian and strategist. When it is reconstructed in this way, Marx's claim that there is a ruling class in a society turns out to have three general aspects, concerned with what the state does, the mechanisms producing this pattern of action, and the possible means of breaking the pattern. In very broad outline, a social group or coalition of social groups is a ruling class politically if government basically does what its long-term interests dictate, if there are definite mechanisms at any given time maintaining this connection between actions and interests, and if this connection cannot be broken by activities that government permits. Thus, with certain hedges and distinctions, the state acts as if it were an executive committee for managing the common affairs of the bourgeoisie, is exclusively guided by their long-term interests ("exclusive political sway"), and will continue to be so guided unless defeated by physical challenges that it does not permit ("the war-engine of capital against labor").[6]

[6] Marx's conception of the state as such, as against his substantive claim about its relation to the rest of society, is an informal precursor of Weber's definition in *Economy and Society*. The state, for Marx, is an organized coercive apparatus, sanctioned by the reigning system of ideas, that dominates the use of force in a territory, monopolizes permission to use force, and does so effectively enough
Footnote continued on following page

The first part of the threefold thesis that there is a ruling class is the claim that, in the social setting in question, government acts in a way that serves the long-term interests of a social group or a coalition of groups, even though those interests do not coincide with those of the rest of society. This is not to say that government never does something that benefits a subordinate group and is, taken by itself, a cost to the dominant group. However, in effect, if not intention, this aspect of government activity must be a means of coping with problems of acquiescence or cooperation that government did not create, problems from the standpoint of the dominant group. Thus, for Marx, the Ten-Hours Bill served the interests of the industrial bourgeoisie, given the need to tame the social upheavals of the Chartist period.[7] This is not to say the costs of provoking working-class violence are always overriding. In the revolutions of 1848, the long-range stakes made provocative interventions essential from the bourgeois point of view.

Apart from the need for concessions, government policies will be affected by another less than ideal circumstance for the dominant group: political leaders are not ideally smart and well-informed. We are inquiring as to whether, in a certain period, the overall course of government action serves the interests of the dominant group as well as can be expected, given

---

that commands of officials, that is, those exercising roles in the apparatus, are typically obeyed. Because of the separateness, centralization and coerciveness of this apparatus, Marx believes that "political power, properly so-called" has class antagonism as its *raison d'être* and is incompatible with classless society, in which "the free development of each is the condition for the free development of all" (*Communist Manifesto*, pp. 352f. See also *Civil War in France*, pp. 555f.; *Critique of the Gotha Program*, p. 394).

Of course, the state, while defined by its coercive function, includes noncoercive functions and offices, as well. This raises an important question for the Marx-Weber conception, of just what institutions to include in the state. To avoid obscuring issues raised by Marx's descriptions of the relationship between the state and the rest of society, I will take relatively narrow, legal specifications of the difference between government and private power to describe the limits of the state in modern societies. Accordingly, "the state" will be used interchangeably with "government." For other purposes, it might be useful to ask whether, for example, the Council on Foreign Relations is part of the state.

[7] *Capital* I, pp. 268ff.

108

the limit of skills and knowledge at the time, and the inevitable absence of perfect fit between political success, on the one hand, and administrative skills and self-discipline, on the other. Louis Napoleon, as Marx portrays him, is often an inefficient and capricious executive. But the bourgeoisie need repressive rule by someone outside the establishment who has broadly based appeal. He is the best available, from the standpoint of their interests. Similarly, Roosevelt's attempts to balance the budget may have been a disaster for all social groups. If they reflected prevailing economic ignorance, these effects do not challenge a ruling-class hypothesis. Nonetheless, in assessing a ruling-class hypothesis, the appeal to human weakness must not be abused. If alleged mistakes imply an implausible level of stupidity or fall into a pattern suggesting the influence of competing interests, we have grounds for supposing that these episodes reflect an independent tendency to fulfill the interests of other groups, apart from the supposed ruling class.

The second aspect of the existence of a ruling class concerns the nature of the connection between government actions and the interests of the dominant group. This connection is not an accident, if that group is a ruling class. At any given time, a variety of definite mechanisms work to maintain this connection. Moreover, unless there is a major shift of extra-governmental resources away from the dominant group, new mechanisms will replace old ones if the latter become inadequate to maintain the connection between government action and dominant social interests.

The diversity of these mechanisms and the fluidity in their replacement in the face of new circumstances are a great difference in form between Marx's ruling-class hypothesis and a conspiracy theory. For example, The Civil War in France contains a capsule political history of France since the Revolution, in which five major shifts in the basic forms of government are acknowledged and ascribed to the changing dictates of the needs of the bourgeoisie as circumstances change and society evolves.[8]

[8] Civil War in France, pp. 552f.

There are some fairly constant mechanisms (none of them conspiratorial) in the bourgeois political repertoire as Marx describes it. The national debt, he emphasizes, means that any change dramatically opposed to bourgeois interests may bring fiscal chaos as its retribution.[9] If politicians are not literally owned by the bourgeoisie, the mass media typically are.[10] The salaries, working conditions, and the whole life style of major political leaders assimilate them to the bourgeoisie, even if they are not of bourgeois origins.[11] However, the ultimate test of whether a group is a ruling class is whether it has sufficient resources that new rules of the political game become effective when old ones will not suit its interests. The rise to power of Louis Napoleon was a central case in Marx's era. A contemporary example might be the dramatic change in mechanisms of government in Chile, when parliamentary democracy no longer suited the interests of a coalition of mineowners, bankers, manufacturers and large landowners.

No doubt, some theorists might label a dominant group a ruling class at a given time, even though it lacks the capacity to use its resources to initiate new rules of the political game. But, as we shall see, an important practical motivation for singling out the question of the existence of a ruling class would then be missing, namely, the effort to test the limits of "going through channels" as a means to social change. Moreover, classical arguments in favor of ruling-class hypotheses would be unavailable, on this alternative reading of the phrase. The hypothesis of a ruling class is often attractive on account of its power to suggest historical explanations for changes in governmental institutions as responses to new challenges to the dominant social group. Finally, by requiring continuity of political dominance throughout relevant periods of crisis, we can test the scope of the dominant group or coalition, perhaps making it relatively exclusive and, hence, relatively determinate in its collective interests. For example, if old-style political leaders are replaced when they cease to serve dominant extra-govern-

[9] *German Ideology*, p. 79.
[10] Ibid., pp. 64f.
[11] *Civil War in France*, p. 554.

mental interests, in times of crisis, that is a basis for supposing that politicians are not themselves a part of the ruling class. In general, we determine which elites are dominant by looking at periods of crisis when the interests of elites seriously conflict. The capacity for continued dominance in these situations of conflict is evidence for the underlying order of dominance in normal times.

Finally, the claim that there is a ruling class is concerned with the *strength* of the connection between what government does and the interests of the dominant group. If that connection can be ended by activities that government would encourage, protect, or, in any case, permit, then there is no ruling class. *Ruling-class* dominance can only be ended by a major shift in extra-governmental resources that must be brought about by "going outside of channels", as those channels would be defined by government responses to discontent. Consider, by way of contrast, one picture of political power in the United States at the turn of the nineteenth century. On this conception, government was serving the interests of big business as a consequence of a variety of mechanisms, shifting in response to changing social circumstances. But the electorate could have changed this situation through electoral processes protected by government, and, in the subsequent decades, they did. If politics at the turn of the nineteenth century had this as-yet latent potential for change, then it would be wrong to say that big business was a ruling class politically, that the representative state was a committee for managing their common affairs, or that the state was a war-engine of capital. These phrases all imply that the state actively intervenes in society according to the interests of the economically dominant group. If, however, the connection between interests and policies can be changed through processes sanctioned by the state, any social bias in government will be a passive reflection of the balance of political influence in society at large. The right metaphor will be not a war-engine, but a weather vane.

This distinction between active and passive bias is a difference between the ruling-class hypothesis and even the most left-wing versions of pluralism, according to which big business is enormously more influential than any other interest group. The Marxist and the left-wing pluralist will often have the same expectations about the course of government policy. What is a concession in the interests of acquiescence, for the Marxist, is a reflection of the minor but real influence of labor, for the pluralist. But they will disagree about the processes underlying the course of government policy. For the Marxist, if a measure significantly serves the interests of workers and hurts the interests of big business, when taken in isolation, it is, as part of the larger social process, a tactical retreat from illegal force or the risk of its ultimate occurrence. Thus, Marxists argue that widespread disruption on the part of North American workers in the late nineteenth century—for example, the Pullman strike, the New Orleans and Pittsburgh general strikes, and the Populist uprisings in the South—played an essential role in the process of reform. In short, without the claim about what it would take to break the tie between social interests and government action, there would be no room for empirical argument between the ruling-class hypothesis and pluralism. On account of the dynamic element in the former, it gives rise to distinctive explanations of reforms and distinctive expectations about government action in times of crisis.

If I have interpreted it correctly, Marx's concept of a ruling class is quite complex. It involves claims about social interests, mechanisms of stability, and techniques for change. This idea of a ruling class does not get its unity from a simple definition or a single test. Rather, it is unified at the level of guiding metaphors and at the level of practical concerns.

In his political theory, Marx is asking us to see the relation between certain social groups on the model of certain relations of dominance between individuals, for example, master and slave, or ruler and ruled. The state is seen as the main coercive apparatus for keeping the superior class in an analogous position. When one considers even the simple-sounding relation of master and slave, it turns out to have a complexity precisely analogous to the three-sided conception of a ruling class. Slaves are constrained in the pursuit of their interests. They are constrained on account of a variety of mechanisms, sometimes changing and by no means confined to the immediate presence of lethal force. They can and have broken those bonds (thousands of North American slaves did escape), but only by risky and illegal actions. Complex as it is, the notion of a ruling class is at least as closely tied to unifying metaphors as the physicists' concepts previously cited, energy, for example.

Even more important, Marx's notion of a ruling class singles out those aspects of the social process that are most relevant to a certain question of political choice: To what extent do most people need to go outside of channels, doing what is risky, discouraged, perhaps punished, in order to bring about significant changes? Suppose you want to bring about a major change in society. To the extent to which there is a ruling class, with interests opposed to such change, there are grounds for pessimism about any strategy based on the expectation that government will tolerate, perhaps even protect, crucial activities for change until they are successful. If, for example, big business is a ruling class, or something like one, many of us have grounds for pessimism about the prospects of bringing about major change solely by voting, by becoming activists within the major parties, by appealing to the consciences or interests of politicians, or by confining agitation to means that police and courts respect. Government will tend to thwart these efforts, where the interests of big business are involved. The obstacles will be based on systematic mechanisms, not just desires, resources and beliefs that current politicians and bureaucrats happen to have. If we do begin to make fundamental gains, government will tend to take them back, in ways we are ill-prepared to resist if we only work through channels.

In short, the concept of a ruling class is most coherent from the standpoint of someone choosing a style of political activism. It is unified pragmatically, like the concept of jade, which covers alloys of quite different chemical composition that are basically interchangeable from the standpoint of jewelers' interests. When so many academic interpretations of Marx underrate the importance of such deliberate political choices

113

in his social outlook, no wonder that he is often seen as lacking a political theory worthy of the name.

THE STATE AND REVOLUTION

In this analysis, the claim that there is a ruling class is in part a claim about change: only widespread illegal and disruptive activities can change the old connection between government action and the special interests of a certain social group. Of course, one such activity is extremely large-scale and well-organized violence directed at control of political institutions, in short, revolution, as the term is usually understood. But apart from revolution, there are other ways in which people have gone outside of channels, for example, in disruptive demonstrations, wildcat strikes, ghetto rebellions and mutinies.

For purposes of defining the notion of a ruling class as a tool of social analysis, the crucial mechanisms of change should probably be understood broadly, so that substantial disruptive action of any of these kinds might serve to break the old tie between government and social interests. If government acts in the interests of one group, does so as a result of definite mechanisms, shifting as circumstances change, *and* will do so unless resources are shifted through proscribed, extragovernmental uses of force, it is reasonable to speak of a ruling class and to apply Marx's metaphors. Moreover, it is useful to have a conception of political power permitting people to accept Marx's basic assessment of political dominance under capitalism even if they do not share all of his strategic views. Presumably, many of the millions of people in the United States who would answer that the government is run for the benefit of a few big interests have at least an informal version of a ruling-class hypothesis, while few are committed to revolution as the way to end dominance by those interests. Conversely, academic political scientists reject the broader ruling-class hypothesis, quite apart from its specifically revolutionary version. The broader usage divides issues in ways that facilitate discussion. I will adopt it, from now on.

114

So far as Marx's particular social theory is concerned, I certainly want to claim that Marx regarded the bourgeoisie, sometimes in coalition with other groups, as a ruling class in this broad sense. Moreover, he regarded this as a normal situation in advanced capitalist societies, not a sign of backwardness or a response to special crises: "The bourgeoisie has conquered for itself in the modern representative state exclusive political sway."[12] It would, however, be misleading to attribute this ruling-class thesis to Marx and to stop there. Or so I will argue. For he has a more specific idea of what it would normally take to break the old tie between government action and social interest, namely, revolution, in the sense that I presented at the beginning of this section. Of course, there might be exceptions to the rule that revolution is necessary, for example, the situation of an unpopular capitalist regime surrounded by large and advanced countries that have undergone successful socialist revolutions. But these are anomalies in the basically revolutionary theory, to be explained away by appealing to the mechanisms typically necessitating revolution, and their impact in the special circumstances at hand. Moreover, revolution, in Marx's view, is necessary for change in economically and technologically mature capitalist societies, not just in backward societies with entrenched and rigid precapitalist elites.

Among Marx scholars, it is very controversial to say that Marx held either the milder thesis, that it is crucial to go outside of channels through widespread disruptive activities, or the stronger thesis, that widespread, well-organized political violence is crucial for change, normally and even in the most advanced capitalist countries. It is time to confront this argument over Marx's meaning.

That Marx was committed to the stronger thesis (and, *a fortiori*, the milder one) would be no surprise to non-scholars whose knowledge of Marx largely consists of the *Manifesto*. There, he says quite explicitly that revolution is necessary in general:

[12] *Communist Manifesto*, p. 337.

115

In depicting the most general phases of the development of the proletariat, we traced the more or less veiled civil war, raging within existing society, up to the point at which the war breaks out into open revolution, and where the violent overthrow of the bourgeoisie lays the foundation for the sway of the proletariat.[13]

This emphasis on revolution is repeated throughout the writings of the 'forties and 'fifties, in statements that are often much more flamboyant. For example:

It is clear that the arm of criticism cannot replace the criticism of arms. Material force can only be overthrown by material force. . . .[14]

Meanwhile the antagonism between the proletariat and the bourgeoisie is a struggle of class against class, a struggle which carried to its highest expression is a total revolution. Indeed, is it at all surprising that a society founded on the opposition of classes should culminate in brutal contradiction, the shock of body against body, as its final denouement?

Do not say that social movement excludes political movement. There is never a political movement which is not at the same time social.

It is only in an order of things in which there are no more classes and class antagonisms that social evolutions will cease to be political revolutions. Till then, on the eve of every general reshuffling of society, the last word of social science will always be: 'Combat or death, the bloody battle or nothing. That is how the question is irresistibly posed' (George Sand).[15]

. . . we tell the workers: 'You have to endure and go through 15, 20, 50 years of civil war in order to change the circumstances, in order to make yourselves fit for power.'[16]

Despite these clear and general statements of the revolutionary view of change, there is an influential interpretation, advanced by Shlomo Avineri, according to which Marx rejected both the strong, revolutionary thesis and the somewhat

[13] Ibid. 344f.
[14] "Critique of Hegel's *Philosophy of Right*" (1843), in Bottomore, *Early Writings*, p. 18.
[15] *The Poverty of Philosophy* (1847) (Moscow, n.d.), p. 152.
[16] Meeting of the Central Authority [of the General Workers' Educational Society], September 15, 1850, *Collected Works* (New York, 1980), vol. X, p. 625.

116

milder one I sketched, in favor of an alternative conception of change which "runs all through his writings."[17] For Avineri, Marx simply is not a revolutionary in the ordinary sense of someone developing a basis for large-scale, organized violent change, though, of course, he is a revolutionary in his ends, since he wants to change the basic structure of society:

In the context of Marx's thought the revolution is never an act of violence using physical power for ends that transcend physical power. A view of revolution based on such a relationship between means and ends will ultimately substitute the means for the end. . . . To Marx the wielding of power as a distinct political means admits that circumstances (and consciousness as one of their components) are yet unripe for change. Where, however, power is applied not through a distinct political structure, it is mostly superflous, as socio-economic development itself has already caught up with the trends now being realized through the dialectics of internal change. The ends of social action are thus achieved without recourse to the threat of physical power. One can summarize Marx's position by saying that for Marx physical power will either fail or prove to be superfluous.[18]

While Marx accepts that industrial workers will sometimes resort to revolution, this can only be a mistake in advanced capitalist countries.[19] There, inherent tendencies of capitalism create means of economic transition through the growth of joint-stock companies and workers' cooperatives, while, in giving rise to universal suffrage, they produce sufficient political means to develop these partial forms of social control into a genuine socialist economy. Marx's description of the rise of joint-stock companies in *Capital* (III, 27, "The Role of Credit in Captialist Production") is "his most comprehensive description of the future development of capitalism and its internal change into a socialized system of production."[20] ". . . [T]he cooperative movement, just like the stock company, indicates for Marx the ultimate trends governing capitalist society."[21]

[17] Shlomo Avineri, *The Social and Political Thought of Karl Marx* (Cambridge, 1968), p. 217.
[18] Ibid., pp. 217f.
[19] Ibid., p. 220.
[20] Ibid., p. 177.
[21] Ibid., p. 180.

"Marx envisions the revolution occurring in the more developed countries through universal suffrage . . . because he sees in universal suffrage the resolution of the conflict between state and civil society."[22]

Avineri accepts that revolutionary tactics are not always mistakes for Marx. They may be appropriate where the gap between "socio-political structure" and "economic development" is large, in "countries with a strong authoritarian tradition, a huge docile peasantry and a late industrial development."[23] It is not clear how Avineri's Marx can admit even these exceptions, since "Marx concludes that any merely political insurrection of the proletariat trying to create politically conditions not yet developed immanently in the economic sphere is doomed to fail."[24] At one point, Avineri suggests that worker-led revolutions in relatively backward countries would be reflections of processes in economically advanced countries; to succeed, the revolutions must soon be consolidated in a worldwide socialist revolution.[25] Later, Avineri suggests that the admission of revolution in relatively backward countries is in tension with Marx's basic ideas: "[T]his historicism may be the most disappointing element in Marx's thought."[26] At any rate, Avineri's Marx rejects the widespread, organized use of violence, or even illegal disruptions, as superfluous at best in advanced societies, a departure from the normal unfolding of capitalist social processes, and, at most, a necessity in special circumstances constituting an explanatory challenge to Marx's general views.

As an interpretation of Marx's outlook all through his writings, this nonrevolutionary outlook cannot survive the clear and general revolutionary statements that I cited at the outset. In Avineri's book, it is defended through readings of an extremely one-sided kind.

[22] Ibid., p. 218.
[23] Ibid., p. 220.
[24] Ibid., p. 194.
[25] Ibid., p. 167.
[26] Ibid., p. 220.

In the interests of fairness, I mostly cited works that are important in Avineri's own view. In his comments on them, he consistently ignores clear and general claims of the necessity of revolution, while elevating tactical advice of a moderate kind to the level of general principle. Thus, while Avineri takes the *Manifesto* to be a valuable guide to Marx's conception of change (see especially pp. 204–8), he neglects the passage about "the violent overthrow of the bourgeoisie" in favor of a detailed examination of ten measures that, Marx and Engels say, would be "pretty generally applicable" "in the most advanced countries" in 1848. Here is Marx and Engels' own estimate of the relative weight of that tactical advice, in their preface to the German edition of 1872:

> The practical application of the principles will depend, as the Manifesto itself states, everywhere and at all times, on the historical conditions for the time being existing, and, for that reason, no special stress is laid on the revolutionary measures proposed at the end of Section II. That passage would, in many respects, be very differently worded today. In view of the gigantic strides of Modern Industry in the last twenty-five years, and of the accompanying improved and extended party organisation of the working class, in view of the practical experience gained, first in the February Revolution, and then, still more, in the Paris Commune, where the proletariat for the first time held political power for two whole months, this program has in some details become antiquated. One thing especially was proved by the Commune, viz., that "the working class cannot simply lay hold of the ready-made State machinery, and wield it for its own purposes." (See *The Civil War in France; Address of the General Council of the International Working Men's Association.* . . .)[27]

In short, the ten measures were marginal, to begin with, and should be revised in a more radical direction in light of the positive lessons learned in political revolutions.

Similarly, Avineri takes the "Introduction to a Critique of Hegel's *Philosophy of Right*" as reflecting Marx's view of the relation between political power and social circumstances.[28] The call to substitute the criticism of weapons for the weapons

---

[27] *Communist Manifesto*, p. 332.
[28] Avineri, *Social and Political Thought*, pp. 193f. See also p. 139.

of criticism is even presented verbatim. But it is glossed as a mild statement that "*praxis* revolutionizes existing reality through human action. This can be achieved by man's sociability and other-directedness."[29] The use of bayonets is other-directed, and perhaps it is sociable, but surely in a very strained and extended sense. As for the statement at the exiles' meeting of September 15, 1850, Avineri rescued it from relative obscurity as evidence of Marx's anti-insurrectional tendency. But this means ignoring the positive reference to the need for "15, 20, 50 years of civil war" and raising to the level of principle the sensible, limited tactical warning that follows: in the face of the failure of the revolutions of 1848–49, it is foolish to embark on a new, doomed effort to seize power immediately.

Of course, many people are fiercely revolutionary in their general statements, but so consistently counsel moderation in tactics that we take them to be opposed to revolution, implicitly and in practice. Avineri's book is the most scholarly expression of a common view that Marx was a nonrevolutionary in his practice. This is especially vivid in Avineri's assessment of "Marx's position in 1848. Despite his seeing in the political upheavals of this year a chance to create the circumstances for a socialist revolution, he consistently opposes all radical attempts at armed insurrection."[30] Of course, Marx does have criticisms of insurrections and their programs, and sometimes warns against doomed adventures, especially after the decisive defeats of the Paris, Berlin and Vienna uprisings. But the main thrust of his extensive advocacy, as editor of the *Neue Rheinische Zeitung*, is mockery of the Frankfurt Assembly for limiting their struggles to words, reminders of the crucial role of armed force in bringing about meaningful change, and the presentation of worker-led insurrections as the road to follow (of course, in a thoughtful and well-prepared way). Here is a representative sample:

The purposeless massacres perpetrated since the June and October events, the tedious offering of sacrifices since February and March,

[29] Ibid., p. 139.
[30] Ibid., p. 194.

the very cannibalism of the counter-revolution will convince the nations that there is only one way in which the murderous death agonies of the old society and the bloody birth throes of the new society can be shortened, simplified and concentrated, and that way is revolutionary terror.[31]

The history of the Prussian middle class, and that of the German middle class in general between March and December shows that a purely middle-class revolution and the establishment of bourgeois rule in the form of a constitutional monarchy is impossible in Germany, and that the only alternatives are either a feudal absolutist counter-revolution or a social republican revolution.[32]

Did we therefore have to advance our social republican tendency only in the last pieces of the *Neue Rheinische Zeitung*? Did you not read our articles about the June revolution, and was not the essence of the June revolution the essence of our paper?[33]

I have a good authority for calling these a representative sample. In the May 19 issue, Marx editorializes on the Prussian government's order that the newspaper cease publication. Marx's summary of the "tendency" of the paper throughout its publication is dominated by the first two passages, quoted verbatim in the editorial, and ends with the statement identifying the June insurrection with the essence of the paper. Nor was Marx's revolutionary activity confined to praise of revolutions from afar. In November 1848, he called for the organization of an armed militia, with special provision of weapons for the poor, and began a provocative campaign for the withholding of taxes. This was the basis for his subsequent arrest.[34]

While Avineri's book is probably the most influential recent argument against a revolutionary interpretation, a more plausible version of the nonrevolutionary view is presented by

---

[31] Issue of November 17, 1848, in *The Revolution of 1848–9: Articles from the Neue Rheinische Zeitung* (New York, 1972), p. 149.

[32] December 31, 1848, ibid., p. 202.

[33] May 19, 1848, ibid., p. 253. Avineri dismisses the June revolution as "the Jacobin-Blanquist *émeutes* of Paris" on p. 194 of his book.

[34] See *The Revolution of 1848–9*, pp. 167f., 227.

Lichtheim and Moore. They accept what naive readers of the *Manifesto* know, that Marx at one time regarded revolution as part of the basic and normal process of change. But they take Marx to have moved to a nonrevolutionary strategy, in response to the failure of workers' uprisings in his lifetime, the growth of the trades-union movement, the widening of the franchise in much of Western Europe, and the deepening of his own social theorizing. More precisely, Moore takes a nonrevolutionary view of the change to socialism to represent the "scientific" trend in Marx's thinking from around the time of *Capital*, coexisting with a "utopian" preference for total, sudden and revolutionary shifts.[35] For Lichtheim, the crucial change is complete, if never announced: "If Marx never expressly repudiated the 'Jacobin' model enshrined in the *Manifesto*, he did not in practice allow it to hamper him. The pragmatic theorist who guided the uncertain steps of the first International, and who preserved its heritage after the catastrophe of the Paris Commune, had finally outgrown the man of 1848."[36] In their sketches of the normal mechanism of change in Marx's mature and scientific view, Lichtheim emphasizes trades-union activity[37] while Moore emphasizes the spread of "cooperative associations within the framework of a capitalist economy."[38]

This interpretation has the virtue of respecting the clear evidence of the earlier texts from the 'forties and 'fifties. What is the state of the writings of Marx's later years? In his later theoretical statements, Marx, far from undercutting the revolutionary thesis, provides a much more thorough rationale for the necessity of large-scale organized violence than he offered in 1848. This is true, in particular, of the most theoretical sections in the French political histories, above all, in *The Civil War in France* (1871). (Defenders of a nonrevolutionary interpretation tend to dismiss the revolutionary tone of the journalistic sections as expressions of comradeship and personal

---

[35] See Moore "Marx and Lenin as Historical Materialists," pp. 222, 226, 233.
[36] Lichtheim, *Marxism* (London, 1965), p. 129.
[37] *Ibid.*, p. 128.
[38] "Marx and Lenin as Historical Materialists," p. 226.

admiration. One would expect the general and reflective passages, then, to provide the needed nonrevolutionary antidote.) In his later reflections on French political history, Marx emphasizes the capacity of the bourgeoisie to use its residual power, when it is losing dominance through electoral rules of the game, to provide crucial support for a more repressive regime. That is the needed response to a question that went unanswered in the *Manifesto*, "Why can't workers triumph, in the modern representative state, by continually electing the lesser of two evils?" In the later political writings, Marx is so far from regarding the peaceful transition to socialism as an outcome of capitalism's maturity that he presents rigidity and repression as the outcome of economic progress in France:

At the same pace at which the progress of modern industry developed, widened, intensified the class antagonism between capital and labour, the State power assumed more and more the character of the national power of capital over labour, of a public force organised for social enslavement, of an engine of class despotism. After every revolution marking a progressive phase in the class struggle, the purely repressive character of the State power stands out in bolder and bolder relief.[39]

While we cannot assume that this is the general trend, for Marx, in every capitalist country, he surely is denying that the bourgeoisie will inevitably, eventually, peacefully succumb to universal suffrage (often won, then lost in France, and freely manipulated by Louis Napoleon), trades unions, workers' cooperatives or the immanent logic of joint-stock companies.

Similarly, the political theory of the *Critique of the Gotha Program*, Marx's last major work (1875) is, if anything, an attack on programs for changing society primarily through elections and other state-protected mechanisms of change.

. . . [A]ccording to II, the German workers' party strives for 'the free state'. Free state—what is this? Freedom consists in converting the state from an organ superimposed upon society into one completely subordinate to it. . . . The German workers' party—at least if it adopts the program—shows that its socialist ideas are only skin-deep. . . . [I]t treats the state rather as an independent entity which

[39] *Civil War in France*, p. 552.

possess its own intellectual, ethical and libertarian bases. . . . [The party program's] political demands contain nothing beyond the old democratic litany familiar to all: universal suffrage, direct legislation, popular rights, a people's militia, etc. They are a mere echo of the bourgeois People's Party, of the League of Peace and Freedom.[40]

The textual basis for the Lichtheim-Moore thesis is a series of brief comments, from 1870 to 1880, in which Marx accepts the possibility that a workers' government might come to power through elections in England, the Netherlands or the United States. The comments are made in articles written for popular journals, interviews with journalists, and communications with an influential English trades unionist and politician, Henry Hyndman. The force of this evidence is blunted by the political context. Marx makes these comments in a period in which he was quite concerned to protect members of the International Workingmen's Association from mounting persecution. Indeed, several have the tone of Marx's defense at his own trial after the failure of the Revolution of 1848: if revolution broke out it was because a violent ruling class attacked reasonable workers.[41]

Still, a really satisfying interpretation would reconcile these statements, as strictly and literally meant, with the arguments for large-scale, organized violence in the major writings of the period. Engels provides the solution in his preface to the English edition of *Capital* in 1886.

. . . [T]he voice ought to be heard of a man whose whole theory is the result of a lifelong study of the economic history and condition of England, and whom that study led to the conclusion that, at least in Europe, England is the only country where the inevitable social revolution might be effected entirely by peaceful and legal means. He certainly never forgot to add that he hardly expected the English ruling classes to submit, without a 'pro-slavery rebellion,' to this peaceful and legal revolution.[42]

---

[40] *Critique of the Gotha Program*, pp. 394f.
[41] Marx was acquitted, and congratulated for his fine speech by the' jury foreman. The Prussian government banished him anyway.
[42] Engels, preface to *Capital* I, p. 17.

124

With memories of Allende's Chile still fresh, Engels' meaning should be clear to us, as it must have been clear to readers who had lived through the triumph of Louis Napoleon or through the defeat of the Paris Commune. It is one thing for a movement with a program threatening dominant social groups to win an election. It is another thing for it to change society. If the changes are as dramatic as the creation of socialism, success in a civil war is required. This may seem to be a comment on politics after capitalism has ended. But brief strategic reflection shows otherwise. A workers' movement whose practice is confined to electoral agitation will hardly be able to put down a "pro-slavery rebellion," with the bulk of material and professional military expertise on the other side. The Chilean and nineteenth-century French examples are poignant, though not conclusive, evidence for this view. Most poignant of all are the histories of the largest socialist movement in the West and the largest one per capita, German and Austrian socialism, respectively, between the two World Wars.

Marx's own response to the defeat of the 1848–49 revolutions was to make such strategic considerations more explicit and emphatic. In the "Address of the Central Committee to the Communist League" (1850), he describes a pattern of revolution in Germany in which workers can expect to be betrayed by liberal bourgeois or petty-bourgeois parties at the time of victory. His proposal is that the basis be laid for independent political *and* military activity well before the ultimate betrayal. "But in order to be able energetically and threateningly to oppose this party, whose treachery to the workers will begin from the first hour of victory, the workers must be armed and organised. The arming of the whole proletariat with rifles, muskets, cannon and munitions must be put through at once, the revival of the old Citizens' Guard directed against the workers must be resisted."[43]

In sum, the primary claim in Marx's mature political theory is that organized large-scale violence is necessary to end bour-

[43] Tucker, *The Marx-Engels Reader*, p. 369.

125

geois dominance. The possibility of socialist electoral triumph turns out to be a relatively secondary question of timing. The way to change society, as he sees it, involves both persuasion and organizing a fighting force outside of the state to take part in a violent class struggle. An electoral triumph may, atypically, precede violent class struggle, but it never supplants it. Surely, it is not seriously misleading to summarize this position as "the necessity of revolution," if the hedge about timing is understood.

I have emphasized Marx's revolutionary side for two reasons. It is the subject of central controversies about Marx's meaning. And it represents the dynamic aspect of the concept of a ruling class which I am trying to extract and apply. In other contexts, it would be important to balance this aspect of Marx's political thought with others. If democratic procedures were not his basic mechanism for change, he regarded universal suffrage as an important gain, identified the success of socialist revolution as "win[ning] the battle of democracy,"[44] and regarded the bloodshed of revolution as an enormous burden only to be borne in the reasonable expectation of enormous gains. Still, the need for widespread, illegal confrontation and disruption must be made a part of the thesis that there is a ruling class. Otherwise, the distinctive contribution of Marx's notion will be lost, in large measure. Or so I shall argue in the next chapter, when I apply Marx's conception of political power to present-day political theory.

TESTABILITY

When Marx's hypotheses are made flexible and abstract, the worry arises that they have been drained of content. How could we test the thesis that there is a ruling class? In the same way as every interesting theoretical statement is tested, by comparing it with the most powerful current rivals to see which is best able to explain the course of events. This is not just

---

[44] *Communist Manifesto*, p. 352.

true of historical or social hypotheses. Experiments or astronomical observations are courses of events as well.

Since ruling-class hypotheses typically characterize enduring social systems, it might seem that appeals to long-term
patterns would be the major empirical arguments. They certainly play a role, especially in establishing the plausibility or
implausibility of rival claims. If, in the course of U.S. history,
major political changes with a profound effect on social interests have always been preceded by violence and its attempted
repression, that is easily explained on a ruling class hypothesis,
but not on the hypothesis that elections are the only important
arena for adjusting conflicts of interest. Still, the detailed investigation of particular historical episodes cannot be avoided
here. A ruling-class hypothesis and its most powerful rivals
are causal hypotheses, not simple predictions of temporal patterns. While one hypothesis may fit an overall pattern better
than the others, several will fit, at least approximately, if accompanied by appropriate auxiliary hypotheses concerning
how people think and respond. For example, in the pattern
just described, violence might have simply served the role of
breaking down moral inertia and putting issues on the public
agenda. The most satisfying tests of these auxiliary adjustments move sociology squarely into the realm of history, investigating actual episodes of change in sufficient detail that
one can see which auxiliary hypotheses best fit the facts.

To have a bearing on the primary general hypothesis that
there is a ruling class, the specific episodes must be chosen by
fair rules of comparison. A specific success in supporting historical explanation counts strongly in favor of a hypothesis just
in case the latter succeeds where its rivals dictate that it is most
likely to fail. Thus it is not very important if the United States
in 1880 looks like a society in which big business is the ruling
class. Who ever denied this? It is important if New Deal reforms are best explained as concessions to working-class militancy, on the part of political leaders prepared not to make
concessions, even to be repressive when the costs to the
bourgeoisie were worth the gains. For the New Deal is sup-

posed to be an example of the direct influence of labor on the state, or (alternatively) of the impact of deepened moral awareness on government policy. When Marxists seek to explain the overall course of the New Deal as a ruling class response to crisis, they argue, for example, that they can provide the best accounts of such episodes of coercion as the Flint sitdown strike of 1937 and Roosevelt's jailing of three Communist Party leaderships during the Lend Lease period. If Roosevelt's social program in the early 1930s, before the sitdown strikes and other ominous unrest, had the significance of his later proposals, that would be a problem for Marxist historians. But it didn't, and the relative conservatism of the "first New Deal" is part of the Marxist case.

Of course, in these comparisons, general hypotheses are matched against the data in light of a variety of background principles used to interpret the data. For example, it is rarely obvious and uncontroversial whether a policy change would serve the long-term interests of the bourgeoisie. Certainly, it cannot simply be read off of the data that protection and co-optation of industrial unionism was the best strategy for the bourgeoisie after 1937. The most one can demand is that ultimate interpretive assumptions be shared by all disputants, keeping comparisons fair. If data are found that favor one alternative when interpreted via shared principles, that is confirmation. But if interpretive principles distinctive to one alternative are used against another, the argument is unfair and no confirmation takes place. Thus, it is not fair for a Marxist to argue against non-Marxist accounts of Lend Lease, while interpreting Roosevelt's statements on the assumption that U.S.-British ties reflect common interests in the context of inter-imperialist rivalries.

This practice of comparison may finally support the eclectic conclusion that a number of rival hypotheses are equally justified. But it may also single out one rival. Darwinian evolutionary theory is one outstanding example of a hypothesis that could only be tested by piecemeal explanatory comparison. And Darwinian evolution won.

STRUCTURALISM AND INSTRUMENTALISM

Among Marxist political theorists, the most important recent controversy over the nature of political power has been the conflict between the so-called "structuralist" and "instrumentalist" approaches. Now that the complexities of the concept of a ruling class are clearer, the debate can be seen to depend on a shared tendency toward oversimplification. This is one of those demoralizing controversies in which each side is largely right, but for the wrong reasons, when it criticizes the other.

Before, I tried to show that Marx's notion of a ruling class is unified by certain leading metaphors and by a concern with certain questions of political choice. Structuralists and instrumentalists are agreed in seeking simplicity at another level, the emphases that should govern projects of research into particular ruling classes. In both approaches, the description of mechanisms for maintaining social dominance is primary. The disagreement concerns the kinds of mechanisms most fruitfully studied, very roughly, the interactions of whole institutional systems for structuralists, the shape of typical careers for instrumentalists. No matter which emphasis one chooses, simplification at this level is, in fact, misplaced. Each approach is apt to deprive investigators of crucial evidence and explanatory options in pursuing questions that are made prominent by Marx's political theory.

Structuralists study the systems of institutions and ideologies through which a capitalist state fulfills its function of coordinating and maintaining capitalist relations of production in the territory in question. Poulantzas' *Political Power and Social Class* and Althusser's "Ideology and Ideological-State Apparatuses" are central works in this tradition. Poulantzas' description of the distinctive functions served by state bureaucracies and Althusser's argument that the public school system has become a central aspect of the state, on account of ideological needs in an era of universal suffrage and organized socialist movements, are representative projects in this style. Instrumentalists, by contrast, tend to study the work situations, patterns of personal interaction, and sources of personal influ-

129

ence that produce the tendency for government officials to act in the interests of the bourgeoisie. Milliband's *The State in Capitalist Society* is widely taken to epitomize this approach. Establishing the predominance of members of the bourgeoisie at the upper reaches of the bureaucracy and in major cabinet positions is a typical instrumentalist project. The labels, it should be added, are somewhat misleading here. Structuralists are certainly interested in processes of change. The label is partly an artifact of French intellectual history, in particular, of the perceived resemblance between Althusser's Marxism and Levi-Strauss' anthropology. The instrumentalists received their label from their critics.

The two approaches are more than matters of taste because each is supposed to describe the questions that should dominate Marxist investigations of political power. According to structuralists, extensive concern with mechanisms of interpersonal influence at the very least distracts social scientists from the important questions about bourgeois dominance, at worst so confuses them that they do not understand those questions at all. This charge often takes the specific form of the accusation that instrumentalist research "leads finally, not to the study of the objective coordinates that determine the distribution of agents into social classes and the contradictions between these classes, but the search for *finalist* explanations founded on the *motivations for conduct* of the individual actors."[45] Instrumentalists accuse structuralists of a flight into abstraction in which essential aspects of Marxist political theory are lost. In particular, Marxist structuralism is supposed to ignore "the importance of empirical validation (or invalidation)"[46] and, also, to overemphasize determination by general structural constraints, ignoring the impact of transitory political forms, fascism, for example, on social history and political strategy.

The general charges are right on both sides, but not for the specific reasons given. The instrumentalist priority on de-

---

[45] Nicos Poulantzas, in an exchange with Ralph Milliband, "The Problem of the Capitalist State," in Robin Blackburn, ed., *Ideology in Social Science* (New York, 1973), p. 243.

[46] Milliband, in ibid., p. 256.

picting networks of influence *is* distorting. This is because an accurate depiction of the networks connecting government action with business interests at a given time does not (at least on a Marxist view) adequately represent the extent of business domination in politics. What is missing is an assessment of the fluidity of the means of dominance, the capacity of a ruling class to mobilize resources not included in the map of influence, with the result that a new pattern of influence is created if the old one won't do. Karl Marx and Theodore Roosevelt would have largely agreed in describing the mechanisms of influence in the United States at the turn of the century. They would have disagreed as to whether honest elections, trustbusting, and the decline of bribery at the higher echelons of government would alter social bias in government action. Without investigations as to what would or could happen in the way of change, the distinctiveness of Marx's hypotheses is missed. These questions of what would or could happen are not resolved by mapping the current network of influences. By the same token, it is a virtue of structuralism that it directs our attention to ways in which new institutions arise to serve old functions of social control.

On the other hand, the structuralist charge that instrumentalists are obsessed with individuals' psychological motivations is quite beside the mark. The mechanisms of influence that are overemphasized by instrumentalists may consist of objective situations and associated interests that do not provide agents with *their* reasons for action or belief, even if they are *the* reasons why they act or believe in ways that maintain the system. To say, for example, that politicians are guided by an objective interest in support by the mass media does not require reading their minds, to determine that they lie when they claim to act on principle. (I discuss these distinctions further at the end of the next chapter.)

If instrumentalists are too concerned with the temporary and concrete, structuralists operate at a level of excessive abstraction. To this extent, the standard charges against them are true. But it is not true, as in the standard indictment, that structuralism is, in principle, unconcerned with empirical data,

131

whatever the practice may have been. Identifying the interests served by institutions is usually a matter of enormous empirical controversy. Nor are structuralists unaware of the variation in institutions through which basic social functions are served. Indeed, the capacity to explain such change is an advantage of the structuralist over the instrumentalist approach.

The flaw in structuralism is, rather, that overemphasis on the function of whole institutions results in the neglect of quite particular kinds of data and explanatory options, which can be of overriding importance when crucial questions are investigated. More specifically, the neglect of patterns of influence means the loss of evidence for hypotheses about the nature of class interests, a central question for structuralists themselves. In addition, inattention to work situations and typical careers within institutions can produce a loss of crucial means for explaining why and in what direction government changes in response to challenges, what should be the main explanatory advantage of structuralism.

To determine whether government policies objectively serve the interests of a social group is no easy matter. In the United States, hundreds, if not thousands, of economic experts alone fiercely debate what policies the interests of big business dictate. Moreover, questions of the fit between policies and interests can play an important role in the dispute as to whether there is a ruling class. For some, the Indochina War is an important instance of the dominance of policy by the international needs of big business. For others, the war was so irrational, in terms of those needs, as to count against the ruling-class hypothesis. To resolve those questions of interests, social scientists need all the evidence they can get. And, especially where long-term patterns are concerned, indirect arguments from the mechanisms of influence can play a vital role. An argument, à la Milliband, that groups such as the Council on Foreign Relations—dominated by old Eastern firms and taking a cool, expert and long-term view of international affairs—have played a leading role in the formulation of foreign policy, would certainly be relevant. In the 1950s and 1960s, the Council and such auxiliary groups as the Rockefeller Brothers Fund made detailed strategic arguments that aggressive counterinsurgency was necessary to preserve United States dominance in less developed countries. If these groups are centrally located in the network of influence, this would support the thesis that bourgeois interests, not autonomous Cold War ideology, often run amok, guide United States foreign policy. And that claim is surely crucial if a ruling-class hypothesis is to fit the United States. More direct structuralist arguments from economic imperatives are important too. But to suppose that the direct argument is always the more convincing here, is not structuralist, but naive. Ascriptions of social interests depend on auxiliary arguments from the whole of social science.

Among Marxists themselves questions of interests that are sensitive to the location of instrumentalist mechanisms are often crucial. No Marxist believes that the fit between bourgeois interests and government action is perfect in the short run. (Or for that matter, in the very long run. Eventually, the bourgeoisie has no winning option.) The most that can be said about the short run is that the institutions and mechanisms of influence create a very approximate fit and that other, feasible arrangements would not as a rule create a better one. Whether government policy is unreasonable, in bourgeois terms, at a given point in time, can be an open and crucial question for Marxists. Thus, whether the Reagan administration's basic policies are a temporary fluke, the reflection of interests of a faction of big business, or the reflection of the interests of big business as a whole, in a time of unprecedented challenges, is a subject of heated debate. What arguments are made or alliances formed will partly depend on the answers. What (if any) mechanisms of influence changed with the elections of 1980, whether, say, the Eastern Establishment was defeated, or rightwing populists gained substantial influence, is obviously relevant to these questions of whose interests are served.

In another way, the instrumentalist map of personal situations is even more directly relevant to Marxist explanations of political change or the failure of change. While the interests served by capitalist institutions are unambiguously bourgeois,

for Marxists, the interests of occupants of roles in those institutions may not be bourgeois and may be quite ambiguous.
Yet the goals, alliances and antagonisms dominating the political process are supposed to be determined by these roles
and the associated interests. To take the most obvious case, in
a capitalist firm, a bourgeois institution if any is, managers are
pulled one way by their work situations and objective interests,
proletarians another, and many white-collar workers are pulled
in several directions at once. Among the groups whose role in
change has been crucial to Marxist political explanations, many
have been groups defined by a position in the political system
itself, for example, soldiers, civil servants and participants in
political parties. According to structuralists, it is usually a mistake to emphasize the role of careers, work situations and personal interests typical of the bearers of these roles, as against
the social interests served by the institutions in which they
function. But, in fact, these instrumentalist concerns are often
essential to explaining large-scale changes in the mechanisms
of government, a crucial project of Marxist political theory in
general, and Marxist structuralism in particular.

Consider, for example, what has become the most important
problem of explaining political change in the twentieth century, the explanation of the Nazi seizure of power. In *Behemoth*,
Neumann explains the Nazi triumph, in essence, as due to the
German bourgeoisie's need for aggressively nationalist and repressive rule, with genuine popular appeal, as a basis for international expansion and labor discipline in the conditions of
the Great Depression. Whatever its ultimate validity, this is
an outstanding example of Marxist political explanation after
Marx, and any theory of the ruling class should do justice to
its power.[47] To support and develop his explanation, Neu-

[47] See Franz Neumann, *Behemoth* (New York, 1944; 1st ed. 1942), especially
the historical "Introduction." Rupert Palme Dutt, *Fascism and Social Revolution*
(New York, 1936) contains other important evidence and elaborations of a
Marxist account, along with some extraneous conspiratorial speculations. It is
a mark of the power of Neumann's argument that it has since been supported
by a variety of studies committed to a contrary perspective. Thus, David
Schoenbaum, in *Hitler's Social Revolution* (New York, 1966), means to show
Footnote continued on following page

mann needed to answer questions such as these: How could big business so dominate German political realities, given the power of the Weimar Social Democratic Party? If the bourgeoisie was the ruling class in politics, why weren't their stewards the conservative nationalists whom they usually supported with their money and their votes? How can the Nazis, with their populist attacks on big business, be seen as representatives of big business? Neumann's answers largely consist of instrumentalist accounts of influences and personal interests, that is, descriptions of the careers, interest and outlooks of typical Social Democratic leaders (often in sharp contrast to those of the rank and file); the influence of big business on the Weimar judiciary and bureaucracy; the interactions of Hitler and his circle with big business, the judiciary and the army (with some sharp contrasts to the Nazi rank and file,); and the careers, outlooks and limitations of traditional conservative politicans. Indeed, these accounts of careers, influences, interests and outlooks dominate the relevant parts of *Behemoth*. It is not just that they are needed defensively, to answer objections from non-Marxist historians. Neumann is describing causal factors that play an essential role in answering central questions about the change in the machinery of government: Why were the Social Democrats incapable of either managing Germany's international expansion or effectively opposing expansionism? Why couldn't conservative nationalists stay in control, when the Presidency, banking and heavy industry were squarely in their camp? His answers often consist of a balance of tendencies characteristic of occupants of a niche in a structure. But the balance is not entailed by any large-scale description of that

---

that the Nazis revolutionized Weimar social arrangements, yet offers abundant statistical confirmation that Nazi Germany developed further all the trends in wealth, income and production characteristic of Weimar. William Sheridan Allen, in *The Nazi Seizure of Power* (Chicago, 1965), often lays the blame on anti-Nazis who opposed the moderate leadership of the Social Democratic Party, but gives much evidence of the uselessness of that leadership in combatting the Nazis. In his recent voting studies, Richard Hamilton, who regards Neumann and Palme Dutt as implausible conspiracy theorists, emphasizes the centrality of the bourgeoisie as leading supporters of the Nazis, in contrast to the standard assumption that the Nazi triumph was a revolt of the lower middle class.

135

structure. If, to put one of Neumann's ideas in *very* crude outline, the Social Democratic leadership was too well co-opted to meet the Nazi seizure of power with substantial force and boldness, but too inadequately co-opted to help manage an aggressive foreign policy, this cannot be deduced from any general account of the nature and function of contemporary institutions.

If instrumentalism neglects the fluidity of mechanisms, structuralism neglects change in its own way. It underestimates the impact of situations, interests and resources that are not entailed in large-scale descriptions of institutions. Yet these extra-institutional details may play a crucial role in transforming political structures. Either the instrumentalist principle of attention to personal situations *or* the structuralist principle of attention to institutional functions can turn one's gaze away from the basic sources of change.

A GOOD QUESTION

As explicated in the previous sections, the thesis that there is a ruling class in society seems to be intelligible. It is intelligible, even plausible, that a coalition of large landowners, big merchants and manufacturers were the ruling class in eighteenth-century England. So it ought to be at least intelligible (whether true or false) that there is a ruling class in the United States today. Moreover, a social group can approach the status of a ruling class on all three dimensions. So it seems an interesting question, *to what extent*, say, big business is a ruling class in the United States today. It is, above all, such questions of degree that I advocate. Everyone accepts measuring the distribution of political power as a task for social science. In these measurements, the question of the extent to which various groups are a ruling class ought to be one yardstick.

Finally, we can investigate some single part of the three-part question, to what extent is there a ruling class. In the course of the next chapter, I will present a variety of reasons, theoretical and practical, for studying the whole, undissected question. But the parts have independent interest, too. One outcome of my subsequent arguments will be that questions of political power that now dominate empirical political theory are inadequate to investigate any one of the three parts. None sheds any light on the relevant question about government actions and social interests. If the question of mechanisms of influence is raised at all, it is raised in a way that neglects the dynamic aspect of the question, the adjustment of mechanisms to changing circumstances. The questions of militance, repression and entrenchment raised by the third sub-thesis tend simply to be ignored.

The question, "To what extent is there a ruling class?" is quite complex and, often, very hard to answer. Yet it is a central question in a great many frameworks for inquiry that have generated important historical explanations. Some examples are Marx on nineteenth-century French history; Neumann on twentieth-century German history; Hill on the English Civil War; Genovese on the United States Civil War; Hilton on English feudalism; Bowles and Gintis on United States educational systems; Lenin, Hilferding and Hobson on imperialism and the background for World War I; Williams on United States diplomatic history; recent explanations of the persistence of racism in the twentieth-century United States;[48] and recent explanations of the Vietnam War as a defense of United States corporate hegemony.[49] I am not dogmatically proposing that these explanations are valid. But they are worth taking seriously. And all depend on the thesis that certain social groups have been a ruling class, or have approached the status of one in large part and to a high degree.

Why is the complex difficult question "To what extent is there a ruling class?" so important in the pursuit of social explanations? In part, because of its explanatory power, as revealed in the writings to which I have alluded. In part, because of its practical importance, in judging whether change requires activism outside of forms that government protects. Not to ask

---

[48] See, for example, Robert Cherry, "Economic Theories of Racism"; and Michael Reich, "The Economics of Racism," in David Gordon, ed., *Problems in Political Economy: An Urban Perspective*, 2d ed., (Lexington, Mass., 1977).

[49] See, for example, Harry Magdoff, *The Age of Imperialism* (New York, 1969.)

to what extent there is a ruling class is to avoid systematic investigation of the issue, how far outside of channels activists have to go.

It is important for my subsequent argument that there be some group in the United States today to which something approaching ruling-class status can be attributed, with at least some plausibility. By this well-hedged claim, I simply mean that some hypothesis of ruling-class or near ruling-class status should be worthy of further investigation and refinement, not outright dismissal. After all, the analysis of the present-day United States and similar societies has, understandably, been the central pursuit of the study of politics, in the United States. If there is no plausible candidate for anything approaching ruling-class status in the United States, then the neglect of the notion of a ruling class is just a reasonable economy. In any case, for exposition's sake, a specific example of a putative ruling class will be needed to illustrate subsequent discussions of how confusions between different questions of power might obscure the existence of a ruling class.

I would propose that at least one group is a candidate for something approaching ruling-class status in the United States, namely, families whose wealth is a source of significant influence on the policies of major firms. High-level executives in these firms and in major corporate law firms are typically led by their situations to make common cause with these wealthiest few. For present purposes, they may all be counted as part of the same group, which I shall label "big business". Whatever the importance for the internal dynamics of corporate life (in my view, overrated) of potential splits between managers and dominant owners, the basic solidarity of actual interests is the important fact for the study of political power.

A number of facts suggest the need to take seriously the possibility that big business may approach the status of a ruling class as I have defined it. In the United States, a mere one-fifth of one percent of the spending units own two-thirds of the publicly held industrial stock.[50] One-half of one percent

---

[50] G. William Domhoff, *Who Rules America?* (Englewood Cliffs, 1967), p. 45.

own one quarter of all privately owned wealth.[51] The richest
tenth receive more money income than the poorer half.[52] One-
tenth of one percent of all corporations own sixty percent of
all corporate assets.[53] At the same time, the careers and needs
of important people in government make this concentration of
economic resources a political resource. Senatorial races, not
to mention Presidential ones, frequently cost over a million
dollars. The media are dominated by three television networks
worth about two billion dollars each. National political leaders
have incomes and life styles similar to big-business people.
Heads of the major bureaucracies typically are members of the
bourgeoisie. In his 1967 study, Domhoff described a pattern
that has certainly continued since. Between 1932 and 1967,
eight of thirteen Secretaries of Defense or War were listed in
that manual of haut-bourgeois prestige, the Social Register, as
were five of eight Secretaries of State, including three corporate lawyers and a partner in a Wall Street bank.[54] It is a
truism of politics and economics that fundamental disagreements between government and big business as a whole would
create dramatic economic difficulties, either by affecting the
government's access to credit of relatively noninflationary
kinds or through the impact of business discontent on investment and unemployment. Note that none of these mechanisms
connecting government action with bourgeois interests entails
a conspiracy in which politicians secretly uphold the special
interests and mandates of big business behind a screen of dis-
honest appeals to the general interest.

If mechanisms of influence are often as one would expect
on the hypothesis that big business is the ruling class, so are
temporal patterns of change. Since World War II, peaceful and

[51] Richard Parker, *The Myth of the Middle Class* (New York, 1972), p. 121.
[52] Ibid., p. 8.
[53] Samuel Bowles and Herbert Gintis, *Schooling in Capitalist America* (New
York, 1976), p. 60. Chapter 3 of their book contains detailed arguments that
the basic distribution of wealth and income has not changed in the United
States in the twentieth century. Gabriel Kolko's seminal *Wealth and Power in
America* (New York, 1962) is still, in many ways, the most perspicuous survey
of inequalities of economic resources.
[54] *Who Rules America?*, pp. 97, 99.

successful initiatives for major shifts in national policy have almost always originated in groups officially sponsored by big business, for example, the Council on Foreign Relations, the Committee on Economic Development, and such specialized groups as the Rockefeller Brothers Fund, the Urban Land Institute and the Trilateral Commission. Periods of reform that have bettered the situations of large groups of working people have almost always been preceded by related outbreaks of illegal violence, including the uprisings of urban workers and of sharecroppers in the 1890s; the general strikes, sit-down strikes and violent labor-management confrontations between the World Wars; and the ghetto rebellions of the 1960s. If reform has been one response, repression has been, too, including the use of the National Guard and support for the Klan and Pinkertons in the 1890s, Wilson's Red Scare, Roosevelt's jailings of Communist Party leaders, Truman's leadership of the post-War anti-communist campaign, and police and National Guard violence in the 1960s.

These facts do not, remotely, demonstrate that big business is a ruling class. In the process of fair comparison that I sketched before, one needs to consider the alternative hypotheses that could account for them, then to sift the rival explanatory frameworks by seeing how well they account for detailed features of specific historical episodes. Still, these facts do make it dangerously hasty to ignore the possibility that big business approaches ruling-class status. By rights, it should be a live option in specific empirical studies. Ways of thinking about political power that make it hard to investigate to what extent there is a ruling class will impoverish social science, rather than clarify it.

There are other candidates for ruling-class status, for example, a triumvirate of stable leadership groups dominating major business firms, national politics and the military. In concentrating on the option of big-business dominance, I do not mean to dismiss these alternatives. It should be clear, in what follows, that the ways in which the hypothesis that big business approaches ruling-class status has been obscured correspond to ways in which the alternative ruling-class hypotheses would be obscured as well. Though I will emphasize just one of these alternatives, the goal of these discussions is to show that the broad category of ruling-class hypotheses has, as a whole, been neglected in illegitimate ways.

CHAPTER FOUR

Questions of Power in Political Theory

DESPITE its great importance, theoretical and practical, the question, "To what extent is there a ruling class?" is a hidden question in the study of politics today. Political scientists do ask where political power lies. Moreover (an enduring legacy of Marx) they do not presuppose that real political power is located at the top of official government hierarchies. But the meanings they attach to the question "Where does political power lie?" do not shed much light on the question of whether or to what extent there is a ruling class. This is true, moreover, not just of the pluralist mainstream and their structural-functionalist allies, but of most dissenters as well.

PLURALISM AND ITS DISCONTENTS

Many theorists take the question of political power to be, "To what extent do various people currently get what they want out of government in the face of opposing interests, where relevant particular issues are concerned?" For pluralists, getting what you want, here, means getting the outcome you *actually* voted for, either literally or, figuratively, by investing time or money in influencing the political process. Bachrach and Baratz, in their influential criticism of pluralism, in effect propose a different understanding of getting what you want, namely, getting the outcome you *would* have voted for if appropriate alternatives had been on the agenda. They are, however, unwilling to depart too far from the situation of explicit choice that the pluralists favor. If you would have voted for an alternative, then its existence is a token of your power, even if your choice would have resulted, in turn, from manipulations of your information or preferences.[1] Critics from the left, Steven Lukes among them, have suggested that the real basis for an assessment of power should be the choice that would be made with adequate information and undistorted deliberations.[2] On the basis of such distinctions between actual inclinations and real interests, Lukes and others take the question of political power to be whether government does what various people would have wanted if their information were the best available and if their insight into their own needs were clear.

On any of these understandings of the question of political power, the basic thesis of Dahl's *Who Governs?* is converted into a truism. Political power is dispersed throughout society, though different bases for political power are differently and unequally dispersed.[3] As Dahl used the term at the time, we live in a polyarchy.[4] In particular, major businesspeople don't always get the outcomes they vote for, the ones they would

---

[1] "Suppose . . . there appears to be universal acquiescence in the status quo. Is it possible, in such circumstances, to determine whether the consensus is genuine or instead has been enforced through nondecision-making? The answer must be negative. Analysis of this problem is beyond the reach of a political analyst and perhaps can only be fruitfully analyzed by a philosopher" (P. Bachrach and M. Baratz, *Power and Poverty* [New York, 1970], p. 49).

[2] See Steven Lukes, *Power* (London, 1974), pp. 23f.

[3] See, for example, the summary on p. 228 of Robert Dahl, *Who Governs?* (New Haven, 1961).

[4] Thus, in *Modern Political Analysis* (Englewood Cliffs, 1963), "'polyarchy' (rule by many)" is a political system "in which power over state officials is widely, though by no means equally shared" (p. 73). Subsequently, both in official definitions and in practice, there is a shift in usage from the description of power relations to the description of governmental institutions. In *Polyarchy* (New Haven, 1971) (see pp. 2–9) and *After the Revolution?* (New Haven, 1970) (see p. 78), "polyarchy" is defined as government with a system of elections involving broad suffrage and competition for offices. In the earlier usage, it is open to question, to put it mildly, whether India, Venezuela, and Pakistan in the 1950s are polyarchies. In the later usage, they obviously are. Yet formal polyarchy continues to be treated as if it has the same tendencies to fulfill social needs and moral demands that substantive polyarchy has. Subsequently, I will suggest that this shift is a symptom of a tendency to convert claims about power that the pluralists explicitly defended in the early 1960s into unstated, undefended, but highly influential assumptions in the 1970s.

vote for if those alternatives were on the agenda, or the ones they would vote for if they were perfectly informed and rational.

This resolution of the question of political power does not matter one way or another so far as the existence of a ruling class is concerned. Of course, there will be polyarchy if there is no ruling class. But the existence of polyarchy, in the indicated sense, is also a consequence of the most plausible ruling-class hypotheses concerning our society.

In general, the best arrangement for a ruling class is one in which government takes on the job of adjusting that class's short-term interests on particular questions to its long-term interest in stability and acquiescence. Big business might have an isolated, short-term interest, if a small one, in my not giving a lecture sympathetic to Marxism. But here (if not in Chile or South Africa), it is now against their long-term interest for a policeman to stop me. The resultant uproar would not be worth the gain. In advanced industrial societies in normal times, the best situation for adjusting the interest in short-term gains to the long-term interest in stability is one in which political leaders are elected and are not usually businesspeople. In such a setting, the most effective ruling-class arrangement is one in which businesspeople often agitate for measures more pro-business in immediate terms than government leaders will accept. The typical major businessperson acknowledges the crucial distinction between institutional interests and issue-by-issue preferences when he says that he is a lifelong Republican, and declares that he would be appalled if the Democratic Party were to disappear.

At least three important needs would usually be served by this political division of labor, if big business is a ruling class. (Similar factors would point in similar directions, where other dominant groups are concerned.) In an industrial capitalist society, it is an extremely important source of stability if most people believe that elections are a means of counterbalancing the obvious influence on society created by the obvious concentration of economic power in the largest firms. This belief would not last for long if a typical Presidential election pitted the Chairman of the Board of Citicorp against the Chief Executive Officer of General Electric. In the second place, big business is routinely divided into competing factions, with conflicting interests that might be crucially affected by government policies. Eastern Establishment versus the Southern Rim, Rockefeller interests versus Morgan interests, manufacturers versus large-scale merchants versus plantation owners are a few historical examples. If the common interests of big business are not to be submerged in these rivalries, it is desirable that corporate factions not typically face the risk that political leadership will personally be held by an active member of an opposing faction. (Correspondingly, a President, such as Nixon, who tilts too far toward one side or another poses a significant threat to stability.) Finally, though major businespeople are fairly good judges of what corporate policies benefit their firms, they are not good judges of most people's attitudes and likely responses to government policies, or good creators of public opinion. Mistakes along these political dimensions may carry a heavy price in social disorder. Yet nothing in the career or situation of a typical leader of big business nourishes the needed talents. There is a need, then, for political leadership to be exercised by people who have succeeded in distinctively political careers, the career politicians who are the prime ingredients in Weber's recipe for a strong, expansionist capitalist nation-state, in "Politics as a Vocation." Given this official leadership by career politicians who are especially sensitive to real social costs in terms of discontent and disorder, business leaders are free to advocate policies more blatantly pro-business than their long-term interests permit. For example, when, in 1973, the Committee on Economic Development called for the virtual dismantling of liberal-arts education for young working-class people, instantaneous implementation would have produced pervasive discontent, hardly worth the savings. In context, this proposal was a rational policy initiative, which became a reality in due time under the ultimate guidance of career politicians.[5]

Given the division of labor between business leaders and political leaders, businesspeople will lose many votes. After all, in this system, the votes of businesspeople will tend to underestimate the bearing of their own need for acquiescence and cooperation in society at large. Moreover, the political interests of particular firms or factions will sometimes depart from the interests of big business as a whole. The wide dispersal of wins and losses in votes over public policy issues does not depend on fixed agendas or misinformation. So, counting vote by vote, people in many social groups often "get what they want out of government" and often fail to do so, on all the standard readings of the phrase, not just the pluralists'. There is polyarchy because there is a ruling class, with government acting as its long-term interests require.

One reason why the question "To what extent do people get what they want from government?" may be unilluminating is that it does not discriminate between two kinds of government responsiveness to social interests. Government may respond to the interests of one group of people only to the extent to which another group needs their cooperation, acquiescence, or obedience. In this sense, the government of the United States is often responsive to the interests of the Politburo of the U.S.S.R. On the other hand, government may respond to the interests of one group beyond the point at which such concern is of value to any other group. The question "To what extent is there a ruling class?" is concerned with whether government attends to interests outside the dominant group only on the first basis, or on the second as well. Despite ferocious disputes between partisans of the three different readings, the question

---

[5] *Who Really Rules?* (Santa Monica, 1978), William Domhoff's reanalysis of Dahl's New Haven data is an extremely detailed and persuasive account of the interaction between business leaders' initiatives in major policy shifts and the special sensitivities and talents of political and media leaders. Nothing Domhoff says contradicts Dahl's finding that big business often lost votes over contested issues in official forums. Yet no one reading Domhoff's book could fail to recognize the real dominance, of a nonconspiratorial sort, that underlies this polyarchy.

"To what extent do people get what they want from government?" does not discriminate between these two bases for getting what you want.

The need to disentangle the two bases for responsiveness is one reason why political theorists need to be political and social historians, choosing among explanations of government responses to crisis. One way to distinguish between the two bases is to look at what government does when it creates or alters institutions affecting the interests of groups outside an alleged ruling class. In the times of crisis in which such changes are made, the conflicts between rival social interests will be relatively acute. The extent to which alternative courses of government action would advance or defeat a group's interests will be, though far from transparent, clearer than in more placid times. Inertia or mere shrewdness in political maneuvering will be a less plausible explanation of the effective choices of dominant political leaders. Do political changes in times of crisis correspond to the changing needs of the dominant group when faced with new challenges? Or do they represent unnecessary, perhaps dangerous concessions from the standpoint of what group? It is often through such debates over history that the two sorts of responsiveness are disentangled. The claim that big business is the ruling class in the United States implies, for example, that Federal protection of union organizing was, in form and timing, the best way of reducing the militancy and unpredictability of unregulated organizing, not an undermining of labor discipline, that the welfare programs of the 'sixties were a response to urban unrest, not to urban needs as such, and that the current shift from welfare spending to defense spending reflects new challenges to the worldwide power of United States corporations, not a spontaneous backlash from earlier reforms. If, on the other hand, the question of whether there is a ruling class is divorced from the relatively familiar and coherent debates over such claims, it may seem unanswerable.

When they announce or prescribe practical responses to immediate crises as against general reflections during tranquil times, pillars of the bourgeois establishment are often close to the Marxist analysis in their emphasis on the government's function of containing discontent. Thus, in the decision upholding the National Labor Relations Act, Chief Justice Hughes portrays the Act as, above all, a response to disorder: "We are asked to shut our eyes to the plainest facts of national life. . . . [H]ow can it be maintained that industrial labor relations constitute a forbidden field into which Congress may not enter when it is necessary to protect interstate commerce from the paralyzing consequences of industrial war?"[6] Much more recently, in the "Report on the Governability of Democracies to the Trilateral Commission," Samuel Huntington, as impeccably anti-Marxist a writer as Chief Justice Hughes, argues for the need for the government to reverse or defy trends in public opinion, which lasted well into the 'seventies, that supported welfare and social-service spending over defense spending, the extension of democracy over respect for authority.

[T]he Defense Shift [public support for defense spending in the 1950s] was a response to the external Soviet threat of the 1940s; . . . the Welfare Shift was a response to the internal democratic surge of the 1960s. The former was primarily a product of elite leadership; the latter was primarily the result of popular expectations and group demands. . . . [A] government which lacks authority and which is committed to substantial domestic programs will have little ability, short of cataclysmic crisis, to impose on its people the sacrifices which may be necessary to deal with foreign policy problems and defense. In the early 1970s, as we have seen, spending for all significant programs connected with the latter purposes was far more unpopular than spending for any other domestic purpose. . . . A value which is normally good in itself is not necessarily optimized when it is maximized. We have come to recognize that there are potentially desirable limits to economic growth. There are also potentially desirable limits to the indefinite extension of democracy.[7]

[6] National Labor Relations Board vs. Jones and Laughlin Steel, *Supreme Court Reporter* 57 (1937), p. 626.
[7] Samuel Huntington, Michel Crozier, and Joji Watanuki, *The Crisis of Democracy* (New York, 1975), pp. 65, 105, 115. The existence of the "Welfare Shift" is documented with extensive survey data.

The Trilateral Commission, organized at David Rockefeller's initiative in 1973, is notable for having included every prominent member of the future Carter administration.

Apart from the conflation of two very different bases for taking desires and interests into account, there is another reason why the question, "Who gets what he wants out of government?" sheds little light on the existence of a ruling class. It fails to give adequate weight to the difference that the existence of certain kinds of political institutions can make to the content of rational, informed political preferences. In a parliamentary democracy, a major businessman will often advocate a measure the immediate adoption of which would not be feasible or would create unacceptable turmoil. In this special sense, his vote does not reflect his real interests, but not because of any manipulation of agendas, information or preferences. Rather, beyond a point, it is not his job but the job of the political system to take feasibility and acquiescence into account. If the Taft-Hartley Act had been enacted in 1945, without a campaign against labor unrest and communists in the unions, the results would probably have been disastrous for big business. It would have been equally disastrous not to press for such changes before they were feasible.

In sum, the questions of political power that I have examined are limited in scope because they are, in a way, apolitical. The distinctive function of government is to create a stable framework for reasonably efficient and peaceful interactions. Because government, by its nature, must be concerned with cooperation, acquiescence and obedience, the questions posed by pluralists and many of their critics cannot tell us whom government is serving. They cannot distinguish between interests that are of primary concern and interests that are problems for coordination, between losing votes that reflect a lack of power and losing votes that reflect the distinctive role of government in maintaining social power.

My point is to distinguish different questions, not to eliminate any. There are important practical concerns that dictate special attention to the question of the extent to which various people get what they want out of government. People engaged in electoral politics, lobbying (including the most benevolent "citizens' lobbying"), or simply trying to persuade the powerful of what morality or reason dictate will want to know where the powerful people are and will find this question their best guide. Similarly, the question of who gets what he wants is a central one for the social critic wondering which people bear individual moral responsibility for the mess we are in. In this context of moral judgment, it may be irrelevant, even misleading, to argue that Presidents and generals are not part of the ruling class. But these are not the only political concerns that ought to be based on rational political inquiry. Knowing to what extent various people get what they want out of government will not help someone who is wondering to what extent the government must actively be resisted for social change to be produced. Thus, it is a pun to say that questions of political power involve the impact of government on interests. In themselves, these questions ask whether government action bears a certain connection to people's interests. In addition, people's interests in politics, from context to context, will dictate which question of power they ought to pursue.

It might seem that I have been unfair to Bachrach, Baratz, Lukes and other critics of pluralism, through neglect of their emphasis on the exercise of power *over* someone else. Thus, in defining power, Bachrach and Baratz propose that a power relation exists between A and B if B acts as A wishes, when he otherwise wouldn't, out of fear that A will deprive him of something.[8] Lukes says, in summary of his view of power, "I have defined the concept of power by saying that A exercises power over B when A affects B in a manner contrary to B's interests."[9] It is above all because notions of power are presented through descriptions of relations of dominance that these writings have such a different tone from Dahl's *Who Governs?* and other pluralist classics.

However, if we are asking, "Where does political power lie?" these differences turn out to be matters more of style than of

[8] Bachrach and Baratz, *Power and Poverty*, p. 24.
[9] Lukes, *Power*, p. 34.

150

substance. In measuring the *distribution* of power, pluralists have always acknowledged that power means getting what you want in the face of opposition. The significant differences among these theorists concern the role of manipulated agendas, information and preferences. These differences, we found, will not close the gap between the assessment of the question of polyarchy and the assessment of the extent to which there is a ruling class.

How can the more left-wing pluralists tell us so little about the existence of a ruling class, when they are so concerned with phenomena of dominance? The answer, once again, is the apolitical nature of their concepts of political power. Knowledge of whether the various As have exercised power over the various Bs may tell us little about power depending on the operation of political institutions. In the Bachrach-Baratz-Lukes conception, blue-collar workers exercise power over businespeople whenever they produce a concession through a threat to strike. Unless we know the role of government in such interactions, this tells us nothing about political power. Of course, we can also ask who has the most power over political leaders, businesspeople or blue-collar workers? But here, the results are apt to be positively misleading if we want to know to what extent there is a ruling class. If big business is a ruling class, one would expect the interests of politicians and businesspeople generally to coincide. Indeed, I will eventually argue that this congruence is essential to a psychologically plausible ruling-class hypothesis. Thus, the conflicts of interest producing instances of power, on the Bachrach-Baratz-Lukes conception, will be rare and will often reflect nothing more than the arrogance or rigidity of individual politicians. On the other hand, if big business is a ruling class, it will be relatively common for political leaders to be roused to an uncomfortable or risky level of activity by the rebelliousness of workers or a new threat of rebelliousness. The course of life that is preferable, given a politician's personal interests, will be disturbed. If we extend concepts of dominance appropriate to one-on-one interactions to the study of politics in society at large, we may

151

find that workers have more power over government than bankers do, precisely when big business is the ruling class.

Lukes insists, "The point . . . of locating power is to fix responsibility for consequences held to flow from the action, or inaction of certain specifiable agents".[10] A similar concern for fixing individual responsibility sometimes seem to underlie Bachrach and Baratz' insistence on the importance of agenda-fixing, as against forthright debate, as a basis for power. No doubt, this is *a* point that locating power may have, and one best served by asking who is getting what he wants in the face of opposition. I hope that I have shown that it is not *the* point, either of all theorizing or of all important strategic discussions bearing on the question of locating power.

THE FATE OF PLURALISM

Pluralists believe that no social group or minority coalition of social groups dominates government in the United States. Political power, in their view, is more dispersed. This is the substantive issue that pluralists try to settle. I have argued that this substantive question must be begged, despite pluralists' intentions to the contrary, if the investigation is regulated by the general conceptions of political power that pluralists recommend.

Many political theorists now believe that such arguments with pluralism are antiquarian. In their view, pluralism has passed away. Most are influenced, in this judgment, by the leftward trend in the views of some pluralists, especially Robert Dahl, the most widely read and one of the most persuasive pluralist writers of the early 'sixties. Most are influenced, as well, by the present tendency for mainstream political scientists to analyze failures of government in the United States and other Western democracies, often attributing these failures to distorting effects of interest-group politics. Thus, the danger that inappropriate understandings of questions about political

[10] Ibid., p. 56.

power will lead to an unjustified preference for pluralism may seem irrelevant to current concerns.

In fact, pluralism is, if anything, more entrenched now than it was twenty years ago. In the early 'sixties, pluralists were at least compelled to make their methodology explicit and to marshal arguments for their beliefs about the distribution of political power. Now, the belief in the wide dispersal of political power is more apt to be a tacit assumption, a framework within which conservative, liberal, even left-wing alternatives are advanced and debated. If mainstream political scientists less frequently advance pluralist definitions of political power in defending a pluralist view of the political process, that is largely because they assume a pluralist view without defending it. Marx's political theory clarifies, by way of contrast, the continued presence of the substantive views characteristic of pluralism. (At the same time, a more specific statement of the essence of pluralism as a theory will make it clearer what substantive disputes are confused or neglected through one-sided emphasis on the question "To what extent do people get what they want out of government?")

In the heyday of pluralism as an explicit and explicitly defended theory, defenders identified the general thesis at issue as the claim that government policy was the outcome of a system of widely dispersed resources for influencing government officials, interacting with the preferences and talents of officials who are not wholly constrained by these influences. Each kind of political resource may be unequally distributed. But the different kinds are dominated by different groups, and a monopoly of one kind would at most enable a group to dominate a few areas of government policy. In particular, the concentration of wealth is not decisive, since universal suffrage makes the weight of numbers an important resource for the non-wealthy majority. The dispersal of different kinds of political resources often gives a political leader considerable options for successful initiatives in support of policies that would not otherwise be proposed as an outcome of bargaining among various social groups. Of course, political leaders may play a more passive role, on account of their particular circumstances, self-interest or personal style.[11]

Within this broad framework, important variations were possible, especially along two dimensions. First, the extent and the moral significance of inequalities in different kinds of resources might be variously assessed. Second, the extent to which political leaders passively reflect the interplay of different influences, and the extent to which they should do so, might be variously judged. One can imagine an extremely conservative pluralism which holds that the bundles of resources on which political influence depends do not differ much, on balance, from person to person, that the inequalities that exist are not pressing moral problems, that major political figures passively reflect the balance of forces among competing groups, and that they should do so. The view that pluralism is passé reflects the fact that few, if any, academic theorists are now committed to this extremely conservative version.

However, the identification of pluralism with this version of it is historically inaccurate and theoretically misleading. There was never a pluralist consensus of this kind. For example, in *Who Governs?*, the official six-point statement of the pluralist view of government has, as its second clause, "With few exceptions these resources [i.e., political resources] are unequally distributed."[12] Dahl is never so naive as to suppose that the average citizen of New Haven has a bundle of political resources about as weighty as the chairman of the board of the First New Haven Bank. Only weight of numbers, through the medium of universal suffrage, balances the resource of wealth. Though Dahl is largely silent, he is certainly not smug about the moral questions that could be raised concerning interpersonal inequalities. Finally, far from being a celebration of "interest-group politics," *Who Governs?* describes how the more passive politics of Mayor Celentano were replaced by the aggressive and independent initiatives of Mayor Lee, a leader portrayed as virtually obsessed with the moral importance of urban renewal, sensibly aware of the distribution of political

[11] See, for example, the summary statement on p. 228 of Dahl *Who Governs?*
[12] Ibid.

154

influence, but concerned to put these facts of political life to the service of a larger vision.

More important than historical accuracy, forgetting the options open to pluralism has meant ignoring its persistence as an unstated, undefended background for important arguments about American politics. This entrenchment of pluralism is illustrated by two books that are leading documents used to support the verdict that pluralism is passé, Dahl's *After the Revolution?* and Theodore Lowi's *The End of Liberalism*.

In *After the Revolution?*, Dahl acknowledges that there are enormous differences in politically effective resources from person to person in the United States, and advocates their redistribution. He recognizes the powerlessness of employees in large corporations, and calls for internal control of corporate policies by employees, combined with external control, where appropriate, by government bodies subject to the more equal distribution of political resources. Nothing here is incompatible with early-'sixties pluralism. Of course, nothing here is incompatible with the hypothesis that big business is something like a ruling class. What discriminates between these outlooks is Dahl's conception of how the recommended changes could be brought about.

Here, pluralist assumptions are crucial. The best means to a radical redistribution of effective political resources is said to be the use of universal suffrage for social change pioneered in European countries.[13] There is no discussion, in this context, of the role of such nonelectoral factors as general strikes, sit-downs, violent or illegal demonstrations and mutinies in these European processes. The evidence that a redistribution of resources and influence resulted is confined to the fact that income (not wealth) is distributed more unequally in the United States than in Britain, Norway and other advanced countries.[14] Although the recommended democratization of industrial firms is supposed to deprive present business leaders of most of their economic power, we are told, "Although sentimentalists on the Left may find the idea too repugnant to

[13] Dahl, *After the Revolution?*, pp. 105–10.
[14] Ibid., p. 112, n. 1.

stomach, quite possibly workers and trade unions are the greatest barriers at present to any profound reconstruction of economic enterprise in the country."[15] The evidence cited is a study arguing for the prevalence of consumption-oriented, family-centered attitudes among affluent workers in England.

It would be very unfair to criticize *After the Revolution?* for failing to marshal substantial evidence in support of an underlying view of the power relations within which change is pursued. The book is avowedly speculative. My point is rather that a general view of political power in the United States is presupposed, without substantial argument. It is the same as the one that was explicitly stated and defended in *Who Governs?*, nine years before.

Lowi's *The End of Liberalism* is influential and typical, among books attributing the failures of United States government since World War II to the substitution of interest-group politics for presidential leadership based on moral appeals to common interests and the creation of well-defined statutes and unified bureaucracies. The book often seems a vigorous critique of pluralism. "Interest-group pluralism," the villain, is said to be the result of transforming pluralism from a political theory into an ideology.[16] Since United States politics allegedly did not conform to this ideology before World War II and will not do so if present failures are corrected in time, the enduring validity of pluralist theory seems cast in doubt as well.

The link between "interest-group liberalism" and real pluralist theory is, in fact, tenuous at best. Lowi's ideal President is not very different from Mayor Richard Lee of *Who Governs?*, writ large. More important, the main strategy of argument in Lowi's book depends on the assumed validity of pluralist theory, as it really was.

The general thesis of *The End of Liberalism* is hardly obvious. In public statements, Johnson and Nixon, the alleged epitomes of interest-group pluralism, made moral appeals to the common interest so sanctimonious that some of us felt vaguely sick. Proceding policy area by policy area, Lowi adopts the follow-

[15] Ibid., p. 134.
[16] Theodore Lowi, *The End of Liberalism* (New York, 1979), p. 36.

ing strategy for showing that an ideology of interest-groups had triumphed nonetheless. He points to failures in the pursuit of stated goals, for example, a drastic reduction in poverty and an effective yet humane foreign policy. He describes a prolif-eration of governmental and quasi-governmental agencies, often tied to particular interest-groups, or officially controlled by representatives of interest-groups, or justified on the grounds that interest-groups should participate more directly in government. This dispersal of authority is said to be the best explanation of the consistent failure to achieve the stated goals.

Such inferences from the best explanation are essential to science. Indeed, they may be the single fundamental form of scientific inference. But it is crucial, in such arguments, that relevant alternatives be considered. One relevant alternative is this: quite apart from organizational forms, basic United States government policy disproportionately tends to serve group in-terests that conflict with the achievement of stated goals. There is no discussion of any policy area in this long and detailed book in which such an alternative is considered. In effect, Lowi assumes that the electoral weight of numbers would guarantee that the interests of most of us would prevail, if we were not, politician and voter alike, misled by the ideology of interest-group liberalism. This vigorous, even outraged attack on one version of pluralist thinking operates wholly within the general framework of pluralist theory.

Ruling Classes and Power Elites

I have suggested that many critics of pluralism share its ov-eremphasis on issue-by-issue tallies of success or failure in par-ticular policy debates. This certainly cannot be said, though, of the major academic alternative to pluralism, the power-structure studies of Hunter, Mills and Domhoff. There, the basic question about political power is, in the first instance, concerned with the social setting, not with the power of in-dividuals: "What are the mechanisms, especially the patterns of informal interaction, by which certain social groups exercise disproportionate influence on government?" Claims that such mechanisms exist are part of the thesis that there is a ruling class. However, the question of the extent to which a group is a ruling class also depends on other questions concerning the nature of its interests and the direction of political change in response to crisis. The most detailed description of mechanisms of influence may fail to answer them.

Though their distaste for elitism is often clear enough, power-structure analysts do not investigate in detail whether the interests of a dominant elite conflict with the interests of society at large. No doubt, many of Hunter's Atlanta businessmen and Domhoff's bankers and corporate lawyers would accept that they have disproportionate influence on government, but claim that this is reasonable and in the public interest because of their special knowledge, responsibilities, and administrative skills. You can read through Hunter's *Community Power Structures* and Domhoff's *Who Rules America?* without finding evidence for or against this view-from-the-executive-dining-room.

In addition, knowledge of mechanisms of influence may not tell us the order of power among the interconnected elites. Is the influence of major businesspeople on government a reflection of their basic control over government, or is it a tribute they are forced to pay to the independent power of politicians? Although this sometimes seems to be just the issue separating power-structure theorists from pluralists, it is actually an unintelligible question within the power-structure framework. The determination of the relative power of the influencers and the influenced depends not on the description of a network of interactions, but on the investigation of what happens when the network is strained or disrupted, who wins and who loses. To the extent to which the power of big business explains the failure of previously successful politicians, the passing away of a whole style of politics or even the replacement of one set of political institutions by another, big business has power over the political establishment and approaches the status of a ruling class. By their nature, such efforts to change the personnel, style or institutions of politics mobilize resources that are not

158

engaged in normal patterns of influence. Obviously, there were many channels of influence running from business to government in the late nineteenth-century United States. What shows that there was also considerable power of business over government is the unhappy fate of political leaders who stepped out of line, for example, Altgeld in Illinois and the Populist government of South Carolina. In these episodes, business resources were employed that differed in degree from those used in the normal network of influence (e.g., the regimentation of the news became much more absolute) and that sometimes differed in kind (e.g., mobs were organized to attack politicians).

Similarly, the study of actual networks of influence does not tell us how strong is the connection between government action and elite interests. For, at any given time, this is a question of what *would* happen, in particular, of whether the connection would be broken by feasible sorts of activism of kinds protected, or, at least, permitted by government. However messy and speculative such claims are, people may need to examine them in a thorough discussion of strategies for change. Suppose we know all there is to know about elite social clubs, conferences, study groups, the constant interchange between the top echelons of business and government and all the other mechanisms reported in power-structure studies. We still may not know how far things can be changed through a strategy of advocating the election of the less pro-business of the candidates, wherever one exists. How would the party bureaucracies and the media respond to unusual successes along these lines? At what point would a candidate, once elected, capitulate to economic disorder based on business discontent? At what point would banks refuse to float government bonds? At what point, if any, would the business community sponsor violent right-wing groups, or support a military takeover, toppling even conservative politicians of a parliamentary sort? These are questions that must be faced when we ask to what extent there is a ruling class, but not when we study current patterns of influence. The Kucinich fiasco in Cleveland may be a small

159

token of the gap between these questions, the Chilean coup a big one.

FUNCTIONALISM AND SOCIAL INTERESTS

The remaining outlook on political power of major importance in empirical political theory is the structural-functionalism explicit, for example, in Easton's writings and implicit in much of Almond and Verba's analysis of the civic culture. Here, government is assumed to be a means of interpreting and coordinating diverse particular interests, in pursuit of a common interest in stability and efficiency. In effect, the study of political power becomes a study of helps and impediments to the achievement of this common goal. The competing functional alternative according to which the patterns of government action are best explained as due to a function of protecting the interests of a dominant elite is, in effect, dismissed without argument. Thus, in *The Civic Culture*, when Mexican and Italian responses to questionnaires display alienation from the political process, this alienation itself, not objective political facts to which it corresponds, is taken to be the main obstacle to effective democracy.[17]

It is interesting that structural-functionalism and pluralism should be the two respectable approaches to political power, in firm intellectual alliance, providing alternative paradigms between which even mildly eclectic theorists unself-consciously shuttle. For in the abstract, the approach and research methods characteristic of each are radically different, quite as different as between such warring factions as the neoclassical and the institutionalist approach to economics or the formalist and substantivist wings of economic anthropology. Structural-functionalist theory studies systems of institutions and cultural values, using surveys and large-scale speculative theorizing to discuss how they approach or depart from an ideal in which each subsystem serves to maintain the stability of the whole. Pluralist theory studies processes of political influence and in-

[17] Gabriel Almond and Sidney Verba, *The Civic Culture* (Boston, 1965), pp. 3–7, 308–18, 368–79.

160

itiative, mapping their course by examining issue-by-issue outcomes, often confined to a few years in a particular city. Here, there is no ideal of long-term equilibrium, or even of an enduring pattern, in the political life of a society. What *is* characteristic of the thinking of both structural-functionalist and pluralist theorists is a common tendency not to take seriously the possible rationality of breaking the rules of the game of a reasonably stable and efficient political system, at least when it is a parliamentary democracy. If such possibilities are dismissed, two natural questions of political power remain: "Who wins and who loses as the game is played?" (pluralism) and "What makes the game stable and efficient?" (structural-functionalism). Thus, when political strategies worth considering are confined to the electoral realm, theoretical questions worth considering are correspondingly limited.

THE CHAINS OF METHODOLOGY

While the academic study of politics does not include the question "To what extent is there a ruling class?", it would be misleading to say that the question is simply ignored. Rather, the possibility that there is something like a ruling class in the United States today is believed to be too farfetched to merit investigation. This general kind of dismissal is not antagonistic to science, but essential to it. The investigation of reality always depends on dismissing some possibilities as too farfetched. But this particular dismissal is premature, based on biased methods of research and a narrow conception of motivation.

First of all, there is a tendency to adopt methods for investigating power that presuppose the nonexistence of a ruling class. Not surprisingly, investigations guided by such methods often make the hypothesis of a ruling class look utterly implausible, if one forgets that the question has been begged. A prime example is the pluralist proposal to measure political power by determining how often people get what they want in a contested issue on the agenda of an official forum. Thus Dahl, in the central empirical argument of *Who Governs?*, meas-

161

ures "the distribution of influence" by examining official decisions on urban renewal in New Haven. The issues considered are essentially those reflected in the deliberations of the Citizens Action Commission, an advisory group consisting of government officials and businesspeople, including "the heads of large utilities, manufacturing firms, banks and other businesses." Power is measured by determining "which individuals . . . most often initiated the proposals which were finally adopted, or most often vetoed the proposals of others." When power is measured in this way, the result is a vindication of the dominance of the Mayor and the Development Administrator, as against the Economic Notables, a result that is said to defeat the hypothesis of "the hidden hand of an economic elite."[18]

In fact, the investigator who assumes that wins and losses in official forums measure power cannot defeat the hypothesis that there is a ruling class. He can only assume its falsehood, by choosing this measure. For empirical findings such as Dahl's (as distinct from his interpretations) are what one would expect if big business *is* a ruling class. One would expect political acts that would threaten big business not to be under discussion in official forums. In one of Dahl's interviews with a top urban development official, in the group who are supposed to overrule the "Economic Notables," the interviewee explains this criterion for taking proposals seriously: ". . . we needed the backing of the financial, industrial, public utility and banking powers. If they were with it, we knew that other people are all for it. . . . But, in other words, a group of earnest people is not going to get very far in urban renewal, in my opinion. I know of only one way to do it, and that is to get the most powerful people in the community."[19] On the other hand, official forums are likely to serve as testing grounds for the feasibility and public acceptability of various options that are all tolerable to big business. Within these limits, political leaders and top administrators, those most alive to questions of feasibility and acceptability, will most often have the last word.

[18] See pp. 122–26.
[19] Cited in Domhoff, *Who Really Rules?*, p. 111.

A rigid methodology may also obscure the connection between government and social interests in another way. Ruling-class hypotheses tend to be identified with implausible conspiracy theories, on account of a basically Weberian preference for subjective reasons, rather than objective interests, as explanations of action. Politicians tell us that they are equally committed to the interests of all. But if the explanation of their behavior should appeal to their reasons for doing what they do, a ruling-class hypothesis would dictate that they are lying, covering up hidden class commitments or ties of outright bribery that are their real reasons for their actions.

In fact, the behavior of politicians and major businesspeople, in the ruling-class approach, is best seen as guided by objective interests that may diverge from conscious reasons, sincerely stated. There is nothing mystifying about the remark that a typical nuclear engineer has an objective interest in viewing himself as a useful professional, which leads him to argue, quite sincerely, for the safety of nuclear power plants even when he should know better. It should seem no more mysterious to say that the objective interests of successful United States politicians lead them to promote the distinctive interests of big business, even when they sincerely appeal to the common interest.[20]

A variety of arguments and investigations, power-structure studies among them, would contribute to a psychologically plausible account of how the typical history and situation of the successful politician make it possible for him to be guided by the interests of big business, while honestly professing commitment to the interests of all. Some important factors reflected in the normal narrative of political success are the need for large campaign expenditures and media support, the sharing of the same personnel at the top echelons of business and public administration, the common school and social ties of those personnel, and the distinctly nonworking-class life style that political success encourages and affords. Corporate executives

[20] I discuss this kind of mechanism and its role in functional explanations in detail in "Methodological Individualism and Social Explanation," *Philosophy of Science* 45 (1978).

and politicians are not the only actors in this drama. Labor union leaders, with their impact on campaign funds, and newspaper editors, with their impact on news coverage, are crucially important, as well. So are the academics who have given an air of plausibility to such theses as that a twelve-hour workday or the defense of the Diem regime was dictated by the national interest. Thus, the tendency to achieve authority in labor unions, newspapers and universities needs to be investigated as well. That militant union locals are routinely taken over and put into trusteeship is at least as important a fact for politics as the legislated structure of public utilities commissions. Finally, more attention should probably be paid to obvious facts that make it enormously risky for a political leader to challenge big business. Governments rely on banks and similar institutions for credit. When businesspeople become demoralized about the future, there is a tendency for millions to be thrown out of work. Because of these facts, a serious violation of big-business interests often could not be managed by a head of government who is not the consciously revolutionary leader of a mass movement.

How do we determine whether major political figures are influenced by such interests, as against the democratic commitments they sincerely profess? We resolve the question of interests and principles with them as with anyone else, by looking at what they actually do, and at the information in the background of their choices. Suppose that United States Presidents since World War II should have known better than to suppose that support for Diem, Reza Pahlevi, and the Somozas benefits democracy. Suppose that such support does conform to the pithy saying of Kennedy's Secretary of the Treasury, "I speak as an investment banker when I say that the less developed countries are our most important investment resource."[21] That is part, though only part, of a case for supposing that political leaders' interests in serving the social interests of big business dominate United States political life.

[21] C. Douglas Dillon, in the *Department of State Bulletin*, May 6, 1958.

Better Theories of Power

If social philosophy is to be truly helpful to social science, it should not just diagnose confusions, but suggest new directions. Understanding how the question of the ruling class has been begged does suggest new tactics and concerns. If political theorists are to take seriously the question of the extent to which there is a ruling class, they must connect descriptions of political structure with explanations of historical change. They must face the fact that disorder and repression have played an important role in the politics of all the Western democracies and have often been a part of processes leading to useful change. They must become aware of the factual assumptions behind the measurements and interpretations they make, not in order to pursue the chimera of methods independent of factual assumptions, but to avoid begging the question when rival hypotheses need to be compared. In sum, political theory, if concerned with the extent to which there is a ruling class, is more historical, more aware of the role of nonelectoral conflict, and less apt to end disputes over underlying theories on methodological grounds.

This expansion of the scope of research into power is to the good if the notion of a ruling class merely captures some significant phenomena left out of account by alternative measures of political power. In addition, there may be a more definite gain, an important fundamental hypothesis further confirmed and accepted. It may be at least approximately true that there is a ruling class in the United States and in other advanced industrial countries. The reader will no doubt have guessed that I think there is such a class, and that it is big business. I hope that the facts I have sketched and the specific studies I have cited make this claim plausible. Yet, though these facts and studies are not esoteric, when eminent and well-informed theorists occasionally confront the question of whether there is a ruling class in the United States, they beg the question through misinterpretation. A ruling-class hypothesis is supposed to imply routine and pervasive political intervention,

165

"the hand of an economic ruling elite in every major domain of public activity."[22] Or it is said to require a conscious "conspiracy among . . . officials to finesse . . . discontent."[23] Or it is consigned to the scrap heap of untestable statements of faith "metaphysical rather than empirical."[24] I hope that the analysis of Marx's theory in the previous chapter makes it clear that a live option is not tested if the idea of a ruling class is assessed in these ways.

Finally, a better understanding of the idea of a ruling class can help us to avoid begging a practical question. Every major movement for reform in the United States has involved people's going beyond electoral politics and protected forms of expression. Within living memories, the tactics include the sit-down strikes and physical exclusion of strikebreakers through which industrial unions triumphed; the illegal demonstrations, many genuinely disruptive, and the ghetto uprisings of the Civil Rights movement, not least the Birmingham ghetto uprising that hastened the Civil Rights Acts; and the sit-ins and mutinies during the Indochina War. Now, many people are deeply concerned with war and the threat of world war to come and with the great and growing gap between rich and poor, white and nonwhite. Is past willingness to go beyond the electoral and the respectable a useful model for people with these concerns? The question tends not to be answered in a detailed and thoughtful way. Students say that 'sixties-type protests are out of style, as if fashions were the issue. Their elders often accept without question the benefits of promoting McGeorge Bundy, Felix Rohatyn and other hallowed figures of the Eastern Establishment into the leadership of movements against war and poverty. Of course, if concern turns into despair, people may also reach hasty and indiscriminate conclusions in favor of violence, as bizarre as the Weather Underground's in

[22] Dahl, *Who Governs?*, p. 70.
[23] Lowi, *The End of Liberalism*, p. 225.
[24] See Nelson Polsby, *Community Power and Political Theory* (New Haven, 1963), p. 23.

the 'sixties. To be brief but not inaccurate, many of us need detailed and strategic discussions of whether and in what ways to do things beside helping liberal Democratic politicians to get elected. In these discussions, the notion of a ruling class is a basic tool.

History

CHAPTER FIVE

Productive Forces and the Forces of Change

INTRODUCTION

OF THE MANY controversies about what Marx meant, the most intense concerns his general theory of history. In dispute is a special topic within this special topic: what is Marx's general theory of basic economic change? Clearly, this part of his theory of history is the foundation for all the rest. For Marx, political and ideological institutions and the climate of respectable ideas have their basic features because those features serve to maintain certain economic relations, what he calls "relations of production." But there is nothing clear about the foundational question of why those relations have their basic features, and why they sometimes change.

The most influential interpretations of Marx's answers to these questions make Marx a technological determinist. On this view, Marx regarded history as the story of how social arrangements adapt to technological progress, facilitating the productivity of tools and techniques. Above all, the development of relations of production is to be explained as ultimately due to the pursuit of more material goods through improved technology.

There have, of course, been dissenters from this view. But they have not offered any decisive criticism or any plausible alternative. Often, opponents accord a larger role to class struggle than technological determinism allows. But they do so without explaining Marx's lifelong concern with the development of productive forces as determining the direction of social change. Worse yet, dissenters from the dominant interpretation often dilute Marx's theory to a thin soup of truisms to the effect that technology influences change and people don't do much thinking if they cannot eat. Marx's practice as a historian is surely more distinctive than that, his general remarks more interesting.

The debate over technological determinism is at the center of the two broad topics of this book, the relation between politics and economics in Marx and the relation between Marx and analytic philosophy. The technological determinist interpretation is by far the most plausible of the many readings of Marx that subordinate the political to the economic. It has been encouraged by positivist assumptions, which have until recently dominated analytic philosophy. Or so I shall argue. Because Marx's historical writings are such a frustrating mixture of fragments of grand theorizing with concrete, elaborate and suggestive narratives, interpreting Marx on history demands, to the highest degree, the style of analytic philosophy, its conceptual resourcefulness, clarity and tolerance for detail.

Refuting a view of such a complex matter as Marx's theory of history means refuting the best version of it, the specification most likely to be correct if the general approach is valid. In the first half of this chapter, I will construct this most defensible version of technological determinism, and argue that it does not remotely fit Marx's historical writings.

In the alternative that I will then develop, what I will call "the mode of production interpretation," basic, internal economic change arises (whenever it does, in fact, take place) on account of a self-transforming tendency of the mode of production as a whole, that is, the relations of production, the forms of cooperation and the technology through which material goods are produced. Because of the nature of the mode, processes that initially maintain its characteristic relations of production eventually produce their downfall. This change need not overcome any barriers to material production. It may do so. Change may be based on developments in the forms of cooperation or in technology, giving access to enhanced productive power to an initially subordinate group, and motivating their resistance to the old relations of production because the latter come to inhibit the further development of that new productive power. But, in this broad mode of production the-

172

ory, change may also be wholly internal to the relations of production. The patterns of control in the old relations of production may make it inevitable that an initially nondominant group will acquire the power and the desire to overthrow the old relations. Unlike technological determinism, this theory fits Marx's practice as a historian. Another difference is that it is a defensible theory of history, Marx interpretation to one side.

Admittedly, a somewhat narrower theory is expressed in some of Marx's general formulations, even though the broader account is entailed by several of his historical explanations. On this narrower account, radical internal economic change is always the result of the first of the two processes that I have sketched, that is, the acquisition of access to increased productive powers by a subordinate group defined by production relations that come to inhibit the further growth of those powers. But even in this narrow theory, Marx is not a technological determinist. The growth of productive powers is not primarily based on an autonomous drive toward technological progress. The enhanced productive powers usually result from changed forms of cooperation, not new technology. The new social relations of production need not be the most productive framework for the development of technology.

For reasons of convenience, I will first develop the narrower mode of production theory, then show why it must be broadened to accommodate the balance of the texts. It will turn out that the standard means of identifying theories in the history of science make the broader theory Marx's essential one. In short, in Marx's essential theory, productive enhancement has no primary role among processes of internal change. In the nonessential narrowing toward which he sometimes inclined, productive enhancement still lacks the particular primacy and the technological character assigned it by technological determinism.

In the choice between technological determinism and the mode of production theory, the stakes are high. In politics, the mode of production theory broadens the material preconditions for socialism, while providing a rationale for revolution as the

173

necessary basis for radical change. In the most abstract realms of methodology, the mode of production theory requires and helps to justify departures from conceptions of explanation and confirmation that have, until very recently, dominated the philosophy of science. I will conclude this book with a demonstration that those conceptions rule out the mode of production interpretation in favor of technological determinism, a sketch of an alternative conception of explanation and confirmation and a suggestion as to how the political consequences of the more standard methodology may help to explain its recurrent appeal, from Hume to the present day.

Marx as Technological Determinist

Many technological determinists have obviously not been Marxists. For example, the anthropologist Leslie White claimed that institutions all evolve in such a way as to maximize "the amount of energy harnessed per capita per year."[1] In his theory, political and cultural institutions can adjust to productive needs quite directly, without any priority for social relations of production. Change that is qualitative, structural, or relatively rapid plays no special role.

What specific version of technological determinism could have been Marx's theory? In effect, the answer to this question has consisted of a technological determinist gloss of a celebrated passage from the Preface to Marx's book *A Contribution to the Critique of Political Economy* (1859). In this passage, Marx says that people's

relations of production correspond to a definite stage of development of their material productive forces. The sum total of these relations of production constitutes . . . the real basis on which rises a legal and political superstructure.

More precisely, this correspondence and support occur in relatively stable social situations.

[1] Leslie White, *The Evolution of Culture* (New York, 1959), p. 368.

174

At a certain stage of their development, the material productive forces of society come in conflict with the existing relations of production. From forms of development of the productive forces these relations turn into their fetters. Then begins an epoch of social revolution. With the change of the economic foundation the whole immense superstructure is more or less rapidly transformed.[2]

Other statements by Marx suggest a technological determinist interpretation, especially in his polemics against Proudhon in the 1840s. However, the passage from the Preface has played a special role. Every classic, systematic exposition of Marxist technological determinism, from Plekhanov's *The Development of the Monist View of History* at the turn of the century to Cohen's recent *Karl Marx's Theory of History: A Defense*, constantly returns to the scaffolding of this passage. (I have not quoted every important sentence in it.) This habit makes some of us suspicious. The passage is part of a short autobiographical sketch. It follows a modest introductory sentence: "The general result at which I arrived and which, once won, served as a guiding thread for my studies, can be briefly formulated as follows." I can think of no other major theorist whose general theory is often reconstructed, in large part, by a close reading of a brief formulation embedded in an autobiographical sketch in a preface to a book that he gladly allowed to go out of print, as superseded by later writings. Still, the central text for technological determinism is one of Marx's few detailed and general formulations of his theory of history. And it does often sound like a systematic presentation of a technological determinist theory. In the interest of both clarity and fairness, I will construct the most defensible version of the technological determinist interpretation by finding the best reading of this passage in which crucial terms are interpreted in a technological determinist manner.

In technological determinism, "productive forces" are best interpreted as tools, techniques and knowledge by which matter is made usable by human beings—tools, techniques, and knowledge meeting two further constraints. Productive forces

[2] Marx and Engels, *Selected Works in Three Volumes* (Moscow, 1973), vol. I, pp. 503f.

175

must be means to overcome physical obstacles, as against the obstacle of resistance by other human beings. On this reading, a gun used to kill deer for venison is a productive force, but not one used to conquer territory. A foreman's knowledge of how to cut sheet metal is a productive force, but not his knowledge of how to maintain labor discipline. This restriction is required by Marxist technological determinism, since the productive forces are supposed to be the autonomous technological factor that, on the whole, explains basic changes in social and political processes, not the other way around. Obviously, the development of means of control over other human beings has, to a large extent, been determined by social and political relations of domination and conflict that the technological factor is supposed to explain.

Also, the most defensible technological interpretation must exclude from the scope of productive forces what Marx calls "modes of cooperation" and Cohen calls by the short and evocative phrase "work relations": relations of cooperation between people engaged in production, defined apart from control over people or means of production. Again, the productive forces must be so restricted, or the claim that they are the autonomous basis for change will be false to history as it obviously is and as Marx obviously sees it. Typically, changes in work relations are due to new relations of dominance. The labor gangs of the Pharoahs, the teamwork in medieval corvée labor on the overlord's demesne, and the dispersal of craftswork through the "putting-out" system in the preindustrial stage of capitalism are a few examples. Moreover, changed patterns of work-relations rarely involve the development of *new* ways to produce efficiently, as they would have to if they were instances of technological progress. Virtually all work-relations are already depicted on the walls of ancient Egyptian tombs.

In the Preface, "the sum total of . . . relations of production" are said to be the basis for political and ideological institutions. Much else is said of them: they find a legal expression in property-relations; productive forces are normally at work within them; they may inhibit the productive forces; an era of social revolution is required to transform them fundamentally. To play these roles, the relations of production are best construed as relations of control over people, labor-power, raw materials or productive forces within the process of material production. People's positions in the network of relations of production define their class. For example, if some people control productive forces and the use for a contracted period of the labor-power of others, while the others sell their labor-power because they lack control of substantial productive forces or raw materials, the former are capitalists, the latter proletarians.

By sharply separating relations of production from productive forces, in this way, Marxist technological determinists can pursue a highly attractive goal of their approach to Marx, the description of general empirical laws in which sufficient causes for change among relations of production are specified in a noncircular way. Though this goal, I shall argue, must be given up, it provides an important motive for maintaining the technological determinist interpretation of Marx's general view in spite of its distance from most of his specific historical explanations.

In the Preface, a network of relations of production is said to change when it fetters the "development of the productive forces." In interpreting this metaphor of fettering, any defensible version of the technological determinist interpretation will have to depart from a strict and literal reading of the Preface. Marx says, there, "No social order ever perishes before all the productive forces for which there is room in it have developed." If we take this to be Marx's strict and settled view, production relations fetter productive forces only when they exclude all further improvements in productivity. A theory of history that insists on this fettering must deny, for example, that feudalism was ever overthrown so long as it permitted any improvement in productivity. The implication for capitalism is just as conservative: capitalism will never change until it is incapable of any improvement in the productive forces. The implication concerning feudalism is historically absurd, as Marx is well aware. The implication concerning capitalism flies in the face of Marx's view that capitalist competition will always stimulate

177

some technological progress, together with the fact that Marx was a socialist.[3]

Marx's extreme statement is an exaggeration to be understood in its political context. It reflects his polemics against Proudhon and the utopian socialists, who studied industrial development only to condemn it and would not realistically assess the material requirements of modern workers' needs. A more moderate standard for fettering is available, which fits Marx's practice much more closely. On this interpretation, the network of relations of production fetters productive forces when some alternative network would better promote the further development of those forces. Following Cohen's usage I will borrow Marx's concise label in the Preface for a whole network of relations of production, namely, an "economic structure." A defensible technological determinist reading of the Preface should understand the claim about fettering, metaphor and hyperbole to one side, as the claim that a basic type of economic structure only lasts so long as it is optimal for the development of the productive forces. It perishes when productive forces would develop more productively in a new structure, even if they could still develop to some extent within the old one.

Presumably, Marx is not proposing to explain every change in an economic structure, down to the smallest detail. In the Preface he is concerned with the disappearance of whole "social orders" or "social formations" and the appearance of new ones. Large-scale changes on the order of the transition from the feudal to the capitalist mode of production are his theme here, as wherever a theory of productive forces is brought to the fore. This less comprehensive aim of only explaining changes in basic type makes a technological determinist Marxism more plausible. But it raises one final interpretative question, the question of what counts as a basic difference in type. The difficulty arises because the statistically preponderant relation

[3] "The bourgeoisie cannot exist without constantly revolutionizing the instruments of production" (*Communist Manifesto*, p. 338). "Modern Industry never looks upon and treats the existing form of a process as final" (*Capital* I, p. 457).

of production need not characterize the basic type of an economy, for Marx. For example, Marx was aware that most producers in sixteenth-century England and in the early Roman Empire were small peasant proprietors.[4] But he treats the respective economies as basically different in type.

Fortunately, Marx states the standard of basic difference explicitly and emphatically in his later writings. "The essential difference between the various economic forms of society . . . lies only in the mode in which . . . surplus labor is in each case extracted from the actual producer, the laborer."[5] Marx identifies the basic type of an economic structure with the main way in which a surplus is extracted from the immediate producers, not with the relation of production that is statistically most pervasive in production as a whole. He does this because of the explanatory project of which the typology is a part. The most basic shifts in economic type are to explain the most basic shifts in political and ideological institutions. And Marx takes control over the surplus to be the most important single determinant of the latter. Once economic structures are distinguished according to the mode of surplus-extraction, the Rome of Augustus and the England of Henry VIII become basically different in type, as they should be in any interpretation of Marx. In one, the surplus is extracted mainly through ownership of slaves, in the other, mainly through political domination of free farmers and craftsworkers.

The most defensible interpretation of Marx as a technological determinist is a gloss of the celebrated passage from the Preface with the crucial terms understood in the ways I have described. The general idea of technological determinism is that social structures evolve by adapting to technological change so as to increase its further productive growth. As a version of Marx's theory of history, technological determinism must answer three questions in ways that give primacy to tools, techniques and productivity: What explains the main features of an economic structure (and, hence, the social system as a whole) during its period of relative stability? What causes the

---

[4] *Grundrisse*, pp. 476f., 487; *Capital* I, p. 671.
[5] *Capital* I, p. 209; see also vol. III, p. 791.

most important changes among the productive forces themselves? What determines the timing and direction of change in
economic structures? The passage from the Preface can plau-
sibly be taken to yield technological determinist answers to
each question. First, a stable economic structure is of its basic
type because that type best promotes the growth of productivity, given the productive forces at hand. Second, the most
important changes among the productive forces are mainly due
to a human drive toward change that is independent of the
desire to dominate other people: the desire and ability to overcome material scarcity. Thus, in the causation of basic changes
in type, the productive forces shape the relations of production
and the commercial, political and ideological processes to
which the latter give rise, to a much greater extent than vice
versa. Cohen usefully compares this primacy with a priority
of the environment in Darwinian evolution, as traditionally
understood: environmental changes are the main influence on
species transformations, not vice versa, though the latter obviously have some impact on the former, as we witness in every
beaver dam. Similarly, in a Marxist technological determinism,
economic structures and their concomitants have some impact
on productive forces (otherwise they could not facilitate their
growth) but the most basic changes in the productive forces
result from their own expansion in people's pursuit of greater
productive efficiency. Third, external influences to one side,
fundamental social instability is the result of the rise of new
productive forces, making a new basic type of economic structure a better means of increasing productivity. Instability continues until the new economic structure is established, the one
best adapted to the new forces.

These three general claims certainly are a general theory of
history that gives genuine primacy to technology and that is
strongly suggested by the passage from the Preface and other
texts. The theory is neatly summarized in Cohen's remark,
"Forces select structures according to their capacity to promote
development."[6] Indeed, in the vast literature on Marx's theory

[6] Gerald Cohen, *Karl Marx's Theory of History: A Defense* (Princeton, 1978),
p. 162.

of history, the version of technological determinism that I have defended as best is closest to the one that Cohen presents in his illuminating book. On some points, especially the definition of "fettering" and the distinction among basic types of economic structures, the account of Marx is, I hope, improved. But the two accounts are very similar. In effect, my underlying argument in the first half of this chapter is that something like Cohen's interpretation is the best version of the technological-determinist account, and that nothing like it is a sound interpretation. Close readers of Cohen will recall from a footnote that he is reluctant to accept the label "technological determinist" because this phrase may suggest that "the course of human history and, more particularly, the future socialist revolution are inevitable . . . despite what men may do," not "because of what men, being rational, are bound . . . to do."[7] But, as I shall soon argue, such technological fatalism is very far from the technological determinism I have described.[8]

THE STAKES ARE HIGH

I have tried to develop the version of technological determinism most likely to be a valid interpretation if the general approach is valid. Other versions are available. For example, Plekhanov inclined toward the strict and literal interpretation of "fettering," according to which a society does not shift from one basic type to another so long as the old arrangement permits increases in productivity. On these grounds, among others, he condemned the Bolsheviks' call for socialist revolution as premature.[9] I have argued that this interpretation is not defensible. But it is not essential to technological determinism. William Shaw, in his recent book, *Marx's Theory of History*,[10]

[7] Ibid., p. 147.

[8] The largely implicit argument with Cohen in this chapter is explicitly connected with his writing in my review-essay "Productive Forces and the Forces of Change," *Philosophical Review* 90 (1981).

[9] Plekhanov's classic statement of his interpretation is *The Development of the Monist View of History*. Lenin gives a pithy summary of the Bolsheviks' side of the debate over the October Revolution in "Our Revolution", *Collected Works in Three Volumes* (Moscow, 1971), vol. III, pp. 767ff.

[10] William Shaw, *Marx's Theory of History* (Stanford, 1978).

develops a technological determinist account in which work relations are included among the productive forces. Though the latter option is attractive in itself (indeed, I will argue for it), I have tried to show that it undermines the project of portraying changes in power-relations as adjustments to the basically autonomous development of productive forces. For many of those who interpret Marx as a theorist of economic breakdown, the connection between structural change and the inefficient use of technology is quite direct. The shift in basic type largely results from the spontaneous perception of the obvious inefficiency of a disintegrating economic system and the productive superiority of the alternative. Long-term ideological and political struggle play a subordinate role.[11] Yet,

---

[11] Such a breakdown theory is at least strongly suggested by some of Engels' later writings. For example, it is a natural interpretation of *Socialism: Utopian and Scientific* (1880), where such passages as these are typical in the account of the materialist conception of history: "In these crises . . . the economic collision has reached its apogee. *The mode of production is in rebellion against the mode of exchange.* . . . The whole mechanism of the capitalist mode of production breaks down under the pressure of the productive forces, its own creations. . . . On the one hand, therefore, the capitalistic mode of production stands convicted of its own incapacity to further direct these productive forces. On the other hand, these productive forces themselves, with increasing energy, press forward to the removal of the existing contradiction, to the *practical recognition of their character as social productive forces.* . . . If the crises demonstrate the incapacity of the bourgeoisie for managing any longer modern productive forces, the transformation of the great establishments for production and distribution into joint-stock companies, trusts and state property shows how unnecessary the bourgeoisie are for that purpose" (*Selected Works in Three Volumes*, pp. 142, 143, 145; Engels' emphases). At the end of this passage, Engels presents this pattern as an epitome of "our sketch of historical evolution." Lichtheim's account of Marx's mature view, in *Marxism*, ties it to spontaneous responses to economic development and, eventually, economic chaos. "Working-class activity provided the only yardstick by which the progress of socialism could be measured. In practice, this meant that the character as well as the tempo of political action had to be regulated by the spontaneously formed aspirations and beliefs of authentic labor leaders" (p. 128). Presumably, these spontaneous aspirations and beliefs tend toward socialism as a result of the economic crises in which "each revolution of the system . . . raises it to a higher level, thus storing up the elements of new and more violent crises, alongside the accumulation of greater riches and an enlarged fund of technical knowledge" (p. 193). In *The Theory of Capitalist Development* (New York, 1970), chap. 11, Sweezy sketches the history of the controversy over breakdown theories in Marxist economics that was sparked by the breakdown interpretation advanced in Bernstein's writings.

as I shall emphasize in developing my alternative to techno-logical determinism, the political and ideological advantages Marx associates with ruling-class status seem to make such transitions through economic breakdown extremely unlikely. Surely, a technological determinist interpretation is more de-fensible if it is not committed to this specific pattern of change.

Above all, the interpretation that will be my target from now on does not make Marx a technological fatalist. This tech-nological determinism is not the inhuman-sounding, histori-cally uninformed position that, given the state of technology, the subsequent development of society would be the same no matter what people thought or desired. What people think and want, including what they think and want under the influence of politics, religion and rational persuasion, may crucially de-termine the direction of change. History changes not despite, but because of these thoughts and desires. But the crucial fea-tures of changes in thought and desire are ultimately to be explained as due to the development of productive forces. For example, the respectable ideas of stable periods are due to po-litical and cultural institutions that derive their basic features from the function of maintaining the economic structure that, in turn, best facilitates the productive forces. The psychologies of people in an epoch of social revolution result from the in-teraction of those stabilizing ideological forces with needs and restrictions stemming from the economic structure and with tensions produced by the conflict between that structure and the productive forces it fetters. The primacy of the productive forces is logical priority in the order of explanation, "explan-atory primacy," as Cohen often puts it.

It might seem that the technological determinism that I have described is so well-hedged and so open to political and ide-ological processes that someone who attributed a different the-ory of history to Marx must be raising a Marxological quibble. In fact, when those who are sympathetic to Marx judge this most defensible version of technological determinism, the stakes are extremely high for social science and for political practice.

For one thing, technological determinism crucially affects the priorities of historical explanation, both priorities in research governing how much time historians should devote to various pursuits and priorities in assessment determining what is a successful explanation and what is not, what is a complete one and what an incomplete one. In a Marxist technological determinism, relations of production are as they are because they promote productivity, given the technology at hand, and they change because a new technology has arisen to which they are ill-adapted. Within this theoretical framework, the most important question for a historian trying to explain the most basic social changes is "How did the new arrangement become the one promoting productivity in society as a whole?" Questions of how the change affected the special interests of different classes and of what power the various classes possessed, though crucial to understanding how the change was brought about, are secondary in understanding why it occurred. This priority of the technological is hotly debated among historians sympathetic to Marx.

As with all debates over the interpretation of Marx, this one has important implications for political practice. Regimes in many countries with little advanced technology, such as Angola, Tanzania and Afghanistan, call on Marxists to support a policy of modernizing technology without instituting socialism, on the grounds that this is a necessary preliminary to socialism. Technological determinism is an important basis for these appeals. The technological determinist emphasis on productivity also has poignant implications for such countries as South Africa and Jordan, where capitalism is pushing per capita GNP ahead by leaps and bounds, despite poverty, degradation and repression. It does not seem that socialism would do a better job of increasing material productivity in these countries, even if it would eliminate much misery. A technological determinist interpretation of Marx suggests a Marxist argument against fighting for socialism now in these countries. "Capitalism is not yet obsolete here" is an argument which is, in fact, advanced by Communist Parties, both Moscow- and Peking-oriented.

184

In addition, the rationale for revolution has a very different position in technological determinism from its situation in the alternative that I shall describe. Granted, a Marxist technological determinist is free to say that the political superstructure stabilizing an economic structure will always be so strong that large-scale organized violence will be essential to basic change. But it is hard to see how the rationale for his or her general theory of the primacy of technology could include a rationale for this general assessment. If anything, an argument that change is based on a universal human drive for efficiency in production will suggest the effectiveness of an alternative to revolution, in which change is brought about by appeals to material desires shared by all classes. (Such a strategy of appealing to obsolescence is common, in fact, among Euro-communist parties today.) Thus, if Marx does believe in the necessity of organized, large-scale violence, this belief becomes readily detachable from the core of his general theory of history. Its position is analogous to Newton's corpuscular theory of light in contrast to his laws of force and acceleration, Darwin's semi-Lamarckian view of the mechanisms of heredity in contrast to his theory of natural selection. On the other hand, the general case for the mode of production interpretation will turn out to be a general case for the necessity of revolution.

In saying that the best version of technological determinism suggests premises for relatively conservative arguments in a generally Marxist framework, I mean neither more nor less than that. In any sensible version of technological determinism, the question of whether fettering has occurred will be debatable, and the time lag between fettering and basic social change will not be precisely and generally defined. In principle, a Marxist inclined toward technological determinism might argue that South African output would grow even more under socialism, or that Tanzanian technology is already advanced enough to be fettered. In the latter case, he or she would presumably add that Western European and North American societies were ripe for socialism, but held back by local and transient factors of a political or ideological kind during the many years in which they were at least as technologically advanced

185

as present-day Tanzania. Similarly, when Marxists discuss the alleged need for revolution, a technological determinist may argue that appeals to the greater output of the new economic structure can never be effective enough to make the violent overthrow of the old ruling class unnecessary. Cohen himself argues that the bourgeoisie will benefit too much from the maldistribution of material goods and power in the old society.[12]

Still, in all these cases, technological determinism puts distinctive burdens of argument on those who take the more radical side in the leading contemporary debates among Marxists. By the same token, technological determinism can be joined with more specific premises to make distinctive arguments for the more conservative side. This is why debates over technology and history in Marx have been so important for millions of Marxist activists. In contrast, the mode of production interpretation has no advantages for the conservative side of these debates. The entrenchment of ruling classes is one of its motivating premises, an entrenchment so deep that revolution would typically be necessary. In the broader version of this interpretation, the fettering of productive forces plays no essential role. Although it does in the narrower version, that version emphasizes the spread of certain work-relations as the most important changes in productive forces. And it is at this level of work-relations that production in so-called "less developed countries" is already highly advanced, in present features and future potential, with pervasive shifts away from family-centered, isolated and subsistence-based work-relations, even when implements worked are relatively archaic.

When all is said and done, though, aren't these effects of alternative Marx interpretations just aspects of Marx worship? Why should historians or activists, as against Marx scholars, care about the interpretation of Marx's general theory? In part, such questions are well-taken. Marx's theory needs empirical defense, and quotation and exegesis do not constitute such defense, the bad habits of some defenders to the contrary. Yet

[12] Cohen, *Karl Marx's Theory of History*, p. 202.

the interpretative debate does have a legitimate role to play in the pursuit of social understanding.

A theory is typically confirmed by the superiority of the explanations it supports. However, one may be reasonably confident that a group of investigators have been led by their beliefs to explanatory successes, but unsure what theoretical beliefs of theirs were responsible for these achievements, and, hence, justified by them. Thus, many biologists have appreciated Darwin's achievements in explaining facts of taxonomy, species distribution and paleontology, but have been unsure how to define the essential theory in *The Origin of Species*. Does it include his account of mechanisms of heredity? Is the thesis of transmutation through gradual departures from the initial type essential or dispensable? These questions have been ingredients of real biological progress, not Darwin-worship. Or, to take a case even more similar to Marx's, where the actual meanings of a theorist are in doubt, what theories were essential to Freud's most convincing achievements? The explicit metaphor guiding Freud and the most creative psychoanalysts of the next generation was that of unarticulated, instinctual energies, harnessed and inhibited by the ego in the service of survival and control. But was this their literal meaning? And, in any case, was this model of drive and inhibition the theory that produced their leading achievements? Or were they accounting for personality development as due to the infant's creation and solution of emotional problems based on love, hate and fear, experienced virtually from the moment of birth? Is the centrality of the Oedipal situation essential to psychoanalytic theory? Or does it reflect an especially salient factor in one cultural context and at a certain level of clinical insight? While these questions can be asked at the level of Freud-worship, they have also been a part of the most important scientific debates in psychoanalysis.

Marx interpretation can and should have the same scientific relevance. On relatively theory-neutral grounds, many investigators accept the basic validity of Marx's explanations of the rise of capitalism in Britain and of the main shifts in modern French political history, Engels' sketch of the origins of the

Reformation, Lenin's explanation of late nineteenth-century imperialism and the coming of World War I, Hill and Arkhangelski's account of the English Civil War, Hilton's explanation of the decline of serfdom in England, or various other concrete achievements of Marxist historiography. Some body of theory seems to be at work in these explanations and to draw support from them. What is it? The debate over Marx's meaning gets its scientific importance from its contribution to this question. Because it is so intimately connected with Marx's practice as a historian, the mode of production interpretation, in particular, locates the best-confirmed core of Marx's general ideas about history.

Marx Was Not a Technological Determinist

The dominant interpretation is wrong. When Marx writes history, he constantly violates the three distinctive principles of "Marxist" technological determinism. In history as he explains it, economic structures do not endure because they provide maximum productivity. Productive forces do not develop autonomously. Change in productive forces, in the narrowly technological sense that excludes work relations, is not the basic source of change in society at large.

It will be convenient to begin with the idea that the development of the productive forces is, in the main, autonomous, with basic changes in economic and political processes ultimately due to changes in the productive forces, far more so than the other way around. Everyone regards the historical parts of *Capital*, volume one, as the paradigm of Marx's practice as an economic historian. There, Marx describes how feudalism was first replaced by capitalism, in Britain. Here are some crucial episodes in this story of the shift from one basic type of economic structure to another, in the course of three centuries. In all of them, the economic structure and the commercial and political processes it generates play an independent role, crucially influencing all important changes in productive forces.

The old nobility is "devoured by the great feudal wars" and replaced by a new nobility of mercantile supporters of the competing dynasties.[13] With this new nobility taking the lead, large landowners respond to Continental demand for wool by expropriating their tenants and converting peasant holdings to sheep pastures.[14] This change does not occur because it makes farming more efficient. Quite traditional methods of sheepherding have simply become more lucrative for landowners. The influx of gold from the New World causes long-term inflation, increasing agricultural prices and decreasing the real rents of relatively well-off peasants with long-term leases and the power to defend them in court. The latter become aggressive capitalist farmers.[15] In manufacturing,

> the discovery of gold and silver in America, the extirpation, enslavement and entombment in mines of the aboriginal population, the beginning of the conquest and looting of the East Indies, the turning of Africa into a warren for the commercial hunting of black skins [hardly: "the development of improved forces of production"!] signalized the rosey dawn of the era of capitalist production.[16]

Rich merchants who benefited from this pillage use their new financial resources to set up manufacturing enterprises, often employing desperate refugees from the rise of capitalism in the countryside. Their large financial resources are crucial to the rise of manufacturing, for nontechnological reasons. It is commercially risky to set up enterprises of a new kind serving new markets. In most branches of production, many wage laborers need to be employed in an enterprise to retain a total surplus attractive to an entrepreneur after each has been paid at least a subsistence wage.[17]

These episodes are not the whole story of the rise of capitalism, as told by Marx, but they are the lion's share. The rise of capitalism eventually includes substantial increases in productivity, through the consolidation of landholdings and the

---

[13] *Capital* I, p. 673.
[14] Ibid.
[15] Ibid., p. 695.
[16] Ibid., p. 703.
[17] Ibid., pp. 292, 305.

economies of scale of the factory system. In a broad sense, these are changes and improvements in productive forces. But these changes are not autonomous. In explaining this paradigmatic change in the level of productive forces, commercial and political processes are at least as important as the general desire to overcome material scarcity through technological improvement.

Actually, the situation for technological determinism is even worse than this. As we have seen, the new work relations in factories and in large-scale farms are not the sort of thing that technological determinism can afford to count as a productive force. Productive forces in the required narrow sense play no significant role in Marx's paradigmatic explanation of basic economic change. However, even if a broader construal could somehow be reconciled with technological determinism, the fact would remain that the main tendencies for productive forces to develop are not autonomous in Marx's account of the rise of capitalism.

Wherever we look in Marx's economic histories, the relations of production and the processes they generate play a basic, independent role in explaining the most important changes in productive forces. At most, there is the balanced interaction that Cohen vividly summarizes and rejects, "a zig-zag 'dialectic' between forces and relations, with priority on neither side."[18] Marx's one extensive discussion of a technological change in a narrow sense of "technological" is his account of the new reliance on machinery in the Industrial Revolution. There Marx gives approximately equal emphasis to the greater efficiency of machine production and to its social advantage to the capitalist, as a means of reducing wages, extending the work day, and instilling labor discipline by destroying bargaining advantages of skilled craftsworkers.[19] Sometimes, the pursuit of more productive tools and techniques plays a distinctly secondary role in shaping epochal changes in tools and techniques themselves. Thus, in discussing the origins of a detailed and interdependent division of labor in society, surely the most

[18] Cohen, *Karl Marx's Theory of History*, p. 138.
[19] *Capital* I, pp. 407–8, 410.

basic influence on the subsequent development of tools, Marx suggests that contact and barter among social groups, not the pursuit of productivity, was its cause.[20] The crucial influence on the shape of technology in late antiquity, the rise of aristocracies employing slave labor on a large scale, is traced, by Marx, to the domestic effects of expansion through conquest, the growth of commerce, and the power of money to "dissolve" traditional social relations.[21]

When we turn from the question of how productive forces change to the question of how they shape stable economic structures, the clash between technological determinism and Marx is just as jarring. According to technological determinism, an economic structure has its basic type because that type best promotes the productive forces. Marx, to the contrary, depicts both slavery and feudalism as structures maintained by the power of an economically dominant class in the face of a feasible alternative, at least as productive. Marx generally describes the feudal aristocracy as a fetter on technology while feudalism was flourishing, an "organized robber-nobility"[22] whose economic obsession is prestigious consumption.[23] Similarly, the basic tendency of the slave-based plantations in the ancient world is regressive, since the masters' aristocratic disdain for technology is matched by their slaves' unwillingness to perform novel or complex work.[24] In both settings, the actual work of production is concentrated in "peasant agriculture on a small scale, and the carrying on of independent handicrafts."[25] Feudalism and slavery do not persist because the productive forces would be weaker if farmers and artisans were to dispense with feudal or slave-owning aristocrats. The whole drift of Marx's comments is to the contrary. They persist because the farmers and artisans lack the means (above all, the unity and discipline throughout broad geographic areas) to overthrow the aristocratic ruling class. Indeed, Marx regards

[20] Ibid., pp. 91f., 332f.
[21] *Grundrisse*, pp. 487, 493–95; *Capital* I, p. 132.
[22] *The German Ideology*, p. 46.
[23] *Grundrisse*, p. 507; *Capital* I, p. 672.
[24] *Capital* I, p. 191.
[25] Ibid., p. 316.

feudalism and slavery as triumphs of military, rather than productive, force in their very origins, "If human beings themselves are conquered along with the land and soil . . . then they are equally conquered as conditions of production, and in this way originates slavery and serfdom."[26]

A third distinctive claim in the technological determinist interpretation of Marx is that fundamental social changes are basically due to changes in the productive forces. Accordingly, one would expect Marx frequently to describe changes in the productive forces in his account of how feudalism became unstable and gave way to capitalism. In my previous sketch of Marx's story of this transformation, I did mention several changes in productive forces in a broad sense of the term, a sense in which the organization of craftwork in factories and the organization of agricultural work in large-scale one-crop farms are themselves productive forces. But technological determinism requires a narrower usage excluding work relations. Marx's writings on the rise of capitalism amount to a consistent, long-standing and explicit denial that changes in the productive forces in this narrow, technological sense were the main stimulus to economic change.

When Marx describes the changes in production that initiated the rise of capitalism, he is almost entirely concerned with the spread of certain work-relations, changes that are not based,

[26] *Grundrisse*, p. 491. Admittedly, feudal and slaveowning overlords may increase actual production by forcing workers to work harder. But the level of technological progress ought to be measured not by the total output of the productive forces, but by their potential output per man-hour when employed most efficiently. A factory's technology does not become less advanced when a successful strike reduces the pace of work. In any case, it is not open to a technological determinist who wants to be a Marxist to make the ability to force people to work an aspect of technological progress. Marx regards it as a major limitation of capitalism that it prevents many people from choosing leisure or more interesting work over increased material output. It is supposed to be an advantage of socialism that workers can and often will collectively decide to shorten the workday or to make work more interesting, even if material production might otherwise increase more rapidly. (See *Capital* I. chap. 10, "The Working-Day"; and vol. III, p. 820.) If coerced intensity of labor were an aspect of technological progress, the technological determinist Marx would be arguing here against his own account of the inevitability of socialism.

192

in his account, on technological innovations. Production by craftsworkers in small, independent, specialized workshops is replaced by "manufacture," production by many interdependent craftsworkers of many specialities, assembled in one place. Farming of diverse crops on small family plots is replaced by one-crop farming on large plots. Technological change is scarcely mentioned. Indeed, Marx's general descriptions of the role of technological change, as against changing work relations, in the rise of capitalism are explictly antitechnological. He says in *Capital*,

with regard to the mode of production itself, manufacture, in its strict meaning, is hardly to be distinguished, in its earliest stages, from the handicraft trades of the guilds, otherwise than by the greater number of workers simultaneously employed by one and the same individual capital. The workshop of the medieval master craftsman is simply enlarged.[27]

In the *Manifesto*, Marx's summary of the change from feudal ways of producing things to capitalist ones is a description of how commercial activity produced changes in work relations:

The feudal system of industry, under which industrial production was monopolized by the closed guilds, now no longer sufficed for the growing wants of the new markets. The manufacturing system took its place. The guild-masters were pushed on one side by the manufacturing middle class; division of labor between the different corporate guilds vanished in the face of division of labor in each single workshop.[28]

Marx does insist repeatedly that the development and subsequent fettering of productive forces is what initiates basic social change. Yet if productive forces are equated with technology Marx dramatically violates this principle when he writes history. Unless Marx had an enormous capacity for inconsistency, he must have been using the phrase in a broader sense.

The narrowly technological interpretation of "productive forces" not only fits Marx's historical practice badly. It also

[27] *Capital* I, p. 305.
[28] *Manifesto*, p. 336.

dramatically conflicts with many passages in which he explicitly classifies modes of cooperation as productive forces. For example, in *The German Ideology* he says,

By social we understand the cooperation of several individuals, no matter under what conditions, in what way, and to what end. It follows from this that a certain mode of production, or industrial stage, is always combined with a certain mode of cooperation, or social stage, and this mode of cooperation is itself a "productive force". Further, that the multitude of productive forces accessible to men determines the nature of society.[29]

He also calls "the social . . . power which arises through the cooperation of different individuals as it is determined by the division of labor" a productive force.[30] In the *Grundrisse*, roughly contemporary with the Preface, Marx says of workteams, "The unification of their forces increases their force of production,"[31] speaks of "the association of the workers—the cooperation and division of labor" as a "productive power [an alternative translation of *"Produktivkraft,"* the word standardly rendered "productive force"] of labor,"[32] and speaks of "the productive force arising from social combination."[33] In *Capital*, he says of "the social force that is developed, when many hands take part simultaneously in one and the same operation," "Not only have we here an increase in the productive power of the individual, by means of cooperation, but the creation of a new power, namely, the collective power of masses."[34] Indeed, he devotes two long chapters to the analysis of modes of cooperation, repeatedly describing them as productive forces.[35]

The prestige of Marx's writings among activists gives the question of defining "productive forces" great contemporary political importance. If changing work-relations, not new technology, may be the means by which productive forces dissolve

[29] *German Ideology*, p. 50.
[30] Ibid., p. 54.
[31] *Grundrisse*, p. 528.
[32] Ibid., p. 585.
[33] Ibid., p. 700.
[34] *Capital* I, pp. 308f. As usual, *power* and *force* are alternative translations of *Kraft*.
[35] See, for example, *Capital* I, pp. 312, 315, 316f., 340, 344.

old economic structures, then Marx's general theories do not suggest that technological progress is a necessary means, or even an effective one, for a regime to advance a technologicaly backward region toward socialism.

In developing my own alternative to the technological determinist interpretation, I will adopt a broader reading of "productive forces." These forces consist of the activities, tools and materials through which material goods are created and made usable, so far as the existence of those activities, tools and materials does not entail, in itself, rights and powers of control over people or things. This conception corresponds to Marx's description of the "elementary factors of the labor-process" in *Capital*: "1. the personal activity of man, i.e., work itself, 2. the subject of that work, 3. its instruments."[36]

A New Glossary

Replacing the technological reading of "productive forces" with the broader one is essential to the new understanding of Marx's theory that I will propose. Abandoning the technological determinist perspective also makes possible a more complete understanding of "relations of production," of a holistic kind. It is not as dramatically different or as essential to understanding where technological determinism goes wrong. But, understood in light of it, my "mode of production" interpretation is truer to Marx's writings and a more useful tool for history and politics.

"Relations of production" cannot be completely defined by equating them with relations of control over people, labor-power or productive forces in the process of material production. Some standard must be offered for individuating different relations of production. Otherwise we will end up with the absurd view that capitalists who control auto factories, capitalists who control oil refineries and capitalists who control ice-cream factories are, by that token, in different relations of production and (what comes to the same thing) different classes.

[36] *Capital* I, p. 174.

Marxist technological determinists try to construct a standard of individuation that does not refer to the political and ideological superstructure, commercial (as against technological) processes, or the effect of social groups on historical change. The task is motivated by a positivist assumption that I will discuss at length in Chapter Seven: Marx's theory of history must provide empirical general laws on the basis of which the main features of political and cultural institutions, the nature of large-scale commercial processes and the dynamics of fundamental social change could be predicted, in principle, given independent knowledge of antecedent conditions. If we individuate relations of production in terms of the former phenomena, then identifying relations of production cannot be an independent basis for saying what those phenomena must have been like. The only remaining tool for distinguishing different relations of production is the distinction of different objects of someone's control, apart from the means and consequences of control supplied by the superstructure. However, to avoid the surplus of distinctions in which auto capitalists, oil capitalists and ice-cream capitalists are put in different classes, the differences in objects producing different relations will have to come from a list of extremely broad and abstract categories, for example: land, human beings, labor-power, material means of production.

This procedure is unsatisfactory in principle. Relations of production are to be distinguished by distinguishing their objects. For example, control over the use of labor-power for a time, as against control over someone's life, is a distinguishing feature, so that proletarians can be distinguished from slaves. But if these differences in content are distinguishing features, why not the differences between the auto capitalists and the oil capitalists? There is no answer based on general principles, in the technological determinist framework. (Note that the oil/auto distinction looks more, not less salient on the face of things if technology is primary.) Moreover, the ahistorical list of abstract differences on which Marxist technological determinists rely in practice looks suspiciously like the distinctions among

sources of revenue and "factors of production" that play a leading role in bourgeois economics and capitalist accountancy—
with the usual understanding that slave-owners' income from
control of human beings is illegal, immoral and outmoded.
Marx's most powerful essays in economic methodology, the
Introduction to the *Grundrisse* and the chapter on "The Trinity
Formula" (land/labor/capital) in *Capital* volume three, are powerful protests against the application of such lists at the deepest
levels of analysis, and throughout the sweep of economic history.

The alternative is greater attention to relatively superstructural phenomena. But such attention can affect the individuation of production relations in a variety of ways. It is important
to distinguish different degrees of interaction here, different
degrees of holism, as it were. For some kinds of interaction
between production relations and other features of society are
quite compatible with the practices of technological determinists. In any case, disputes over such interaction are too often
clouded over with loose charges that one side is insufficiently
dialectical or the other is replacing science with metaphysics.

In the lowest degree of interaction, one constructs a certain
typology of relations of production because one believes that
the differences in type are the most important for explaining
political, cultural, commercial and historical phenomena. Naturally, technological determinists are dialectical to this degree,
and quite coherently so. They would not be technological determinists to begin with if they did not think that their larger
taxonomy—technology/relations   of   production/superstruc-
ture—was the best tool for explaining the most important phenomena.

In characterizing Marx's practice, when he individuates certain relations of production, I will emphasize higher degrees
of interaction, which do conflict with the technological-determinist style of individuation. In these cases, the distinctions
on which Marx relies cannot be described adequately and explicitly without referring to means or consequences of control,
including political means or consequences. Two different

197

grades of holism might be distinguished here. In some cases, one could describe a feature of the relation in question, singling it out from all others, without referring to relatively superstructural phenomena. But one would then fail to describe any central factor responsible for the distinctive accompaniments of that relation, in Marx's view. Thus, one could single out the relation characterizing the "Asiatic mode of production" as control over the irrigation system, and technological determinists, most notably Karl Wittfogel, have done so. But, as we shall see, Marx himself is concerned with a different feature, involving the political relation between a central bureaucracy and dispersed villages. The apolitical definition would not describe the essential nature of the relationship, the property causally underlying its other important features. It would be like defining capitalism as the system in which most education occurs outside the family, or the system in which hard liquor is consumed in great quantities. All and only the items in question are singled out, but their essential nature is not described. Finally, at the highest level of interaction, there just is no description singling out the kind of relation in question that does not refer to distinctive means or consequences of control. For example, I will argue that feudal overlordship cannot be distinguished from capitalist ownership without referring to the political means of dominance.

In general, positivism has made philosophers and social scientists too ashamed of partly circular theories, sometimes connecting by definition kinds of phenomena they causally relate. I hope that the following partial survey of Marx's historical typology will shed some light on a subject that is largely neglected, as a consequence, the kinds and uses of nonvicious circularity in science.

Outside of his analysis of capitalist society, Marx's most important and distinctive concept of a production relation has been his conception of feudal overlordship, the economic relation characterizing feudal society, in his view. Marx locates "the transition from the feudal mode of production" in the midseventeenth century in England, with the Civil War and the

198

Commonwealth serving as the watershed.[37] This late date for feudalism is a paradox, if social relations are defined in relation to a fixed list of objects of control. By 1600, corvée labor, in which the overlord controls a fixed part of the tenant's working life, had been extinct in England for about two centuries. Even rent in kind had largely been replaced by money-rent. Until we consider the political means by which control is maintained, the commercial objectives of the controllers, and the tendencies of class positions to promote change, what we see is an economy dominated by production under long-term leases, in independent workshops, or in cottage industries catering to merchants. In short, we have an impossible beast, feudalism without feudal overlords.

Marx's own procedure is to associate feudalism with a social relation between overlord and serf that he defines very broadly, in terms of force that determines the level of surplus-extraction from the subordinate, and of a capacity for self-subsistence that limits the effectiveness of this force:

It is evident that in all forms in which the direct labourer remains the "possessor" of the means of production and labour conditions necessary for the production of his own means of subsistence, the property relationship must simultaneously appear as a direct relation of lordship and servitude, so that the direct producer is not free; a lack of freedom which may be reduced from serfdom with enforced labour to a mere tributary relationship. The direct producer, according to our assumption, is to be found here in possession of his own means of production, the necessary material labour conditions required for the realisation of his labour and the production of his means of subsistence. He conducts his agricultural activity and the rural home industries connected with it independently. . . . The specific economic form, in which unpaid surplus-labour is pumped out of direct producers, determines the relationship of rulers and ruled, as it grows directly out of production itself and, in turn, reacts upon it as a determining element.[38]

[37] *Capital* III, p. 334. See also *Capital* I, p. 703; "The Bourgeoisie and the Counter-Revolution," *Selected Works*, vol. I, p. 319; *German Ideology*, p. 77; *Communist Manifesto*, p. 137; review of Guizot, *Why Has the English Revolution Been Successful?* in K. Marx and F. Engels, *On Britain* (Moscow, n.d.), pp. 89ff.
[38] *Capital* III, pp. 790f.

In this conception, as Marx develops it, someone is a feudal overlord if he or she extracts a surplus from direct producers through the relatively direct exercise of military and political power, rather than the exploitation of market advantages, leaving the producers otherwise in control of their own productive forces. Thus, the terms of sixteenth-century leases reflect the political dominance of the gentry over the countryside, rather than purely economic advantages. In manufacturing, the benefits of monopolies granted by the royal court and of guild .privileges yield most of the surplus. Though the distinctive means of control is probably the essential feature, differences in commercial capacities and objectives also distinguish the late feudal situation from a capitalist one, for Marx. While possessing their own tools, and lifelong or very long leases, which are traditionally renewed on the old terms, most actual farmers are not free to·sell "their" land. The overlords, for their part, are largely interested in prestige and personal luxury, rather than commercial expansion through competition. Finally, Marx emphasizes the different tendencies to change society of the late-feudal overlords, as against superficially similar, but more genuinely capitalist figures. For example, the great merchants who regard the employment of craftspeople as simply another object for the investment of surplus funds are sharply distinguished from ambitious craftspeople who become entrepreneurs. The latter cannot rely on monopolistic advantages and political privileges, but take on extra help as part of an effort to expand production and achieve economies of scale. The commercial activity of the former, in contrast, "cannot by itself contribute to the overthrow of the old mode of production, but tends rather to preserve and retain it as its precondition."[39]

In short, Marx, avoids the impossible category of feudalism without feudal overlords because he characterizes social relations of production by reference to political means, commercial objectives, and dynamic roles. Moreover, the distinguishing features are derived from the detailed study of particular his-

[39] *Capital* III, p. 334. See the passages cited in n. 37 above for other sources of the conception of the feudal mode of production presented in this paragraph.

torical processes, not from some fixed list of abstract factors of production, derived from reflection on the production process in general.

The definition of feudal overlordship is an especially dramatic and important example, both because the story of the rise of capitalism is so central to Marx's theories and because the claim that certain countries are feudal or semi-feudal has been politically important in arguments that they are not yet ripe for socialism. There are, however, other cases in which Marx's usage is also governed by the whole social context in which production occurs. Though plantation owners in the antebellum southern United States owned slaves, he regards them as a species of capitalist, because they pursued profits in a capitalist world economy.[40] The plebeians of Rome are, in his view, a fundamentally different class from the proletarians of modern times because larger social processes restrict them to a disorganized, parasitic way of life.[41] In traditional Chinese society, a surplus from relatively isolated and self-sufficient villages is extracted by a highly mobile and far-flung bureaucracy that dominates the coordinating functions required for stable and effective production. Here, if the definition of production relations can make no reference to political control, the bureaucracy stands outside of the economic structure and we have yet another impossible beast for Marxism: a class-divided society without a ruling class. To the contrary, Marx explicitly identifies relations of production with certain political relations, in this specific type of society:

Should the direct producers not be confronted by a private landowner but rather, as in Asia, under direct subordination to a state which stands over them as their landlord and simultaneously as sovereign, then rent and taxes coincide, or rather, there exists no tax which differs from this form of ground-rent. Under such circumstances,

---

[40] *Capital* I, pp. 253f. In *Theories of Surplus-Value*, vol. II, pp. 303f., Marx writes (the emphasis is his): ". . . [T]he business in which slaves are used is conducted by *capitalists.*"
[41] Letter to the editorial board of *Otechestvenniye Zapiski* (1877), in Marx and Engels, *Basic Writings on Politics and Philosophy*, ed. L. Feuer (Garden City, 1959), p. 441.

there need exist no stronger political or economic pressure than that common to all subjection to that state. The state is then the supreme lord. Sovereignty here consists in the ownership of land concentrated on a national scale.[42]

In Marx's theory, what counts as a relation of production must be discovered through a theoretical and empirical investigation of stability and change in actual societies. This is one of the reasons why his theory is, in Engels' phrase "not a doctrine, but a method,"[43] a framework for developing explanations, not, in Marx's own derisive phrase, "a general historico-philosophical theory the supreme virtue of which consists in being super-historical."[44]

Relations of production *are* relations of control over productive forces, labor-power or people in the process of material production. However, from society to society, relations of production may be individuated according to their objects, or the means of control, or the uses to which control is put. Which distinctions define distinctive relations of production depends on which are crucial in the explanation of subsequent radical change (along lines that I will soon be sketching), and in the explanation of the shape of stable institutions (of the form, "These institutions are as they are mainly to stabilize these relations of production.") The claim that relations of production are the basis for political, ideological and commercial processes is the claim that stability and change in the latter realms is basically to be explained in the former ways. But the distinctions between relations of production that figure in these explanations cannot be defined in advance.

Among many critics of Marx, his theory is held to collapse into circularity if identifications of relations of production inevitably depend on hypotheses concerning their interactions with the alleged political superstructure. For example, Plamenetz and Acton have argued that this circularity is so obvious and devastating in Marx that his theory of history is unworthy of

[42] *Capital* III, p. 791.
[43] Engels to Sombart, March 11, 1895, *Selected Correspondence*, p. 455.
[44] Letter to *Otecehestvenniye Zapiski*, p. 441.

further empirical test.[45] In fact, it is typical of the most interesting scientific theories that phenomena which are connected by way of explanation are also connected, to some extent, by definition. Thus, the revolution in chemistry begun at the time of Dalton depends on a distinction between true compounds and mere mixtures that presupposes part of Dalton's atomic theory. That genuine chemical substances are only created by rearrangements of atoms at the molecular level is entailed by Dalton's way of identifying processes of genuine chemical creation. The cornerstone of Dalton's chemistry was the hypothesis that elementary substances combine to form new substances in fixed, simple numerical ratios. Partisans of the traditional chemistry, based on the notion of mutual affinity, pointed to a variety of processes displaying no fixed ratio which had always been seen as the creation of new chemical substances by compounding. Often Daltonians could only reply by claiming that mere mixtures, not genuinely new chemical substances, were produced. And there is no general way to explicate the distinction, as they drew it, that does not presuppose the atomic view of chemistry. It is just a reassuring fiction of elementary school textbooks that the distinction between true compounds and mixtures can be drawn in a theory-neutral way. Not all (Daltonian) mixtures are unstable, or separable by mechanical means. Many solutions and alloys are examples to the contrary, crucial to the debate over Daltonian chemistry.[46]

Because Daltonian chemistry individuates its subject matter in this self-serving way, a variety of Daltonian claims that sound like testable hypotheses cannot be tested except through the assessment of the theory as a whole. That solutions of salts are not compounds is a case in point. By the same token, there will be cases in which the atomic theory of chemical combination permits the same observations and explanations as rival

[45] J. P. Plamenetz, *German Marxism and Russian Communism* (London, 1954), chap. 2, sec. 1; H. B. Acton, *The Illusion of the Epoch* (London, 1955), pp. 164ff.

[46] See Thomas Kuhn, *The Structure of Scientific Revolutions* (Chicago, 1970), pp. 130–34. Aaron Ihde, in *The Development of Modern Chemistry* (New York, 1964), pp. 98f., describes in more detail the most sustained attack on the law of definite proportions, by the distinguished and innovative chemist Berthollet.

theories, even though in the latter theories, these cases violate the law of fixed ratios. Still, Daltonian chemistry could be justified, without circularity, because of the many cases in which comparison was possible. There were many fixed ratios of combination that, all agreed, cried out for explanation, and that only the new chemistry could explain. Eventually, all came to see that certain regularities in conductivity and in the behavior of gases were best explained in a Daltonian framework. The cases whose status was in dispute, mere mixtures for Dalton, true compounds for his opponents, became relatively unimportant compared with the realm of the achievements of Daltonian chemistry.

Similarly, there may be cases in which the more holistic Marxism renders immune from test a claim that might have seemed disputable. Probably, the claim that production relations determined the basic shape of political control in ancient China is a case in point. Some cases in which the mode of production is primary, in the version of Marx that I will soon elaborate, will be cases in which noneconomic processes are primary for non-Marxist historians, because the more holistic Marxism sometimes individuates economic structures in terms of political means of control. Still, from society to society and historical episode to historical episode, Marx's theory of history usually favors different explanations from its current rivals. It is to be tested by means of these comparisons, not dismissed by revealing a circularity that potentially, though not actually, might render all comparison impossible.

When technological determinists respond to dismissals of the latter sort with a rigid analytical distinction between relations of production and political processes, they accept shared methodological premises that they should reject. Here as elsewhere, technological determinism and *a priori* anti-Marxism are two different aspects of the same positivist methodology. I hope I have shown that the resulting treatment of relations of production is an unfortunate basis for interpreting Marx or for explaining history in a plausible Marxist way. Still, the reader who is unconvinced can attach a less holistic reading to "re-

lations of production" and discover an alternative to technological determinism in the interpretation that follows.

THE MODE OF PRODUCTION INTERPRETATION

There is a familiar picture of Marx as a superb practicing
historian whose general theories departed enormously from his
historical insights because he got involved in politics. If Marx's
theory were technological determinism, we would now have
grounds for accepting this diagnosis of Marx's sad case. But
two alternative interpretations are available that make Marx's
theoretical statements largely of one piece with his historical
explanations. The first, which I will present in this section,
fits all of Marx's general theoretical statements and nearly all
of his specific explanations. In it, economic structures have
great causal independence, while the growth of productive
forces (in the broad, nontechnical sense) remains the basis for
internal change. It is the general theory of history to which
Marx explicitly commits himself. The second theory, which
I present in the next section, fits all of his specific explanations
and fits almost all of his general statements to a large extent,
if not entirely. It is a broadened version of the first theory,
one in which the growth of productive forces is not the only
internal source of change. This is the theory that guided Marx
in practice when he wrote history.

In Marx's view, both stable social structure and dramatic
social change are ultimately based on the mode of production,
the activities, facilities and relationships, material *and* social,
through which material goods are produced. The mode of production consists of productive forces in the technological sense,
productive forces, such as work relations, in my broader sense,
and relations of production. Although it plays no fundamental
role in technological determinism, the concept of a mode of
production is used throughout Marx's general statements concerning history, including a notable passage from the Preface:
"The mode of production of material life conditions the social,
political and intellectual life process in general."

205

Different features of the mode of production are primary, depending on what is to be explained, the features of a stable society or the occurrence and direction of change. For stable societies, the basic type of economic structure is primary; for social change, productive forces (in the broader sense) are.

The most important features of a relatively stable society are largely explained by the needs and powers of what Marx calls "the ruling class," the group in the economic structure that, through its control of productive forces, mainly controls the surplus product of direct participants in production.[47] Because of ruling class dominance of the surplus, political and ideological institutions will operate to maintain the economic structure, at least so far as it benefits this class.[48] In Chapters Three and Four, I analyzed the political aspect of this kind of dominance. For present purposes, the political and ideological aspects are equally important. The distinctions—for example, between stabilizing mechanisms and conspiracies, objective interests and conscious reasons—that helped to clarify the former aspect of dominance apply to both.

This framework for explaining features of a stable society creates a pressing problem about social change, all the more pressing for a revolutionary like Marx. If a society is dominanted by a ruling class combining economic, political and ideological power, how can processes internal to the society change its economic structure into another basic type, marked by the dominance of a different class?

---

[47] My interpretation will be directed at societies in which class divisions have already appeared. Technological determinism is obviously unsuited to account for Marx's discussions of pre-class societies. There he emphasizes two sources of change, neither constituting technological progress: conquest and exchange among social groups. See *Grundrisse*, pp. 471–513; *Capital* I, pp. 91f., 332f.

[48] *The German Ideology* contains several neat descriptions of dominance by a ruling class; for example, "The ideas of the ruling class are in every epoch the ruling ideas, i.e., the class which is the ruling *material* force in society is at the same time its ruling *intellectual* force. The class which has the means of material production at its disposal, has control at the same time over the means of mental production, so that, thereby, generally speaking, the ideas of those who lack the means of mental production are subject to it" (p. 64); "The state is the form in which the individuals of a ruling class assert their common interest" (p. 80).

With respect to this question of change, the productive forces are primary. Like Hegel before him, Lenin after him, and practicing scientists all the time, Marx treats primacy as relative to the question being asked.

A relatively stable economic structure may permit people to use new kinds of productive forces, or to employ old kinds in greater numbers, as they pursue greater control over material goods. This opportunity for change may have unforeseen revolutionary consequences. Although permitted, the additional productive forces may come to be fettered, in that the old economic structure discourages their effective use or further development where a new one would not. For example, as entrepreneurs were well aware in seventeenth-century England, the large fixed investment required for large-scale, one-crop agriculture or setting up a factory is discouraged by the risk that the investment may come to nothing because some court favorite has been granted a royal monopoly. At a certain point, these fetters on productive forces may be broken, and a new, better-suited economic structure set up, on account of quantitative or qualitative factors, usually both. Quantitatively, it may be that the new productive forces would be so much more productive in a new economic structure that a class that would dominate the new structure can organize successful revolution against the ruling class, based on a widespread hope for greater well-being. Qualitatively, it may be that the new productive forces—in particular, the new work relations—are of a kind that gives a nondominant class new power to seize control of the surplus, quite apart from potential increases in the size of the social product. Marx gives approximately equal emphasis to both the quantitative and the qualitative factors in his account of how socialism will triumph. The deepening industrial depressions and increasingly violent wars characteristic of advanced capitalism limit society's ability to provide material well-being with the productive forces capitalism has developed. At the same time, the large-scale unity, discipline and coordination produced by capitalist work-relations give workers, for the first time, the ability to seize and control the productive forces. For example, both of these factors are emphasized in the famous descriptions of the triumph of socialism in the *Communist Manifesto*[49] and *Capital*.[50] Marx emphasizes the quantitative factor in his account of the rise of the bourgeoisie, who had been well-organized internally in feudal society but needed the ties to larger groups afforded by the promise of heightened well-being through liberation from feudal constraints on production. He emphasizes the qualitative factor in his description of how a Greco-Roman aristocracy arose through the strategic advantages of larger farmers within the traditional apparatus for conquest, colonization and trade.

Typical members of a subordinate class want to improve their well-being, powers and opportunities, both in absolute terms and relative to the ruling class. Yet, as fetters tighten on developing productive forces, they limit the possibilities of improvement within the old economic structure of a subordinate class whose status depends on the development of those forces. As we have seen, the changes in productive forces that result in this fettering may, at the same time, give the subordinate class a new ability to change society, attacking the superstructure that maintains the old economic structure and setting up a new, nonfettering structure over which that class presides. Since this process involves the overcoming of fetters on the new productive forces, the new society will be more productive than the old. In sum, if change occurs from internal processes, it occurs when the productive forces have developed in such a way that (a) the old economic structure inhibits their further effective use, producing a new motive for structural change, and (b) the economic bases of class power are transformed, enabling a formerly subordinate class to set up a new economic structure, under its dominance, better adapted to the productive forces.

Purely for convenience, I will call the interpretation I have just sketched the "mode of production interpretation." Before, I summed up the technological determinist interpretation by describing its distinctive answers to questions about stability and change: What explains the main features of a stable society?

[49] *Communist Manifesto* p. 345.
[50] *Capital* I, p. 715.

What causes the most important changes in the productive forces? What determines the nature of basic changes in economic structures? The difference between the two interpretations is reflected in the different answers they yield.

According to the mode of production interpretation, the character of a stable society is explained by the economic dominance of the ruling class. In itself, this is perfectly compatible with the technological determinist interpretation, indeed implied by it. But there is a further element in technological determinism that is absent from the mode of production interpretation. There is no suggestion that a stable economic structure does a better job of promoting productivity than any alternative. Alternative economic structures, at least as productive as the triumphant one, may be ruled out by incapacities arising from the class situation of people who are quite adept at material production. This accords with Marx on feudalism and slavery. For example, so far as productivity is concerned, a structure dominated by peasants and artisans would have been at least as effective as the feudal economic structure. But sustained unity and collective discipline over large geographic areas would have been required to break the bonds that the overlords forged from the surplus they controlled. The social relations of peasants, by focusing loyalties on the family and the village, guaranteed that the needed class solidarity would not arise.[51]

According to technological determinism, the course of development of the productive forces is to be explained, in the main, as due to an autonomous, general human tendency to use technology to overcome natural scarcity. The mode of production interpretation makes no such claim of explanatory primacy, either with the broad usage of "productive forces" it typically employs, or with the narrow usage characteristic of technological determinism. The zigzag dialectic it permits between changes in productive forces and nonderivative social processes is required by all of Marx's concrete discussions of major transformations of the productive forces. Moreover,

[51] See *German Ideology*, p. 45; *Communist Manifesto*, pp. 114–19; *Capital* I, chap. 32.

209

since it does not make a universal tendency to advance technology the sufficient cause of social change, the mode of production interpretation allows for the possibility that an economic structure might generate powers and attitudes that preclude substantial increases in productivity. This possibility is realized in Marx's account of ancient India and China.[52]

In the technological determinist interpretation, what initiates radical social change is change in the productive forces, conceived in a relatively narrow, technological way. The subsequent era of revolution ends with a society that is optimally productive, given the new productive forces. In the mode of production interpretation, changes in productive forces initiate social change. But productive forces are conceived in a much broader way and include work relations. Marx's paradigmatic explanation of social change, his discussion of the rise of capitalism, requires this broader reading. Moreover, the new society need not be optimally productive. Since it overcomes fetters on production, it will be more productive than the old. But further alternatives, at least as productive as the triumphant one, may be ruled out by differences in power based on historical differences in class situation. This is the possibility implied by Marx's discussions of feudal and slave societies.

An interpretation that unites Marx's general outlook on history with almost all of his specific historical explanations is surely preferable to one that splits him down the middle. I have argued that the mode of production interpretation is preferable on this ground. In addition it fits several of Marx's general statements better than the technological determinist interpretation, and it is compatible with the rest.

Marx's first detailed descriptions of his theory of history occur in *The German Ideology*. There, Marx and Engels begin their most important summary of their theory of change with the sentence: "The form of intercourse determined by the existing productive forces at all previous historical stages, *and in its turn determining these*, is civil society."[53] Quite uncontroversially, "civil society" here means the social relations of pro-

---

[52] See *Grundrisse*, p. 486; *Capital* I, pp. 140, 330.
[53] *German Ideology*, p. 57; italics added.

duction. At the outset, it is presented as the causal partner of the productive forces, not their servant.

While Marx quietly let the Preface go out of print, he encouraged and often supervised the reissue of the *Communist Manifesto* throughout his lifetime. The general statements about history there emphasize the social aspect of production and do not give primacy to the technological. They are epitomized by the sentence introducing Marx's sketch of world history: "The history of all hitherto existing societies is the history of class struggle."

Marx's theoretical work was dominated by the writing of *Capital*. That work contains general statements about the nature of society and change that invite a nontechnological determinist reading, for example:

The specific economic form in which unpaid labor is pumped out of direct producers determines the relationship of rulers and ruled, as it grows directly out of production itself and, reacts upon it [i.e., production itself] as a determining element. Upon this, however, is founded the entire formation of the economic community . . . thereby simultaneously its specific political form. It . . . reveals the innermost secret, the hidden basis of the entire social structure.[54]

Among the general statements by Marx that appear to support the technological determinist interpretation, the Preface is the most important and is highly representative of the rest. In showing how it can be accommodated to the mode of production interpretation, I hope I will provide the interested reader with ways of accommodating similar passages in *The Poverty of Philosophy*, the 1846 letter to Annenkov and elsewhere.

Most of the Preface is obviously compatible with either interpretation. Two sentences do resist the mode of production interpretation. At one point, Marx says, "No social formation ever perishes before all the productive forces for which there is room in it have developed." Literally understood, this is no

[54] *Capital* III, p. 791. See also vol. I, p. 209, and the summary of the rise of capitalism in *Theories of Surplus-Value* (in effect, the fourth volume of *Capital*), vol. I, p. 389.

part of the mode of production interpretation. However, as we have seen, it cannot be part of Marx's considered judgment. Marx did not believe that capitalism is, or feudalism was, incapable of any technological progress at the moment of its death. This sentence, and similar ones from Marx's criticisms of Proudhon, must be a hyperbolic statement of the claim that a social formation is viable so long as it does not inhibit the development of productive forces, threatened once fettering begins. And this claim is very much a part of both interpretations.

Marx introduces his summary of his notion of history with the sentence: "In the social production of their life, men enter into . . . relations of production which correspond to a definite stage of development of their material productive forces." In his book, Cohen notes, and rightly so, that this strong statement gives some kind of primacy to the productive forces. It certainly does in context, since no converse statement of the correspondence of productive forces to relations of production follows. But need this primacy be of the kind required by the technological determinist interpretation?

There is something special about the development of productive forces in the present interpretation of Marx. It is always fettering of the productive forces that puts basic, internal change on the agenda, and basic, internal change always enhances productivity at first. It would be quite reasonable to summarize this by claiming that an economic structure corresponds to a stage of development of the productive forces.

Working in the other direction of causality, there is no universal phenomenon that would justify saying that productive forces correspond to a stage in the development of economic structures. If the mode of production interpretation is right, structures do select forces quite as much as forces select structures. More precisely, this possibility is left open by Marx's general theory and realized in his specific explanations. And sometimes the impact of the structures is as direct and straightforward as the phenomenon of fettering. Thus, in the Industrial Revolution, class struggle quite directly contributes to the adoption of industrial techniques by employers. But more frequently, the influence of the economic structure on the shape of the productive forces is indirect, mediated by commercial and political processes to which the structure gives rise. For example, new commercial needs and opportunities and new competitive pressures arise from the pursuit of interests determined by the old economic structure and lead to changes in the productive forces. The development of Continental markets for wool and rich peasants' exploitation of inflated food prices and fixed rents are cases in point. The other, even higher barrier to the statement that forces correspond to structures is the fact that technological determinism is not all wrong. Of course, there are important cases in which changes in productive forces do result from the use of human know-how to overcome natural scarcity. Because the story of the impact of structures on forces is so mixed, the claim that forces correspond to structures is not an appropriate summary.

Marx's statement about the correspondence of structures to forces is a synopsis of a specific scenario for change in structure, but not an assessment of the balance of ultimate causal influences. Even though no mechanism for shaping forces is as direct and universal as fettering, the following can be true: the nature of basic changes in forces is as much to be explained as due to structures and the processes to which they give rise as the nature of changes in structures is due to forces; productive forces include work relations; a stable structure may be far from optimal for the productive development of forces.

A BROADER VIEW

The above version of the mode of production interpretation is meant to account for all of Marx's general statements about historical change, and almost all of his explanations of specific historical episodes. However, Marx sometimes offers specific explanations suggesting an even broader view of history, in which the growth of productive forces, broadly defined, is not the only internal source of fundamental change.

The *Grundrisse*, in effect Marx's notebooks for *Capital*, contains an especially clear case of such an explanation, together

213

with a fairly general description of the kind of mechanism for change on which these explanations rely. There, Marx examines the change from the early Roman society of independent household farms into a later society characterized by sharp class divisions among nonslaves.[55] His speculation is that the earlier economic structure maintained itself by means that guaranteed its destruction in the long run. As population grew, new households were given farms as a result of conquest and colonization bringing land, slaves and tribute. This process of expansion gave increased power to the richer farmers who dominated the army and the administration of public resources. They also specially benefited from the growth in trade produced by territorial expansion, since richer farmers are better able to switch to the raising of cash crops. Eventually, the better-off farmers used their accumulated control over land, slaves and the political apparatus to become a new ruling class of large-scale absentee landowners. Other farmers became their exploited tenants, if they were not dispossessed entirely. "Thus," Marx concludes, "the preservation of the old community includes the destruction of the conditions on which it rests, turns into its opposite."[56]

The Preface and several other general statements about history make contradictions between the economic structure and the productive forces the basis for change. But in this explanation of change in the ancient world, contradictions within the earlier economic structure are themselves sufficient to bring about change. The earlier economic structure is maintained through processes that ultimately destroy it, quite apart from changes in the productive forces, even in the broad sense of the term. Indeed, Marx explicitly distinguishes the actual process of change, in which the maintenance of household farming by conquest proves self-destructive, from the process of change through productive growth. After the previously quoted remark about the preservation of the old community turning into its opposite, he adds,

[55] See *Grundrisse*, pp. 487, 493–95, 506.
[56] Ibid., p. 494.

If it were thought that productivity on the same land could be increased by developing the forces of production etc. (this precisely the slowest of all in traditional agriculture), then the new order would include combinations of labor, a large part of the day spent in agriculture, etc., and thereby again suspend the old economic conditions of the community.

The growth of productive forces is an imaginable but unlikely alternative source of basic economic change, here.

Marx's speculation about the ancient world requires a broader outlook than that of the Preface. Social structure and social change are still based on the mode of production. The institutions of a stable society are still means of preserving ruling class control. Basic internal change still occurs because the mode of production as a whole encourages processes that eventually give a social group the ability and desire to destroy it, and create a new one. But this process of self-destruction may take two forms. As in the Preface, productive forces may grow until they encounter fetters. Alternatively, the economic structure may maintain itself through relations of power over people and productive forces that eventually enable a group to accumulate the power to remake society. Since these power relations (e.g., nonslaves' collective control of means to acquire new land and slaves for household farming) are themselves a part of the economic structure, an economic structure may be said to change as a result of conflict with itself, as well as with the productive forces. I will call this view of history the broader mode of production interpretation.

Although the *Grundrisse* discussion of class divisions in ancient Rome is uniquely clear and detailed in this regard, several other passages also appeal to the mechanisms for change characteristic of the broader view of history. The earliest is a brief discussion of ancient Rome in *The German Ideology*[57]—in effect, a highly condensed version of the *Grundrisse* passage. A few years later, the *Communist Manifesto* traces the rise of capitalism to ultimately self-destructive conflicts inherent in the feudal economic structure. Escaped serfs form the basis of an urban

[57] *German Ideology*, p. 44.

bourgeoisie that unites with monarchs in the expansion of international trade and colonization, which so strengthens the bourgeoisie that it can dominate and transform society.[58]

In the *Grundrisse* as a whole, a long, self-contained discussion of precapitalist economic structures (roughly pp. 471–515 in the Nicolaus edition) is dominated by the idea that the total set of social relations of production may dictate the direction of social change, including change in those relations themselves. The possibility that these relations may be ultimately self-transforming is formulated in general terms in at least three passages.[59]

In *Capital*, the explanations of some crucial episodes of economic change suggest the broader mode of production interpretation, in that they appeal to a self-undermining tendency of an initial pattern of control over production. Capitalist manufacturing is initially characterized by a pattern of capitalists' control over factory buildings and raw materials, and workers' control over tools and technical knowledge. This pattern generates class struggles in which capitalists are driven to use their monopoly of surplus wealth to create a new, industrial pattern. In this pattern, workers are deprived of old bargaining advantages, since they use capitalist-controlled machinery requiring relatively little technical knowledge.[60] Similarly, Marx speculates that a self-transforming pattern of control might have given rise to class divisions. A classless society organized into communities of farmers and artisans, independent but trading with each other, may acquire class divisions as contact between communities leads to increased reliance on large-scale production for trade, rather than subsistence farming and small-scale barter.[61] Finally, the self-destructive tendency of the feudal economic structure is implied by Marx's description of the first stage in the rise of capitalism: "The old nobility had been devoured by the great feudal wars. The new nobility was the child of its times for which money was the power of all

---

[58] *Communist Manifesto*, pp. 336f. See also *German Ideology*, pp. 82–85.
[59] *Grundrisse*, pp. 487, 493, and the previously quoted remark from p. 494.
[60] See *Capital* I, pp. 407–10.
[61] *Capital* I, pp. 91f., 332f.

MARX'S MODELS AND MARX'S CONTEXT

powers."[62] The literal self-destruction of the old aristocracy and the rise of mercantile supporters of the great royal houses were not the result of productive growth. They were the result of a tendency toward civil war inherent in the feudal economic structure, where a surplus is mostly extracted through dominance over land and its tillers by means of military force possessed by independent family groups.

In a sense, the narrower theory was never part of the essential core of Marx's view of history. The rationale for the claim that productive growth is the only basic internal source of change is that only productive growth and fettering can serve as an internal basis for the overthrow of a ruling class. But all of Marx's actual arguments to this effect are directed against efforts to locate a basic source of change outside the mode of production—for example, in independent cultural innovations or in military triumphs.[63] He never constructs an argument against the possibility that an economic structure might be inherently self-destructive in the long run. When he initially formulates this possibility, in the *Grundrisse*, it is to defend it. The logic of his argument does not require that productive forces be primary, whatever his own conclusions may sometimes have been.

MARX'S MODELS AND MARX'S CONTEXT

Which is Marx's theory of history, the broader or the narrower mode of production theory? In practice, the broader one is. When Marx develops an explanation that seems only to fit the broader theory, he is prepared to adopt it despite apparent conflict with the narrower one. Indeed, in at least one passage,[64] he acknowledges that explanations appealing to the self-destructive tendency of an economic structure may be superior to explanations appealing to the growth of productive forces

---

[62] *Capital* I, p. 672.
[63] As usual, *The German Ideology* contains vivid summaries of crucial arguments. See, for example, pp. 64–68 (on cultural change), 89f. (on military conquest).
[64] *Grundrisse*, p. 494.

in the case at hand. At the same time, the narrower theory is Marx's explicit general theory of history. Marx's most general statements about the nature of history make the growth of productive forces the basis for change.

Several compelling influences help to explain Marx's explicit appeals to a relatively narrow model that he freely abandoned in practice. One is the influence of Hegel. One of the several paths that led Marx to his mature views was an initial commitment to Hegel's philosophy of change in general, historical change in particular, and Marx's subsequent criticism of it in light of Feuerbach's materialism. The paragraph in the Preface that includes the celebrated sketch of history is, in effect, a description of this path. The simplest conversion of Hegel's philosophy of history into something materialist supports the narrower mode of production model rather than the broad one. For Hegel, peoples achieve and lose world-historical significance as their institutions embody, and then inhibit, the achievements of mind striving for freedom through reflection. Substitute "the achievements of people struggling for freedom from natural scarcity through production" and a basis for the narrower model, or for technological determinism, results.

The ease with which Hegel yields a productive forces interpretation, once converted to materialism should, if anything, make us suspicious of such interpretations of Marx. Though Marx pays tribute to Hegel, throughout his writings, for Hegel's emphasis on internal contradictions as a source of change, he warns us, especially in *Capital*, to interpret his theories in light of his practice, not by taking literally "flirtations" with Hegelian ways of speaking.[65] Moreover, other paths to his mature view of history had independent significance and are also alluded to in the Preface autobiography, as well as in Marx's transitional works of the 1840s: political activities as a muckraking journalist, the study of writings from and about the French Revolution, and the study of English political economists. Finally, nothing is more common in the history of science and of literature than the presentation of a new ap-

[65] *Capital* I, p. 29.

218

proach in forms derived from a great predecessor, by someone who is departing farther from the predecessor than those forms suggest. The use of mechanical models in nineteenth-century field theories, Newton's geometrical presentation of the calculus, and Einstein's initial retention of space and time as distinct magnitudes are a few examples. Revolutionary thinkers use traditional models to organize their descriptions of new terrain.

In the second place, as Engels notes in later biographical comments, Marx's political activities often dictated a heavy emphasis on the role of productive forces, not merited by less pressing theoretical concerns. In the 1840s, Marx was concerned to distinguish his views from those of Left Hegelian idealists, who considered the material needs of working people either not at all or with disdain. During the rest of his life, the anti-Marxist tendencies in the European workers' movement that had the widest influence were, broadly speaking, anarchist, based on the ideal of an egalitarian, decentralized society of independent producers. In these controversies, Marx needed to emphasize the role of modern productive forces. For example, he needed to convince people that the material needs of modern workers could not be fulfilled in the anarchist utopias, which were incompatible with modern industrial technology; that technology had doomed small producers, the social underpinning of anarchist movements, to a marginal status; and that the workers' movement should take advantage of the positive and revolutionary aspects of industrialization rather than simply condemning its costs. Small wonder, then, that Marx's formulations come closest to self-caricature when he is attacking the historical speculations underlying Proudhon's anarchism: "The hand-mill gives you society with the feudal lord; the steam-mill, society, with the industrial capitalist."[66]

Finally, Marx's reluctance to abandon in theory a model that did not constrain him in practice may have resulted, in part, from his commitment to a general principle regarding change. That principle is the assumption that social evolution always

[66] Karl Marx, *The Poverty of Philosophy* (Moscow, 1973), p. 95.

involves progress, at least of a certain limited kind. This equation of evolution and progress is entailed by the narrower theory, in which evolution always facilitates productive growth. It is not entailed by the broader theory, since an economic structure destroyed through self-generated conflicts need not give birth to a more productive society. The transition from the Roman Empire to feudalism might be an actual case of such self-destruction without productive progress.

Marx's autobiographical comments in the Preface suggest that the equation of evolution and progress had been extremely fruitful in his own development. It guided most of the best social science in his era. He might, then, quite reasonably have been reluctant to adopt a new theory of change in which the idea of progress is not so central. Moreover, since he was using a very broad notion of productive forces, he may well have hoped that explanations that seemed to depart from the narrower mode of production theory could be reconciled with it, on further analysis. The political problems of the workers' movement, which always directed his theoretical interests, did not make it urgent to pursue this hope, or to choose between the broad and the narrow theories, should reconciliation fail.

In the late twentieth century, by contrast, the general equation of social evolution and progress is no longer the dominant working hypothesis of the best social science. The political context has changed as well. At least in the so-called "less developed" countries, a frequent argument of self-described socialists against fighting for socialism now is, "The productive forces aren't ripe." This argument has much less initial plausibility in the broad mode of production theory than in the narrow one. On the broader view, even where capitalism does not inhibit productivity, it may have created a working class with the need and the power to overthrow it. In sum, Marx's reasons for continued ambivalence between the two theories are no longer good excuses.

CHAPTER SIX

The Mode of Production and History

SOME OBJECTIONS

IN THE REST of this book, I will mostly discuss the two largest problems with the broad mode of production interpretation as a theory of history: How can one show, even tentatively, that a historical theory this vast and general is true? What are the implications of the bad fit of the theory with standard models of explanation and confirmation in the philosophy of science? Before doing so, I want to face some other objections, small enough to be answered briefly, at least in a preliminary way, but important enough to clarify Marx's basic theory of history, as I have interpreted him: Is this the kind of implausibly holistic theory that gives structures a life of their own? Is it too concerned with power-relations to be materialist? Is it too vague to be a theory worthy of the name? Is it too well-hedged to be falsified? What is the force of the restriction to internal causes?

Holism. In stating the mode of production theory (by this phrase, I will mean the broad version, from now on), I have stayed close to Marx's formulations in the *Grundrisse*. In the internal transformation of an economic structure, processes that originally maintained the basic type of the structure ultimately lead to a change in basic type, because of the nature of the mode of production. It might seem that such a theory is too structural, imposing not just the normal holism of many good structural explanations, but an excessive holism in which structures manipulate their parts like puppets.

By a structural explanation, I mean one that explains a phenomenon by describing large-scale structural features rather than a chain of individual causes through which constituents of the structure interact. Its holism is not excessive if we have reason to believe that the structural causation is realized in some appropriate causal interactions among the constituents. Thus, Neumann's explanation of the Nazi seizure of power appeals to the impact of large-scale social interests and circumstances. If it is right, then a variety of alternative individual causal chains would have sufficed—for example, if Hindenburg had not been naive about his ability to control Hitler, the Nazis would have come to power some other way. Yet, at least if we accept that people's objective interests can shape their behavior without being formulated in conscious deliberations, we may suppose that some individual causal chain in which people's responses were governed by their individual psychologies did connect the social situation Neumann describes with the political outcome he seeks to explain.[1]

By way of contrast, many readers find that Hegel's theory of history is excessively holistic. In excessive holism, we have reason to believe that chains of individual causes do not exist where they must to connect the structural features with the phenomenon those features are supposed to explain. In Hegel, when a people has made the idea of freedom more rational and concrete, and then reached an impasse, this makes another people come along, raising the work to a higher level. Since the latter people usually had insufficient or inappropriate cultural contact with their world-historic predecessors, we usually have reason to believe that no appropriate personal interactions linked the two enterprises. A structural feature, the development of the idea of freedom in history, is manipulating constituents like puppets where it should be realized in their interactions.

If historical and psychological knowledge otherwise supported technological determinism, it would not be excessively holistic. The mechanism at the level of individual action would be a desire for more efficient production, and frustration when

[1] See "Methodological Individualism and Social Explanation," *Philosophy of Science* 45 (1978), pp. 402–14, where I discuss in more detail the underlying distinctions between explanation and the description of causes, and the sort of necessity conveyed by talk of what would have happened anyway through an alternative chain of causes.

the power of others inhibits this growth. On the other hand, the mode of production theory might seem excessively holistic, like Hegel's. In particular, the alleged tendency of certain economic structures to self-destruct sounds like a structural feature that guides people's behavior externally, if it is not shorthand for the utterly banal claim that structures collapse when people's situations lead them to fight in very large numbers.

The worry about excessive holism is best answered by putting the mode of production theory in a more psychological way, where psychology is understood to comprise both people's reasons for acting and objective interests guiding their actions, in the manner sketched in Chapter Four. At a given point in time, people's location in the economic structure and in the network of work-relations, and the nature of the productive forces to which they have access all influence both their resources and their priorities in the use of their resources. This is no more mysterious than the claim that many people will put family loyalties first in a society in which most work is done by people in families who have hereditary control of land used for subsistence purposes. The mode of production theory attributes internal change to combinations of resources and priorities due to people's location in the mode of production, together with the actions to which those combinations lead. Initially, the pattern of resources and priorities largely maintains the old economic structure. Otherwise, there would be no economic structure to speak of. Eventually, a pattern of resources and priorities arises that leads to the destruction of the structure. Typically, perhaps always, this involves a series of intermediate steps, in some of which people, led by initial resources and priorities, act so as to land in new locations in the mode, leading to new resources and priorities. As Marx says of the workers' movement, these people, by their actions, "create new circumstances *and* men."[2]

It is because actions governed by one conception of economic self-interest can lead to a new conception of economic self-interest that the mode of production interpretation can answer

[2] *Civil War in France*, p. 558.

a fundamental objection to historical materialism that might be called Weber's Challenge. In *The Protestant Ethic and the Spirit of Capitalism*, along with a narrative history of the most fragmentary and questionable kind, Weber poses a highly insightful objection to any effort to explain a transformation of economic life on the basis of phenomena of economic life. Economic structures, he points out, are not all associated with a single basic set of priorities governing economic activity, say, the desire for as much efficiency as possible. Rather, different structures are associated with different priorities that keep people from disrupting the dominant economic pattern. In particular, feudal societies are dominated by a traditionalist economic outlook, in which customary ties of mutual protection are given a high priority, and economic goals are fulfilled once a customary standard of living is reached. For capitalism to arise, entrepreneurs have to break with the traditionalist outlook, tailoring employment and prices to the market and maximizing profits and capital accumulation. Only then will the modern situation arise in which traditionalism would mean bankruptcy. In general, a new economic structure must be founded by people with a new economic outlook. How, then, can an internal change in structure ultimately be attributed to economic activity itself?

This is a good question, even if Weber's own story of traditionalism dissolving from the charisma of a few religious "virtuosi" and the religious anxieties of their followers is not a good alternative explanation of change. As we shall see, technological determinism cannot withstand Weber's insight into the social determination of economic priorities. But the mode of production interpretation can. In his economic histories, Marx frequently refers to processes in which actions motivated by one set of economic priorities lead to new situations producing new economic priorities. Consider one significant chain of events that replaced the traditional emphasis on mutually protective ties in economic life. Before the feudal wars that culminated in the Wars of the Roses, people with significant control over others' labor-power did not end those others' traditional access to means of subsistence for mere commercial advantages. In the feudal wars, the dispersal of military control over land and its inhabitants led to conflicts in which many of the old overlord families killed each other. The leading families, that is, the rival dynastic houses, promoted their merchant supporters into the nobility, based on traditional tactical considerations. For the first time, many people whose lives were shaped by (traditional, urban) commercial priorities, not by the commitment to maintain a large and loyal following, were in control of great tracts of land and much labor-power. At the same time, the development of the wool trade with the Continent, based on quite traditional commercial pursuits, added yet another novel element to the situation of the new nobility: the opportunity to make enormous profits by converting subsistence agriculture to the raising of sheep. If they had been the old nobles, they might not have taken advantage of the opportunity; if they had stayed urban merchants they might well have disapproved of massive evictions from afar; but as it was, the new merchant-nobles dispossessed their tenants in a dramatic break from the old priority on the maintenance of customary obligations. In short, "the rapid rise of the Flemish wool manufacturers, and the corresponding rise in the price of wool in England, gave the direct impulse to these evictions. The old nobility had been devoured in the great feudal wars. The new nobility was the child of its time, for which money was the power of all powers."[3]

Did a new location in the mode of production really produce a new set of priorities here, de-emphasizing the maintenance of traditional ties? Or were people with old priorities just presented with new opportunities, which they exploited without psychological change? In principle, Weber's Challenge could be answered exclusively in the latter style. It would be naively idealistic to suppose that an economic outlook protecting a structure in given circumstances would produce conservative activity in all circumstances. Traditionalist members of the old nobility might well have dispossessed their tenants if as grand a gain as kingship was likely. After all, King Richard was not

[3] *Capital* I, p. 672.

respecting traditional obligations of kinship when he had his nephews drowned. Still, there are many cases in which a genuine psychological change probably does result from a new location within the mode of production, perhaps including the case at hand. A *pre*-Tudor merchant would no doubt have protested that dispossessing one's tenants for gain would be horrible, if presented with later possibilities as a hypothetical case. Why suppose that he must lack normal self-insight just because he or similar people will later come to act in accordance with different priorities? Anyone who can imagine genuine moral corruption of character can imagine a genuine change in priorities based on a shift in situation. Certainly, the mode of production theory does not lead to the absurdities that Weber had in mind, with the Pharoah Tutankhamen accorded the same basic economic priorities as Andrew Carnegie, with the sole concession that each had different options to choose from.

Why suppose that internal processes of change are exclusively governed by the mode of production in the way just sketched? Later, I will offer a detailed case for the plausibility of this model. For now, the important fact is that this eventual answer will not conflict with our general beliefs about how people act. Very roughly, the argument will be that cultural processes are not an ultimate source of change because ideology is so rigid, while the mobilization of force is not effective unless based on new social processes because force is too dispersed outside of a ruling class. Put more psychologically, people have so great a capacity to fool themselves and others when major interests are at stake, and coordination, endurance and mobility count for so much when physical force is used in conflict, that the ruling class needs to be undermined through other processes, based on social arrangements it initially permits. Only the mode of production remains as a source of such processes. This may be right or wrong, but it does not appeal to anything mysterious in the interactions among human beings.

Materialism. Marx's theory of history is often said to be economic, as opposed, in particular, to the political emphasis of many non-Marxist historians. Indeed, "economic determinism" or "the economic interpretation of history" are traditional euphemisms for the Marxist theory of history.

If the mode of production interpretation is right, such labels as "economic determinism" are utterly misleading. Marx's emphasis is not on the economic as opposed to the political. Political phenomena are fundamental in his theory, in at least three ways. An economic structure may be stable, not because the class dominance defining it is more efficient than any alternative but because the situations of social groups give only the ruling class the coercive capacities to dominate politically. In feudalism, the lords of the manor dominate, not because undominated peasants would have been less productive but because the lords' and the peasants' locations in the mode of production give the former so much more coordination, mobility and concentrated leadership in the use of force. In the second place, the relations of production defining an economic structure must sometimes be individuated in terms of distinctive and distinctively political means of control. The bureaucratic ruling class in ancient China is one example, the overlord class defining feudalism, in Marx's conception of it, is another. Finally, fundamental episodes in structural change, not just in the ultimate revolution but at the start of the process, may be distinctively political activities in which conflicts latent in power-relations are played out. In the feudal wars, lords did not compete in agricultural output. They killed each other in dynastic conflicts.

In all these ways, Marx does give political processes fundamental important when he writes history. Indeed, one would expect a mode of production theorist often to emphasize just the same events as traditional historians, albeit for different reasons. And that is precisely Marx's practice, much to the surprise of readers who have been introduced to his writings through economic determinist interpretations.

This limitation on economic determinism is very different from the very sensible hedges suggested by Engels' letters on his and Marx's theory of history. In those letters, Engels makes it clear that this theory of history is subject to important qual-

227

ifications about the stringency, time scale and directness of the underlying causes. The underlying causes are supposed to explain the most important social institutions and processes, in their most important features, not every detail of social life that is important to some degree.[4] They explain why a phenomenon occurred sooner or later in a society, rather than not occurring. They are not meant to explain why a phenomenon occurred just when it did and not at some other time.[5] The underlying causes may work indirectly, by means of other causes that they explain in turn. Religious movements and military triumphs may be necessary causes, so long as they are explained in terms of the underlying factor.[6] If economic determinism is modified in these ways, that is all to the good, but quite inadequate. The prior question is whether the ultimate causal factors, whatever their determining power, are economic as opposed to political. A theory in which they are is not Marx's, whatever hedges are then introduced.

If Marx had labeled his conception of history "economic," his more political practice might be part of another case for a split between theory and practice in Marx. But in fact, his repeated and emphatic rubric is "the *materialist* conception of history." And despite the role of politics, the mode of production theory is thoroughly materialist, in several dimensions.

In the first place, the mode of production that regulates processes of change is, of course, the mode of material production: the tools and techniques with which material goods are produced, the relations of cooperation through which people produce material goods, and relations of control over tools, techniques, land, labor-power and people employed in the production of material goods. Change is due to the pattern of resources and priorities and the consequent actions that are

[4] See, for example, Engels to Bloch, September 21, 1890, *Selected Correspondence*, p. 395, and Engels to Schmidt, October 27, 1890, pp. 397ff. In the latter, Engels makes the nice point that the content of his and Marx's social theory precludes precise determinations since the social division of labor distributes different social functions, resources and interests among different social groups, whose relative influence cannot be measured precisely.
[5] See Engels to Borgius, January 25, 1894, ibid., p. 442.
[6] See Engels to Mehring, July 14, 1893, ibid., p. 435.

228

explainable in terms of people's location in this quite material mode. Suppose, on the other hand, that a change in basic type was due to a religious movement, arising from the personal charisma of a religious leader and due to religious feelings that had no explanation in terms of the mode of production. Or suppose that a basic change was due to the military successes of a politically ambitious military genius, and that the occurrence, sooner or later, of such a socially transforming military process was not explainable in terms of people's location in the mode of production. Suppose, in short, that Weber's Calvin or Carlyle's Napoleon existed. Then there would be a counter-example to this materialist conception of history.

In the second place, the economic structure, the relations of control over resources used in material production, has a unique status in the mode of production theory. Institutions are to be explained in a certain logical order. A new economic structure is explained as due to conflicts in the mode of production. The rest of the social order is explained by showing how political and cultural institutions derive their main features from their role in stabilizing the economic structure. Two easy mistakes, suggested by any simple summary of Marx, can make this strategy of explanation seem worthy of the name "economic determinist." The truly large-scale institutions in the second, superstructural phase of explanation are those one would naturally call political or cultural, as opposed to economic. (Not that this is true on a smaller scale. The National Labor Relations Board in the United States and the East India Company in the early British Empire are superstructural, too.) It might seem, then, that Marx's strategy is to explain political by nonpolitical, economic arrangements, at least in his largest explanatory projects. But this is to forget that the economic structure may itself include what we would naturally call political institutions (the ancient Chinese bureaucracy) and, in any case, may be defined in terms of distinctive means of control of a political sort (feudalism). In sum, once the economic structure is explained, then further large-scale institutions that are political as against economic are explained by their role in stabilizing the economic structure; but this strategy should not

229

be taken to imply that the structure being stabilized is itself political as against economic.

Also, the logical order of explanation, here, might be taken for the chronological order, leading to an overly rigid separation of the political from the economic. First, the new economic structure emerges from the mode of production. Then, in the period of political revolution, the new structure is consolidated through suitable political and social institutions. Before the period of revolution, the old ruling class is in control, capable of discerning and eliminating rival political and cultural arrangements before they become widespread and enduring. So (an economic determinist might argue), the economic *as against the political* must be the subject of the first and more basic phase of Marx's explanatory strategy.

In fact, this order in time does not correspond to many of Marx's patterns of explanation. Sometimes, the new economically dominant class must, by its very nature, arise from political processes consolidating its social power. His explanation of the origins in conquest of the feudal ruling class are a case in point. In any case, the dominance of surplus extraction that gives a ruling class its rule and produces a change in type in the economic structure may result from, not just be consolidated in, political revolutions. In these revolutions, the ascendent class allies with other subordinate groups to set up new regimes, then turns upon them. That is Marx's view of the English Civil War and the French Revolution.

There is no conflict between the nonpriority of economic structure in temporal order and its priority in the logical order of explanation. When evolutionary biologists explain nonadaptive features of a species, for example, the redness of human (as against lobster) blood, they first explain the associated adaptive features, for example, tracing the origins of the hemoglobin mechanism as the means of oxygen-transport for vertebrates. Then they note that the nonadaptive features are physically tied to the adaptive ones. This is not to attribute to biologists the view that vertebrates first came to have hemoglobin-type blood and then this blood turned red.

230

I have emphasized the materialism of mode-of-production explanations of change. The explanations of stability are material as well. The stable dominance of a ruling class is explained by its location, and the location of the other classes, in the mode of material production. Suppose, by contrast, that the "native intelligence" of the people in the ruling class is said to be the explanation, or that certain religious ideas of obedience are given ultimate explanatory status. That would be a genuine departure from the materialist concept of social stability.

The mode of production theory is distinctively materialist, as compared with rival approaches, including many current in Marx's day. It is not, to the same degree, distinctively economic. Since the phrase "economic determinism" has come to be accompanied by contrasts between the economic and the political, it is profoundly misleading. It would be better if the phrase were dropped, or used, like "Social Darwinism," as a label for a standard misinterpretation.

Theories Worthy of the Name. The mode of production interpretation strikes some people as too vague to be a theory worthy of the name. Of course, this might or might not count against it as an interpretation, depending on whether Marx meant to offer a theory in any strict sense. He does make fun of those who "use, as one's master key, a general historico-philosophical theory."[7] It is much more characteristic of Engels to speak of the materialist conception of history as the materialist "theory."

In fact, these textual points about the use of "theory" are moot. The mode of production interpretation does describe a theory worthy of the name. At the same time, it is not the sort of pattern for generating explanations of historical trends that Marx is attacking when he mocks the pursuit of the historico-philosophical master key.

Why might the mode of production interpretation be thought vague, once its terms are explicated? The distinctive terms of the interpretation are no vaguer than any sensible

[7] Marx to the board of *Otechestvenniye Zapiski*, in Feuer, *Basic Writings*, p. 441.

historical theory's should be. They are often the same and are defined as precisely as those in technological determinism, which does not strike readers as excessively vague once explicated by such insightful advocates as Cohen. The vagueness, probably a misleading label here, is at the level of distinctive laws, not of distinctive concepts.

According to a widely shared expectation as to what a theory should do, a theory should be a source of empirical laws on the basis of which certain phenomena can be deduced from the occurrence of certain antecedents. More precisely, the laws are logically entailed once the theory is joined with statements of facts that are acceptable to all or observed to be the case.

The model, here, is the derivation of Kepler's laws for successive planetary positions from Newton's theory, or the derivation of the Boyle-Charles gas laws from the molecular theory of gases. In Marx's phrase, Newton's theory really is a master key for unlocking empirical laws describing astronomical sequences.

The mode of production interpretation does not do this job. When one tries to extract from it an empirical law describing when change occurs, one ends up with something like: basic change in economic structure occurs when the mode of production gives rise to conflicts severe enough to produce such change. And that is not an empirical law but a tautology, as surely as the principle that anyone who is an uncle is male. Even the more specific scenario of the narrow mode of production theory yields only such tautologies as: if fettering of productive forces is sufficiently severe to give a subordinate group the desire and the means to overthrow the old economic structure, the structure will change. "Sufficient" cannot be explicated in any other terms than "sufficient to bring about the structural change."

Really, it is misleading to speak of this lack as "vagueness." "Tropical habitats have a great diversity of species" is a standard, highly vague, but empirical law in ecology. It is vague because of the numerous borderline cases in which habitats are not tropical as against subtropical, and speciation isn't highly, as against not highly, diverse. The Marxist principles just stated are not vague empirical laws. They are not empirical laws at all. And that is the feature people are responding to with the charge of "vagueness." For no one would think it a charge against a general theory of history that it "only" yielded principles as good as the ecological one.[8]

Later I will discuss in detail the positivist conceptions of explanation and confirmation that underlie the notion of a theory as a master key to empirical laws. And I will look at some further attempts to fit Marx's account of history into this pattern. It is enough for present purposes to see that the mode of production interpretation describes as much of a theory as a body of ideas that everyone calls a theory, unless overwhelmed by prior commitment to positivism: Darwin's theory of evolution.

The theory of evolution provides no empirical law describing conditions in which a new species arises. If one tries to extract such a law one ends up with principles such as this: when the selective advantage of the traits associated with new genetic material are great enough in a population, it comes to pervade the gene pool; if enough new traits accumulate, a new species emerges. (Here I use post-Darwinian jargon that accurately evokes ideas in *The Origin of Species*.) In these principles, "enough" in the antecedents means enough to produce the changes described in the consequents. The principles are pure tautologies. The most perfect knowledge of past populations and environments will not overcome these barriers, above all the absence of noncircular specifications of "enough selective advantage." Darwin concludes the chapter on selective advantages in *The Origin*, a chapter consisting wholly of after-the-fact reconstructions and thought-experiments about

[8] Still, there is a similarity between the Marxist principles and the ecological one (and a difference between all of them and "All uncles are males.") All the principles subjected to charges of vagueness contain descriptions of antecedent or consequent states whose application from case to case would differ among linguistically competent observers. For "tropical" the differences are primarily due to the inherent nature of the corresponding category. As a matter of fact, tropicality just is a vague matter. For the "this will result if this is strong enough" principles, the differences are primarily due to people's disagreeing on what is powerful enough to bring about an effect, based on different background beliefs.

the impact of advantageous traits, with a characteristic candid disclaimer:

It is good thus to try in our imagination to give any form some advantage over another. Probably in no single instance should we know what to do, so as to succeed. It will convince us of our ignorance on the mutual relations of all organic beings; a conviction as necessary, as it seems to be difficult to acquire.[9]

In constructing mathematical models, modern population geneticists sometimes attach numbers to selective advantages, producing formulas with the general look of Newtonian laws. But the "laws" are tautologies.

Nonetheless, Darwin offers a real theory. He describes the causal mechanisms that produce a certain kind of change, when it occurs. He describes the scenarios for such changes, considering and arguing against alternative accounts of the level at which variation occurs, the kinds of selective advantages at work, and the conditions for their effectiveness in transforming a species. He argues against rival accounts of the origins of the unquestioned data at hand. None of this need produce a master key to empirical laws.

Of course, Newton, too, describes a repertoire of causal mechanisms governing certain phenomena, in his case, mass and motion phenomena. Describing a causal repertoire is what a scientific theory does, in general. Sometimes, scientists have reason to believe that the phenomena they seek to explain are only governed, to a significant extent, by a single causal factor (cf. Newton, celestial mechanics and gravity). Or they may take the phenomena to be governed by a multiplicity of factors,

[9] Charles Darwin, *The Origin of Species*, ed. J. M. Burrow (Baltimore, 1968), p. 129. For recent statements basically to the same effect, see Richard C. Lewontin, *The Genetic Basis of Evolutionary Change* (New York, 1974), pp. 42, 236. With a few species, especially among the wonderfully malleable *Drosophila*, the effects of artificial selection in the laboratory on many sub-specific traits are fairly predictable. But elsewhere, apparently analogous processes of limited, artifical selection are quite unreliable, often to agronomists' dismay (see ibid., pp. 88f.) In any case, when we move from artificially controlled to natural settings, the task of predicting the course of evolution remains quite hopeless a century after Darwin. Lewontin discusses some relevant difficulties on pp. 234–39 and 266–71.

234

whose relative effectiveness is regulated by general empirical laws (cf. the multiple forces in post-Newtonian physics). In these cases, the master key to empirical laws may be provided by the theory. But often the phenomena to be explained are produced by mutually countervailing factors whose relative weight is not described by any general laws. This is true of the balance of factors for inheritance and for variation, in Darwin's view. Then, the description of the overall mechanism may yield no empirical law with which the phenomena to be explained can be deduced from antecedent conditions. Surely, social evolution is at least as complex as biological evolution. So the mode of production theory is precisely the kind of scientific theory one would expect, for this subject matter.

It is harder to locate technological determinism among these types of theories. Its leading principle of change is: "When fettering occurs, a change in the economic structure to a productively optimal one results." No reasonable technological determinist supposes that any small amount of fettering produces structural change, or that the change occurs immediately or with a time-lag that can be described in precise and general terms. So, at a minimum, the characteristic principle must be construed as a vague empirical law, like the one about species in the tropics, containing vague terms like "substantial" and "soon." It would then be a vague theory but on the Newtonian model. Yet this reading has distinctive costs. So long as the appropriate severity of fettering is described in terms which, though vague, make no reference to the occurrence of subsequent structural change, there seems to be no reason why this particular severity of fettering should be enough. So it might seem better strategy to render the "law" tautologous and fit the theory to the Darwinian model.

I will soon be arguing that technological determinism is not a plausible account of internal structural change on either reading. If that argument is accepted, the issue of which version should be adopted is empty. Neither should. However, I will also be arguing that the expectation that all theories will fit the Newtonian model is an important motivation for preferring technological determinism as interpretation and as historical theory. The kind of theory that technological determinists mean to advance is, in the main, a source of vague but empirical laws of change, a vague "master key." Perhaps the most important fact, for now, is that technological determinism needs to be vague, too, either vague in its concepts or tautologous in its descriptions of when change occurs.

Falsification. A theory as flexible as the mode-of-production theory may seem too flexible to provide definite guidance about empirical facts. In other words, it may seem unfalsifiable. This worry is all the more acute if the theory goes tautologous when we try to extract principles saying when change will occur.

Often, the worry about falsifiability reflects powerful general assumptions about the nature of testing, which I will discuss later on. For now, I will take it as a straightforward request for strategies that could, in principle, defeat the mode of production theory, strategies appealing, in part, to specific historical facts that might be regarded as data.

Marx is claiming that internal structural change, when it occurs, is due to people's location in the mode of production. For present purposes, we may assume that this claim does not conflict with shared general background principles about how people behave. The worry about falsifiability concerns the possibility of conflict with specific historical facts.

In general, a theory of Marx's kind is defeated by showing that a rival account of the underlying mechanisms fits the facts better. Given shared background principles, the actual facts as a whole are more likely on the basis of some rival than on the basis of the defeated theory. That is how the Darwinian rival defeated Lamarckian evolution and the theory of the individual creation of each species.

However, such a general prescription is not very helpful in practice, when we are looking for tests that might overthrow a particular theory. Every theory has its problems, particular cases in which data are more to be expected on the basis of some rival hypothesis. For example, on the basis of present-day astronomy, but not of certain primitive systems, one would not expect the night sky to be dark. (The expected mag-

236

nitude of light from the stars is too great.) Often, one supposes that the present-day defeat simply reflects present-day ignorance of relevant facts or auxiliary theories. (That is why the term "falsification" itself oversimplifies, suggesting that conflict with the facts is lethal as such.) It is true that a hypothesis is overthrown, at least for the time being, if a rival better fits all the data on balance. But no one has developed a usable recipe for balancing successes and failures, here. Absolutely general virtues for hypotheses, for example, predictive accuracy, scope, causal depth, and fruitfulness, are so diverse that we would need a general rule for adjudicating trade-offs among them. No such rule has been developed.

Fortunately, when we are interested in whether a particular hypothesis can be defeated, we can often take advantage of the structure and history of the debate about it, that is, the assumptions about how reality is apt to behave that are shared by all sides, and the history of investigation and argument that establishes certain specific and controversial claims as the well-researched "home territory" of the hypothesis. In the case at hand, Marx's account of the rise of capitalism in England is clearly the home territory of the mode of production theory. For it was Marx's central concern in this theorizing and the one that motivated his theoretical innovations. The kind of defeat that would most definitively overthrow his theory is, above all, the superiority of a rival here, where the best explanations are most likely to embody his theory's mechanisms if, indeed, his theory is true. Also, Marx's main concerns and central claims, together with relevant shared beliefs about human conduct, make his hypotheses most vulnerable to two kinds of rebuttal. On the one hand, episodes that are generally regarded as cases of internal structural change might better be explained as due to factors independent of the mode of production. On the other, people might turn out not to behave in ways that Marx's mechanisms for change require. Whatever the problems of detail in *The Protestant Ethic and the Spirit of Capitalism*, Weber's anti-Marxist arguments are extremely useful in illustrating the form such refutation might take, when these two kinds of worries are directed at Marx's home territory.

If *The Protestant Ethic* is fleshed out with *Economy and Society* and the *Sociology of Religion*, Weber's rival explanation is basically this. The Protestant Reformation was due to the charismatic leadership of "religious virtuosi" (Weber's term) personally responding to abiding religious tensions in Christianity. Resources and motivations ultimately due to locations in the mode of production cannot explain the socially significant features of the Reformation. In Calvinism, the rank and file in succeeding generations could not live with the doctrine of predestination without believing in more definite and tangible signs of grace than the founders allowed. The urgency of their quest is to be explained solely in terms of religious psychology, which is also the ultimate cause of their solution: worldly success through methodical accumulation of capital is a sign of grace. This religious tranformation of ascetic Protestantism was an important cause of the rise of capitalism, since it provided a necessary psychic stimulus for overcoming the barriers, practical and psychological, of the traditionalist way of life.

As history, Weber's book utterly lacks the richness and depth of volume one of *Capital*. Marx describes a variety of processes in which traditionalism is overcome, most unconnected with Calvinism and several occurring before Calvin's birth. Weber never considers in any detail alternative explanations of the facts he does mobilize, above all, Engels' explanation of Reformation phenomena as an ideological transformation due to the changing situation and interests of the nascent bourgeoisie.[10] Yet, whatever its specific defects, Weber has offered a clear pattern for one reply to Marx that could succeed: an argument for the independent operation of processes outside of the mode of production in producing a basic internal change in a case that Marx's theory ought to account for with relative ease if it is right.

[10] See preface to the English edition of *Socialism: Utopian and Scientific*, in Marx and Engels, *Selected Works in One Volume* (New York, 1968), pp. 387–89.

238

Elsewhere, Weber's argument takes a somewhat different pattern. He insightfully identifies certain assumptions about human tendencies in the way of action and belief that are required by Marx's mechanisms. And he argues that there is clear evidence that these tendencies do not exist to the extent that Marx requires. Here, general psychological principles are the main subject matter, and the crucial cases need not be instances of internal structural change. Above all, Weber emphasizes Marx's assumption that people are more apt, in the long run, to change in religious outlook in ways that adapt to activities derived from the mode of production than they are to change economic activities in ways that adapt to religion. He argues that "it will suffice for our purposes" to call attention to contrary facts from England's North American colonies. There the spirit of capitalism was present before the capitalist order. Though the South was colonized by entrepreneurs, only in the more Calvinist North, especially in colonies founded by preachers, did "calculating profit-seeking" flourish, even in the economically primitive territory of backwoods Pennsylvania.[11]

Weber's particular argument is, again, not very convincing. Obviously, this is not the clear case that would suffice for his argument against "the more naive historical materialism,"[12] since relevant appeals to cultural influence and time-lags are standard in Marx's explanatory framework. The colonists brought with them such capitalist psychologies as they had, from a capitalist society. It is obscure why Weber thinks tobacco plantations in the South are less concerned with calculated profit-seeking than shops in New England. The tendency of the backwoods economy to revert to subsistence agriculture, much to the despair of colonial land tycoons, is simply neglected. But, again, the general strategy is insightful and clear. In principle, a situation could be found in which many people, influenced by the same locations in the mode of production, come to pursue radically different economic activities, in ways that can only be explained by appeals to religious differences.

[11] Max Weber, *The Protestant Ethic and the Spirit of Capitalism* (New York, 1958), pp. 55f., 75.
[12] Ibid., p. 55.

That would be a substantial argument against Marx's theory. In effect, it would be the reverse of an important Marxist argument that takes seventeenth-century England as a laboratory of religious psychology. In that environment, people started out with the same sacred book and religious tradition. With the sincerest religious conviction, they came to interpret the book in dramatically different ways, of the deepest social and religious significance. The differences in where people turned religiously fit their location in the mode of production fairly well, a phenomenon recorded at least as early as Hobbes' *Behemoth*. The differences do not fit any large-scale variation of any other sort that one would normally take to be decisive. For example, farm workers had a much greater tendency to move in a messianic direction, even where there were highly eloquent preachers of a sober Anglican or Presbyterian tendency. Somewhere, a neat case of the opposite kind might exist. If so, it would count heavily against the mode of production interpretation.

Of course, arguments against Marx's theory need not attack the same kinds of targets as Weber's did. Indeed, given the actual state of the facts, the most plausible empirical objections may be entirely different. I will eventually describe just such an objection, based on the balance between internal and external causes of change. However, the worry about falsifiability is at a high level of abstraction from the actual data: is it imaginable that empirical arguments might defeat this theory? The best answer lies in a description of imaginable data so clearly counting against the theory that it is defeated, at least in the absence of equally clear evidence counting against its rivals. The two Weberian patterns are the appropriate recipes for such clear evidence, given Marx's own emphases. The point can be made more vividly by tampering with Weber's examples to make them exclude the mode of production theory even more definitively. Suppose North America had been settled by English colonists before Marx's story begins, say, around 1400. The social backgrounds of settlers in all the colonies are the same. However, some colonies are dominated by immigrants from towns with local sects of an ascetic Protestant kind. The characteristic economic activities in the respective colonies diversify, with a few becoming miniature capitalist societies. Those are the ones influenced by ascetic Protestantism. They are backwoods colonies, insulated from advances in the mode of production. In this just-so story, North America provides a laboratory yielding clear evidence against Marx's theory. If the real tests are less clear, that is because real history is not as neat, not because Marx's historical theory is itself unfalsifiable.

Internal/External. I have characterized the main subject matter of the mode of production theory as basic *internal* change, that is, change in basic type due to factors internal to the society in question. Just how the line between internal and external should be drawn is one of the hardest and the most important questions in analyzing Marx's theory of history. Both the fettering model of the Preface and the self-destructive reproduction model of the *Grundrisse* are presented as locating the sources of change inside the transformed society. That Marx was concerned to be an internalist of some sort is strongly implied by his vigorous contrasts between his model for change and theories that emphasize conquest. "This whole interpretation of history appears to be contradicted by the fact of conquest."[13] Moreover, an assessment of the extent of Marx's internalism has been politically urgent when Marxists have debated the possibility of socialism in the less economically advanced countries. Yet the texts give no clear and uncontradicted indication of how Marx separates internal from external factors and the scope he gives to each. While he does have interesting clarifications of the meaning of his theory for less advanced capitalist countries, it is hard to extrapolate from them any general moral as to the role of external factors in basic social change.

It might seem easy to draw the line between the internal and the external. Divine history to one side, factors from outside a society that might, in principle, affect its structure seem

[13] *German Ideology*, p. 89.

to be of two kinds. There are geographically external factors, such as conquest or cultural influence, having to do with interaction with people from other societies. And there are factors from outside the social process as such—for example, climatic shifts or epidemics—having to do with changes that are not ultimately the result of socially organized human activity. A definition of Marx's main subject matter that is "strict internalist," as I shall use the phrase, excludes all structural changes significantly due to either kind of process from the mode of production model.

In practice, I will concentrate on the status of geographic externality, since this is both Marx's main concern for the epoch of recorded history and the emphasis of the most important rival theories. Also, I will begin with the question of what should count as internal for purposes of defining the subject matter of the mode of production model. But later, I will consider the related question of the extent to which historical change as a whole is internal for Marx.

The problem with strict internalism is that it seems to exclude not just some but all the basic changes in history, as Marx sees it. Consider the following examples, already described in other contexts. His one account of how class divisions might have arisen emphasizes exchange and consequent division of labor due to contact between societies. In the explanation of rigid class divisions among nonslaves in the ancient world, processes of conquest and commerce are primary. Feudalism is attributed to conquest by invading Germanic tribes. The account of the rise of capitalism involves the growth of international trade, together with the later conquest and exploitation of non-European societies. Even the rise of socialism is likely to be affected by intersocietal influences, in Marx's view. He says, in the *Manifesto*, "The Communists turn their attention chiefly to Germany . . . because the bourgeois revolution in Germany will be but the prelude to the immediately following proletarian revolution."[14] Obviously, backward Germany was not expected to develop its mode of production

[14] *Communist Manifesto*, p. 362.

to the same point as Britain or France in the months or few years suggested by "immediately." Rather, aspects of mature capitalism in the most advanced countries had been exported to Germany (above all, a small but concentrated and politically sophisticated proletariat had arisen in such centers as Cologne), while the German elites, for their part, remained divided and largely archaic compared with those of Britain and France. In sum, were Marx offering us a theory of strictly internal basic change, he would seem to be offering us a theory of nothing, on his own account.

The final problem for strict internalism, the possibility of socialism's first developing in less advanced countries, has, of course, been a subject of heated debate, especially among Russian Marxists and those responding to the Bolsheviks' victory. A certain looser understanding of Marx's internalism helps to reconcile Marx's acknowledgment of this possibility with his general theory. It clarifies the internalism of that theory, even though it does not, in the end, go far enough in extending the limits of the internal.

For simplicity of exposition, it is often useful to assume that the territorial extent of a society, in Marx's model, is the same as the extent of the mode of production whose evolution governs that society's transformation. I have made this simplifying assumption in my own formulations of the mode of production theory: it was said to involve a scenario in which processes that initially serve to maintain the economic structure of a society eventually destroy it because of the nature of *its* mode of production. But it would be a kind of nationalist superstition to suppose that societies really must be windowless monads in an explanatory model that emphasizes the mode of production. In particular, capitalist societies are part of an international capitalist mode of production, in which economic structures of the capitalist type are stabilized within many nation-states. The societies in this system may be crucially affected by interaction with other societies. Such interactions can, in principle, be explained as ultimately based on the modes of production in the respective interacting societies. After all, everyone explains the rise and fall of British influence on South

America in just this way, to take a simple example. So the mode of production theory had best be understood more broadly. The processes transforming a society are governed by the mode of production of which it is a part, a mode that may comprise other societies. The larger mode includes the local ones and the interactions to which they give rise, in the given geographic relations. This was precisely Marx's basis, throughout the mid-'forties, for saying that the dynamics of capitalism made socialism an imminent possibility in Germany:

[T]o lead to collisions in a country, this contradiction [between the productive forces and the economic structure] need not necessarily have reached its extreme limit in this particular country. The competition with industrially more advanced countries, brought about by the expansion of international intercourse, is sufficient to produce a similar contradiction in countries with a backward industry (e.g., the latent proletariat in Germany brought into view by the competition of English industry).[15]

Indeed, a related tacit assumption might as well be lifted at the same time, namely, that all societies within a mode of production will have an economic structure of the same basic type. There might be a stable system of territorially distinct, mutually influencing societies, in which the influences are governed by those local modes, and in which the modes embody basically different structures. This may be Marx's idea in his discussions of Germany, since he takes Germany to be semi-feudal, at best. A similarly diverse system is also suggested by his idea that the Italian core did little to transform social relations in the periphery, under the Roman Empire.[16] In any case, a stable but variegated mode is an open possibility for a mode of production model. Since Marx, such systems have been well-studied by anthropologists, who often find it necessary to fit mobile societies of pastoralists or "slash and burn"

[15] *German Ideology*, p. 89. See also "Contribution to the Critique of Hegel's Philosophy of Right," in T. B. Bottomore, ed., *Early Writings*, (New York, 1964), pp. 48f., 58f.
[16] *German Ideology*, p. 90.

farmers into a larger system including the more sedentary agriculturalists whom they routinely raid.[17]

While both technological determinism and the mode of production theory can be broadened to encompass multi-societal systems, this broadening is much less ad hoc in the mode of production model. If the basic mechanism for change is fettering, then intersocietal factors will be outside of the basic mechanism, except for a very special phenomenon, the exporting of new technology. But if all economic resources and priorities to which the mode of production gives rise are part of the basic mechanism, the admission of the larger modes is, in itself, the most natural understanding of the theory of change.

This broadening of internalism is quite expansive, indefinitely so in geographic terms. But it has structural limitations that seem to exclude processes that are important for Marx. If different societies are part of a mode of production, their interactions ought to be relatively stable and enduring, and guided by the local modes of each. Put another way, it would be extremely misleading to attribute structural change to a sudden interaction in which the distinctive structure of the changed society is mostly destroyed, and to call this an explanation based on a large-scale mode of production. But the first wave of European imperialism, so important to Marx's account of the triumph of capitalism in manufacturing, was often of this kind. And his model for change should certainly fit his account of the rise of capitalism. Moreover, so far as Marx shows, the conquests that gave birth to the Greco-Roman aristocracy and the Germanic invasions on which he bases feudalism are closer to one-shot cataclysms than to the final form of a previously stable pattern. Yet Marx claims to be able to reconcile his theory of history with the apparently contradictory fact of conquest.

[17] Edmund Leach, *Political Systems of Highland Burma* (Cambridge, Mass., 1954) is the classic study of how the structure and dynamics of one such mode of production can only be understood as part of a larger mode. ("Mode of production" is not Leach's phrase, but it fits, as previously defined.) Another well-studied interaction is the Nuer-Dinka raiding relation in the Sudan. See E. E. Evans-Pritchard, *The Nuer* (Oxford, 1940), pp. 125–32, 218–20.

It might now seem that strict internalism might as well be defended, by showing that intersocietal conflicts only seem to make a difference for structural change. This is Marx's tactic at times in the discussion of conquest in *The German Ideology*, a very rich and very messy passage that is his most extensive defense of his emphasis on the internal:

Here we must limit ourselves to the chief points and take, therefore, only the most striking example [of conquest]—the destruction of an old civilization by a barbarous people and the resulting formation of an entirely new organization of society. . . . Nothing is more common than the notion that in history up till now it has only been a question of *taking*. . . . [E]verywhere there is very soon an end to taking, and when there is nothing more to take you set about producing. From this necessity of producing, which very soon asserts itself, it follows that the form of community adopted by the settling conquerors must correspond to the stage of development of the productive forces they find in existence; or, if this is not the case from the start, it must change according to the productive forces.[18]

Here, and in the parallel passage in *Capital*, Marx seems to be saying that conquest produces no basic change in social structure. Of course, conquest is a pervasive fact in history and does put different people in the top niches of structures. But it does not affect the evolution of the structures themselves. The appearance to the contrary is due to confusing the enormous impact on individuals' destinies with impact on the structures defining the kinds of destinies available. In fact, the social structure reemerges intact after the conquest, like the Chinese Empire after the Manchu invasion, or it changes in directions it would have followed in any case. The latter must be Marx's conception of the transition to feudalism, in these comments. For he certainly took feudal society to be basically different from that of the Roman Empire, whatever his doubts about the impact of the invasions.

This dismissal of the invasions is an unsupported speculation, at best. Moreover, it isn't clear how strict internalism could be made to fit other scenarios in Marx, where interaction

---

[18] *German Ideology*, pp. 89f. Much of this is repeated in *Capital* I, pp. 84f.

is the main explanatory factor—the account of the rise of class societies, for example, or of the origins of aristocratic domination in Greece and Rome. There is no need to pursue these problems much further, though. For Marx himself contradicts his speculation a few sentences later: "The feudal system was by no means brought complete from Germany, but had its origins, as far as the conqueror was concerned, in the martial organization of the army during the actual conquest, and this only evolved after the conquest into the feudal system proper through the action of the productive forces found in the conquered countries." Since feudalism, here, depends in part on the invaders' military organization at the time of conquest and in part on their native mode of production as it influenced that organization, the new economic structure would not have arisen anyway, without the impact of external factors on the old imperial territory.

As happens so often in analyzing Marx's theory of history, we need to descend to his concrete practice to understand the abstract concepts that guide it. Marx offers a number of historical explanations that any open-minded reader would regard as explaining change from within the changing society's mode of production, even though interactions with external phenomena are involved and strict internalism is violated. An appropriately broad understanding of the general focus on the internal may emerge by considering why these particular explanations are naturally seen as internal.

Consider Marx's explanation of the rise of the Greco-Roman aristocracy. Here, a strategic location in an apparatus of *conquest* is the main reason why families who are initially just better-off become a genuine ruling class. Since strenuous interaction with outsiders (the conquered) is required, strict internalism is violated. But at the level of explanation, as against the level of causal interaction, the whole process is based on the structure of the expanding society. The military process, in Marx's analysis, is necessary for the expanding society, say, the early Roman Republic, to reproduce its economic structure. In other words, the process of conquest is due to resources and priorities explainable in terms of locations in the Roman

247

Republican mode of production. Marx follows a similar pattern, in which a mode of production necessitates violations of strict internalism, in his explanation of the aggressiveness of the barbarian conquerors of Rome: "With the conquering people war itself is still . . . a regular form of intercourse, which is the more eagerly exploited as the increase in population together with the traditional and, for it, the only possible crude mode of production gives rise to the need for new means of production." Here, conquest is again explained as a necessary means of reproducing the economic structure, given the paucity of resources and of possibilities of innovation.[19]

We naturally regard the account of the rise of the Greco-Roman aristocracy as explaining it in terms of the Greco-Roman mode of production, even though the resistance of people outside the mode, the eventually subjugated people, is causally essential. Why is this? Presumably, because the distinctive features of those people's societies and their responses can go without saying at the level of explanation. No change or peculiarity that is in need of explanation characterizes their essential role. Marx only relies on such standing truisms as that people usually put up a fight before conceding their land and their freedom. Thus, to say that the process of conquest is explained by the structure of the Greco-Roman society, even though people beyond the border played an essential role, is as natural as saying that a fire was due to a short circuit, even though the presence of oxygen was causally necessary as well. (If the fire took place in an unmanned spaceship, however, one might very well mention the surprising presence of oxygen.) I followed this ordinary usage above, in saying that explanatory factors could be internal when causal interactions were not.

In general, a process of change is internal, for Marx, if it is explainable as due to the social system of the society in ques-

---

[19] *German Ideology*, p. 89. The phrase, "a regular form of intercourse," also suggests that traditional Germanic patterns of warfare might be part of the economic structure of the larger system in which the tribes traditionally lived, that is, part of the traditional system of control over productive forces. For "form of intercourse" is Marx's phrase for an economic structure in this period. In this respect, his Germanic tribes would be analogous to Leach's Kachin and Evans-Prichard's Nuer.

tion. While interactions with people or phenomena outside the system may be crucial, the crucial ones are not governed by external changes or abnormalities standing in need of explanation.[20]

Sometimes, in categorizing historical theories, it is also useful to call changes internal when they can be explained as the outcome of factors internal to another, conquering society. The transformation of traditional Etruscan society was due to factors external to it. But if the internalist explanation of Roman expansion does all the work of explaining this change, it can be put among the processes that fit a general theory of internal social change.

Finally, to this broadening of the internal, add the previous insight that the relevant system of social processes and institutions need not be limited to the governing territory in which basic change takes place. The result is the sense of "internal" in which Marx claims that basic internal change is governed by the mode of production. Of course, the claim that a change is internal in this sense will sometimes be controversial. But this assumption is often shared by rivals to Marx's explanations, so that it is no barrier to direct comparison. Weber, for example, is as much an internalist as Marx. Their disagreement is over the primacy of the mode of production. Also, the tactic of saying that a process is external, and beyond the scope of the mode of production model, had better be used sparingly by a Marxist where basic changes are concerned. For the model is to be justified by showing that it does generate superior explanations of a variety of basic changes.

In the newly extended sense, almost all of the cases in the list that threaten strict internalism are cases of internal change. Most, but not all. In particular, the transition to feudalism is basic, but not internal, since distinctive features of both the Roman Empire and the Germanic tribes contribute to the

---

[20] "Crucial interaction" means crucial for explaining the occurrence of structural change sooner or later. That the Spanish discovered gold in Peru stands in need of explanation. But presumably Marx believed that the Age of Discovery would have produced an influx of riches, with the crucial consequences for the rise of capitalism, sooner or later. Such an influx is a normal result of the large-scale conquest of weaker peoples.

structure of the outcome, in Marx's view. If Marx was only offering "a materialist conception of internal history," it would follow that feudalism is beyond the scope of his theory. But, of course, Marx offers a conception of history as a whole. So a final question about Marx's theory must be faced. What is he saying about the role of modes of production in the cases (and he admits they exist) in which basic change is not internal?

Again, the best strategy is to reconstruct the theory from the practice. The main case of admittedly noninternal basic change is the rise of feudalism. In *The German Ideology* and the *Grundrisse*, Marx offers the following account of this process.[21] The eventual fall of the Roman Empire, as against the form of the society growing up on its ruins, was determined by an internal contradiction in the Roman mode of production, internal in the sense just described. The ruling aristocracy was sustained by conquest and co-optation of elites at the periphery, based on the exploitation of the farming population in the Italian core. As the borders expanded, the exploitation at the core grew more intense, until the exploited population could not sustain the burdens of empire. As for the feudal successors to Roman society, the Empire made a twofold contribution to their mode of production. On the one hand, Roman productive forces were more productive, coordinated and technologically advanced than those of the invaders. When "very soon there was an end to taking," they could not be managed through the invaders' native structures of control. On the other hand, the imperial strategy of co-optation meant that Rome's "connection with the provinces was almost exclusively political and could, therefore, be easily broken again by political events."[22] By the same token, many aspects of Roman production were highly vulnerable to disappearance in conquest as based "merely on their association and on the community."[23] Roman plantation agriculture and the system of raising grain at the periphery and importing it into the center are cases Marx must have had in mind. Thus, out of the wholesale military defeat of Rome,

[21] *German Ideology*, pp. 45f., 89f.; *Grundrisse*, pp. 471–91.
[22] *German Ideology*, p. 90.
[23] Ibid.

no Germanic version of the Manchus would arise, a new dynasty presiding over the old system. The result would be a system far more decentralized than Rome's, though more coordinated and productive than the Germanic tribes'.

The invaders' mode of production explains their aggressiveness, in ways sketched above, and, of course, helped to shape the structure of the invading armies. To the final result, the Germanic invaders contributed both that military structure and aspects of their native economic structure. Or rather, both affected the final result.

The outcome of the drama of conflict and Roman defeat was a system of separate but similar societies, in which sedentary agriculturalists were exploited by overlords specializing in the mobile and coordinated use of physical force. The relations among the overlords were initially fairly egalitarian, in ways derived from the Germanic mode, but governed by interpersonal obligations and hierarchies, adaptations of the apparatus of conquest to the task of exploitation.

This account is almost as sketchy in the texts as it is in my brief summary.[24] It is very far from a paradigm of Marx's practice in historical explanation. But it is a useful paradigm of how Marx tries to give a certain primacy to internal factors even when a process of change is not internal as a whole. The crucial contributions of each party to the interaction are governed here by the respective modes of production. To put it another way, the outcome is enormously sensitive to variations in the modes, even if we keep constant the fact that one society is being invaded and defeated by others. Once we have explained how the initial modes of production contributed to the process of interaction, most of the work of explaining the ultimate result is done. Most, but not all. For example, some of the hierarchical structure of early feudalism is attributed to chains of command shaped by the conquest itself. In the explanation of the latter relations, military imperatives of the conquest would play an independent role.

[24] Also, there are some differences between the two main texts. The *Grundrisse* places more emphasis on the native Germanic mode.

Marx's total theory of history has two parts. First, basic internal change results when processes initially maintaining an economic structure destroy it, because of the nature of the mode of production. This is Marx's main theme, in part because he was close to the era in which the whole planet was internal to a single mode of production. My main purpose has been to analyze this claim. In the next section I will be concerned to defend it. Second, when basic change is not internal, it is mainly to be explained as the result of processes of self-reproduction and consequent processes of interaction governed by the modes of production of the respective societies. It isn't clear that this possibility of noninternal basic change extends much further than feudalism for Marx. Still, it is an important option.

In defining the second option, I introduced a vague matter of degree, the question of whether a change is mainly explained on the basis of modes of production. In principle, this vagueness could make it impossible to tell whether an explanation relies so fundamentally on external interactions that Marx's theory must exclude it just on that account. In practice, though, the rivalries are usually clear, especially where the rise of feudalism is concerned.

For a clear rival, consider Marc Bloch's account of the origins of feudalism.[25] In his explanation, early feudalism is the result of true Dark Ages, a millennium of virtually constant invasion. Under this pressure, farmers, artisans and merchants are dependent on military specialists for their defense. The warriors come to dominate, as a result. Their interrelations are governed by the organization and ideology suited to a life of constant battle against desperate, unpredictable and utterly alien enemies. Apart from a certain minimal capacity for agriculture, crafts, and transportation, and certain weaponry, the creation of this society is relatively insensitive to features of the societies preceding it. Usually, Bloch appeals to processes that would characterize any basically sedentary society constantly threatened by invasion, but strong enough not to succumb. Even-

[25] See Marc Bloch, *Feudal Society* (London, 1965.)

252

tually, the invasions stop, owing to factors beyond the control or knowledge of the invaded lands. The warrior culture of early feudalism is routinized and ritualized, giving birth to classical feudalism. Here, the main work of explanation explores the mode of defense. Modes of production are not the main ultimate determinants of structural change. If Bloch is right, then the rise of feudalism is not mainly due to internal processes, in the way Marx supposes.

I have tried to make the mode of production theory clear enough for one to see how it might be tested. But many clear statements are clear falsehoods. The next task is to see how a case might be made that this theory is true.

Is History like That?

Often unintentionally, technological determinism has contributed to Marxolatry. Arguments that Marx's texts imply some form of technological determinism can be extensive and plausible, if ultimately invalid. But there is no plausible argument that Marx, so interpreted, is right. No doubt, people have always wanted to cope more efficiently with nature in material production. But there is no general reason to suppose that this desire is always powerful enough to destroy social structures that reduce efficiency. Certainly, apparent counterexamples abound and were familiar to Marx. In the Roman Empire, traditional China, traditional India and the indigenous societies invaded by European colonialism, technologically inhibiting social forms seem to have endured for centuries, even millennia. Moreover, there are general reasons for supposing that the drive for technological improvement is not always supreme. People may want more efficient production and its fruits, but they also want to avoid death, torture, prison, social opprobrium, harrassment, shame and the many other costs of violating an established social order. Even when specific conservative mechanisms are not at work, potentially revolutionary innovations are always risky at the outset. To become pervasive, they must answer to widely felt, acutely deprived

253

needs. Yet a relatively low technological level seems to answer, by and large, to the needs felt in many societies. The reconstructions of traditional Iroquois, Asian and Slavic societies, which Marx so avidly read, portray people who are no more dissatisfied with relatively inefficient technology than Marx's parents were dissatisfied with an absence of flush toilets, which would deeply trouble us today.

Even if Marx's writings did argue that the drive for efficiency was strong enough to change inhibiting social structures from the seventeenth century onward, there would be not the vaguest hint of an argument that this should generally be so throughout history. Indeed, Marx's mature theory of wages under capitalism undermines such arguments. While he claims that capitalism, on the average, does no better than provide workers with necessities, he points out that the needs defining what is necessary have a historical element depending on the history of class struggle and the perception of the differences between workers and their employers.[26] By emphasizing the historical relativity of needs, Marx brings into the foreground one of the questions that technological determinism is least equipped to answer, "How does a need for better technology arise?"

Does the mode of production theory, for its part, have a justification, as more likely than not to be basically true, given the facts at hand? Apart from whatever resistance the facts offer, there might seem to be problems of principle in justifying a theory so vast and relatively nonpredictive. The mode of production theory describes mechanisms for basic internal change in all class-divided societies, if not all societies. Obviously, the historical record is too incomplete to yield data for it in every single case specific enough to substantiate the theory. But what would count as a fair sample of all cases of basic internal change? Moreover, the theory does not yield empirical laws saying that in circumstances of certain general kinds changes of certain general kinds occur. How can a theory be justified except by confirming such laws?

[26] See *Capital* I, p. 168; *Wages, Price and Profit*, pp. 71f.

In fact, the best bet at present is, I think, that the mode of production theory is basically true. I will present a case for this bet, up to the point at which it must go beyond the limits of a single book, the detailed investigation of particular historical episodes. Here, I will describe the role of case studies, and refer to some that are especially important ones given the nature of present historical disputes. Because of the need to refer to case studies presented elsewhere, the case will not be complete. But it should be complete enough to show that there is no obstacle in principle to the justification of the mode of production theory, even though it is highly general, yields no empirical laws from which change could have been predicted, and is full of hedges concerning "basic" change, the "main" explanation, and changes' taking place "sooner or later." There is no reason to relegate the theory to the modern historian's graveyard, the realm of metaphysical articles of faith.

A general theory of underlying mechanisms needs to be justified at two levels. On the one hand, general considerations have to be offered, giving reasons (which are never conclusive) for supposing that the theory does hold in general. On the other hand, the theory needs to be applied to concrete problems of explanation. It must be shown to be a better basis for solving these problems than the best current rivals. Darwin's theory of evolution is a good example of this double process, precisely analogous to Marx's theory. On the one hand, Darwin appeals to general considerations and widely known phenomena that make it plausible that his favored mechanisms are responsible for species change or implausible that an alternative could do the job. For example, the first two chapters of *The Origin of Species* are dominated by an argument from widely shared beliefs to the plausibility of the general claim that new species can arise through natural selection. Artificial selection by breeders of domesticated plants and animals gives rise to new varieties, with distinctive features that breed true. No one has shown that the species-variety distinction is any more than a matter of degree. So it is plausible that new species can arise by the selection imposed by the natural process of the struggle to survive and propagate. This plausibility argument is so important for Darwin that it motivates the choice of the very phrase "natural selection."[27] On the other hand, Darwin shows that his theory provides a better basis than its rivals for explaining quite specific facts of taxonomy, geographic distribution and the fossil record. Moreover, Darwin's theory is like Marx's in its limitations. He does not purport to describe the circumstances in which species change must occur, that is, to sketch a noncircular account of when selective pressures and mutating factors are "powerful enough." Crucial ideas are vague, including the whole notion of a species and the scope of natural selection itself, which Darwin takes to be merely the main factor in evolution.[28]

At the general level, the argument for the mode of production theory rests on a plausible estimate of the extent to which a ruling class dominates society. Once the unconsumed surplus product of immediate producers is controlled by a minority, enormous social power develops. The material advantage, together with the leisure, mobility, coordination and resources for co-optation that accompany it, are the basis for a near monopoly of control over organized force. Since intellectual and ideological work are furthered by freedom from manual work while, among those engaged in intellectual work, "even a philosopher of the future cannot live on air," the economically dominant class has enormous influence on the production and propagation of ideas. Moreover, in any class-dominated society, attacking the ruling class is not, for any significant number of people, a means of making a living, though it does jeopardize one's living.

How can change occur, nonetheless, on the basis of internal processes? It does not seem that the production and criticism

[27] "Can the principle of selection, which we have seen is so potent in the hands of man, apply in nature? . . . Can it, then, be thought improbable, seeing that variations useful to man have undoubtedly occurred, that other variations useful in some way to each being in the great and complex battle of life, should sometimes occur in the course of thousands of generations? . . . This preservation of favorable variations and the rejection of injurious variations, I call Natural Selection" (Darwin, *Origin*, pp. 130f.).

[28] See, for example, ibid., p. 74, acknowledging the probability that heritable drooping ears have evolved in domestic animals purely from disuse.

of ideas can function as the ultimate source of basic change. Contradictory, irrational ideologies have persisted for generations, even millennia, in the face of intellectually compelling criticism. People seem capable of beliefs that fly in the face of the best arguments and evidence when such belief serves basic interests, including an interest in avoiding risky and hopeless defiance. At the political level, the inevitable blunders and local defeats that suspend for a time the appartus of coercion do not seem sufficient to produce radical change. With their coordination, mobility, reserves of power and reliance on familiar social and intellectual impulses, ruling classes have successfully regrouped and counterattacked, from Spartacus' uprising to the fluorescence of urban communes in the Middle Ages to the *jacqueries* of Bourbon France. There are always bases for discontent in a class-divided society. The question that an explanation of change must answer is how the discontent is joined to the power and the desire to overthrow the ruling class. Explicit political organizing and the mobilizing of revolutionary force do not provide the answer if they do not reflect pervasive processes at another level leading to the changes in unity and desire. Without that pervasive reshaping of society, the ruling class can nip movements for change in the bud before enough people are organized to compensate for the stabilizing advantages of the ruling class.

One part of the social system remains as a source of internal mechanisms of change, the mode of material production. The means of reproducing the material basis for the old relations of production, under the pressures of natural scarcity and human recalcitrance, may have as an inevitable but unintended consequence, crucial shifts in power, together with the creation of new felt needs. Since they radically change resources and interests, these processes can produce new powers and felt needs that eloquence and logic could not have created. Since they pervade a whole society, they can be the basis for large-scale, coordinated revolutionary activity. Since these changes are the necessary yet unintended consequences of the means of maintaining the old society, the ruling class does not nip them in the bud. The processes of change arising from the mode of production can invest a subordinate class with enough mobility, discipline and security to provide a fighting chance to overthrow the ruling class. In short, while ideology is too rigid and purely political processes too easily isolated, the mode of production is fluid, pervasive and unforeseeable in its destructive effects. It alone can merit Marx's encomium to the transforming power of underlying social processes, "Well-grubbed, old mole!"[29]

I have already described several ways in which a mode of production could be self-transforming. I will simply add that this "what else could it be?" argument for locating internal change within the mode of production depends on flexibility in distinguishing the social relations of production from the political superstructure. If means and consequences of control could not be used to define relations of production, further factors for change would be available, located in the political realm as against the mode of production. Organized means of controlling human recalcitrance are always, in a certain broad sense, political. Yet such means, employed to control the surplus product, may be ultimately self-transforming. The *Grundrisse* account of the rise of class divisions among nonslaves is a case in point. Here, the holistic understanding of "relations of production" and of basic differences in type among economic structures is not optional.

This general argument is not, of course, conclusive, any more than Darwin's general arguments are. Such appeals to background beliefs only establish the plausibility of a general claim. (Without more knowledge of genetics than anyone had at the time, Darwin could not rule out the possibility that domesticators only concentrated in certain populations items from an immutable array of genotypes.) What is needed is a series of specific arguments establishing the superiority of the general theory as a basis for explanations of why actual phenomena occurred in the domain in question. In particular, these detailed arguments ought to show that an explanation supported by the general theory is superior to the best sup-

[29] *Eighteenth Brumaire*, p. 514.

ported by the most powerful current rival theories, superior in light of data assessed using principles shared by the rivals. Without these detailed and specific comparisons, some rival will always remain justified, at least among those investigators who find its premises especially attractive. On the other hand, unless the more general argument is available, the specific explanatory triumphs will be significant as isolated accounts of the episodes in question, not as evidence for the presence in general of the theoretical mechanisms.

Especially important as subjects for detailed explanatory comparison are standard problems that have long occupied investigators working in rival frameworks. If an advocate of the new theory strays too far from such problems, there is a danger that his or her successes will be, in a sense, fortuitous. They may reflect the fact that he or she has chosen a question that happens to yield easily to the general theory for special reasons, or the fact that theorists in rival frameworks have not yet applied their talents to this nonstandard problem. This willingness to confront standard problems using a deviant theory is one basis for Marx's scientific power. It pervades *Capital*, and helps to explain his commitment to that work, even as his strategies for the workers' movement shifted toward political struggles, foreign affairs and the overcoming of ethnic and racial antagonisms. Much of volume one is occupied with the great standard problem of history writing in his time: to explain the shift from feudalism to modernity in Western Europe. Volume two is occupied with problems of large-scale instability and cyclical fluctuation in a capitalist economy, which were the theoretical scandal of economics since the first general industrial depression in 1825. Much of volume three is concerned with testing Marx's theories of technology, class struggle and profit against a problem that had challenged the best efforts of the best economists in the previous generations: why had there been a long-term decline in the average rate of profit since the eighteenth century? Similarly, Marx's historical writings, apart from obvious political concerns, are occupied with such testing-by-comparison. For the most urgent task of political history had become the effort to explain the instability

259

and frequent *bizarreries* of French political history since the Revolution. That is the importance of what would otherwise be a minor tour de force, the effort in *The Eighteenth Brumaire* to explain what all regarded as an anomaly, the rise of a mediocre stockmarket swindler to Emperor of France.

Apart from its importance in the judgment of Marx's theory, the epistemological role of these writings can be crucial in identifying their very meaning. Consider, for example, Marx's discussion of the tendency for the rate of profit to decline. On the usual interpretation, the tendency is important to Marx because it is inherent and universal. So the mechanism he identifies and the trend he seeks to explain ought to be characteristic of twentieth-century capitalism as well. (In fact, the rate of profit in the United States in this century seems fairly stable over the long run. The capital/labor ratio seems not to have increased in the way Marx describes.) On the present view of the logic of his overall argument, the trend that so concerns him can be a particular historical phenomenon that major nineteenth-century investigators acknowledge and seek to explain: the tendency of the rate of profit to fall with industrialization, for example, its decline in England from the eighteenth century up to Marx's time. He argues that his theory of profit offers a superior explanation of this trend by connecting it to parallel historical developments, the increased capital/labor ratio characteristic of industrialization and the ability of the growing trades-union movement to maintain the ratio of social labor providing for workers' material demands to social labor providing for capitalists' demands concerning consumption and productive expansion. The general significance of the argument is not that it establishes an inherent tendency of capitalism (in contrast, say, to the repeated industrial crises that *are* inherent for Marx). Rather, the general theory of profit is supported by using it to solve a standard, recalcitrant problem of historical explanation. Marx describes his achievement in this spirit in his letter to Engels of April 30, 1868.[30] He calls it "one of the greatest triumphs over the pons asinorum of all

[30] *Selected Correspondence*, p. 194.

previous economics." The only standard problem to which he could be alluding is the need to explain the profit trend that I have described, a task that had challenged the best efforts of Ricardo, Malthus and many others.

Of course, not everyone today accepts the basic validity of Marx's explanations of the historical developments that most occupied him. Apart from dogmatists, very few would take those explanations to be right in every detail. But the enduring power of Marx's main historical explanations is quite striking. In no case has a basically contrary explanation, in which Marx's is fundamentally wrong, triumphed among the majority of *non*-Marxist investigators. At certain focal points of historical inquiry, for example, the rise of capitalism in England, the political turmoil of nineteenth-century France, the origins of the English Civil War and the rise of the modern labor movement, Marx's basic ideas are closer than any rivals to being the standard hypotheses after a century of controversy.

If the detailed explanatory achievements using his theories were only Marx's, that would be grounds for deep suspicion of those theories. This unique success would best be explained as due to the historical shrewdness of an individual manipulating an inadequate theory. As the eminent positivist philosopher of science C. G. Hempel noted, with Marxism as his implicit concern:

Occasionally, the adherents of some particular school of explanation or interpretation in history will adduce, as evidence in favor of their approach, a successful historical prediction which was made by a representative of their school. But . . . an adherent of a quite metaphysical "theory" of history may have a sound feeling for historical developments and may be able to make correct predictions, which he will even couch in the terminology of his theory, though they could not have been attained by means of it. [These are] pseudo-confirming cases . . .[31]

In fact, the broad mode of production theory has been the basis for a variety of explanatory achievements by people other

[31] C. G. Hempel "The Function of General Laws in History" (originally 1940), in *Aspects of Scientific Explanation* (New York, 1965), p. 239.

than Marx, even though Marxist historiography has usually not been a respectable enterprise, just as the Marxist theory of ideology would lead one to expect. Some important examples are Engels on the Reformation and the German Peasant Wars, Lenin and Hilferding on nineteenth-century imperialism, Hill and Arkhangelski on the English Civil War, Hilton on class struggles in the Middle Ages, De Sainte Croix on the decline of Rome, and Meillasoux, Thurnwald and Fried on the rise of class societies.[32] It should be noted that Marxist investigators other than Marx are sometimes doing a necessary job that Marx did not attempt. In defending a theory it is important to look not just at standard problems, but at the cases most favorable to the other side, where a rival theory is most likely to succeed if it is actually valid. In the case of the mode of production theory, religion plays a crucial role. Here, large-scale ideological changes seem to have occurred without a material basis and seem to have motivated coordinated, risky activity with radical objectives. On this subject, probably for reasons of temperament, Marx is far behind Engels, who sketches a compelling account of the Reformation and its consequences, within a broad mode of production theory. Hill's work on Puritanism continues this enterprise.[33] Also, Marx's

[32] Among the more recent writers, see, for example, Christopher Hill, *The English Revolution* (London, 1940); Rodney Hilton, *The Decline of Serfdom in England* (New York, 1972); G. E. M. De Sainte Croix, "Karl Marx and the History of Classical Antiquity," *Arethusa* 8(1975), pp. 7–41; Claude Meillasoux, "Essai d'interprétation du phenomène économique dans les sociétés traditionelles d'auto-subsistance," *Cahiers d'études Africaines* 4 (1960) pp. 49–67; R. Thurnwald, *Economics in Primitive Communities* (London, 1932); Morton Fried, *The Evolution of Political Society* (New York, 1967). Like most Anglophones, I only know of the untranslated Arkhangelski from the strong descriptions of his contributions scattered through Hill's writings.

[33] See, for example, Engels' preface to the 1898 edition of *Socialism: Utopian and Scientific*, and Hill, *Puritanism and Revolution* (New York, 1968). Very recently, the Islamic Republic of Iran has become the leading example in arguments for the primacy of religion over factors emphasized by Marx. If Marx's theory were technological determinism, this would be a troubling counterexample to psychological assumptions his theory requires. For the vast majority of Iranians now accept a dramatically reduced material output. But these same developments are hardly surprising on a mode of production model. The most numerous of the groups who rebelled against the Pahlavis were farmers

Footnote continued on following page

discussions of precapitalist societies are extremely fragmentary. And there, one would expect the independent role of ideology to be especially important. Recent work on social change in the Middle Ages, the decline of the Roman Empire, and the rise of class societies has helped to fill this gap.[34] Finally, even within capitalist society, the defense of the mode of production interpretation is complicated by the falsehood of a simplifying principle in the *Manifesto*: that capitalism tends to reduce the importance of national and racial divisions. Marx dramatically abandoned this view in later years. In a previously quoted letter of 1870 he writes, "Every industrial and commercial center in England now possesses a working class *divided* into two *hostile* camps, English proletarians and Irish proletarians. . . . This antagonism is artificially kept alive and intensified by the press, the pulpit, the comic papers, in short by all the means at the disposal of the ruling classes. *This antagonism* is the *secret of the impotence of the English working class*, despite its organization."[35] In Marx's speeches and manifestoes for the International Workingmen's Association, international affairs, for example, the Irish struggle for independence, Russian efforts to dominate the Continent and the Franco-Prussian War, determine the larger strategic choices of the workers' movement. Still, a detailed materialist discussion of interna-

and craftspeople dispossessed or threatened by the rapid intrusion of agribusiness in the countryside, of industry and large-scale marketing in the cities. Many became an unemployed or underemployed subproletariat around the big cities. Like Marx's peasants, their short-term interests drew them toward the past, even if their long-term interests pointed toward alliances with industrial workers, the base of the Iranian left (cf. *Communist Manifesto*, p. 344; *Eighteenth Brumaire*, pp. 515–19). The mullahs' unequivocal support comes from bazaar merchants whose interest is unequivocally a return to the past. Since all organized left-wing groups chose to ally with Khomeini in the revolution, the outcome hardly reveals a tendency for religious revival to overwhelm the influence of the mode of production. Nor is the social tendency of present-day Iran dictated by the internal logic of Shi'ism. Khomeini's most important ideological rival was the most important Ayatollah in Shi'ism, Shariatmadari. For similar considerations, see Nikki Keddie, *Roots of Revolution* (New Haven, 1981), chaps. 7 and 9.

[34] See Hilton, De Sainte Croix, Meillasoux, Thurnwald and Fried, in the works cited in n. 32 above and elsewhere.

[35] Marx to Meyer and Vogt, April 9, 1870, *Selected Correspondence*, p. 222; Marx's emphases.

263

tional antagonism and racism is missing. Yet these antagonisms might seem an independent source of change. This gives special importance to more recent theories of imperialism and of the persistence of racial antagonisms in advanced industrial societies.[36]

The detailed explanatory investigations that employ the mode of production theory can only be assessed through equally detailed arguments. So I will simply offer a verdict that the interested reader will, I hope, take seriously in assessing the theory: despite over a hundred years of general academic disrepute, the basic features of the explanations supported by this theory have survived remarkably well, and the theory has been remarkably fruitful; the successes are significant enough to make the approximate truth of the general theory, as against the rivals, a good bet. It certainly is striking, and not especially controversial, that the original rivals to Marx's general theory have become quaint museum pieces. That history is the story of the triumph of the forces of intelligence over the forces of superstition, or the story of heroic individuals remaking society through force of will is not a significant working hypothesis today.

In contrast, the distinctive ideas of Marxist technological determinism have not been put to work, to any significant extent, in any reasonably successful detailed study of any major historical question by an investigator sympathetic to Marx. Of course, it is easy enough to show that many of these studies are compatible with the distinctive ideas of technological determinism. The processes studied are seen as means by which the superstructure defending an outmoded economic structure is destroyed; somewhere else must lie the ultimate, techno-

[36] The importance of international antagonisms makes Lenin's and Hilferding's writings on imperialism crucial to the development of the mode of production theory. Among recent writings on racism within a broad mode of production framework, Michael Reich's and Robert Cherry's are especially informative and clear. See Cherry, "Economic Theories of Racism" and Reich, "The Economics of Racism," in David Gordon, ed., *Problems in Political Economy*, 2d ed. (Lexington, Mass., 1977); and Michael Reich, *Racial Inequality* (Princeton, 1981). Alan Gilbert discusses Marx's deepening emphasis on international relations in "Marx on Internationalism and War," *Philosophy and Public Affairs* 7 (1978).

logical explanation of why it was outmoded and of why the processes of change occurred. Or the processes in question are conflicts produced by the economic structure, but conflicts not of the same kind as the ultimate sources of the structure or the ultimate sources of its passing. Or the questions answered concern matters of timing or short-term phenomena or relatively small-scale features that are entirely outside the scope of technological determinism. In this way, the distinctive features of technological determinism can be defended from an assault that treats as a counter-example Lenin's work on imperialism, or for that matter, Engels' research on the German Peasant Wars, or Marx's utterly and obviously nontechnological *The Eighteenth Brumaire of Louis Napoleon*. (How curious, if Marx was a technological determinist, that Engels repeatedly singled out this work as the epitome of Marx's historical method.)[37] This defense, however, devastates itself in the end. The distinctive ideas of technological determinism turn out to be immune from criticism using the classical achievements of Marxist historiography because they are indifferent to the latter. Thus, they can neither be undermined *nor* supported by them. A crucial level of justification, application in a series of specific explanatory achievements, is missing. The broad mode of production theory is, however, applied and tested in these studies, though sometimes to a greater, sometimes to a lesser extent. It provides relevant estimates of the power, resources and flexibility of a ruling class, and a relevant model of how power-relations governing material production may guarantee conflicts that ultimately destroy them. Because the ultimate sources of change are not wholly apolitical, the classical studies shed light on them, are not "merely" political or merely concerned with the superstructure.

In addition, many of the particular studies to which I have referred really do undermine technological determinism. This can be said of Marx's own work on ancient Rome and traditional India and China. Here are some more recent examples,

[37] See Engels' preface to the 1885 edition of *The Eighteenth Brumaire, Selected Works*, vol. I, p. 397; Engels to Bloch, September 21, 1890, *Selected Correspondence*, p. 396; and Engels to Schmidt, October 27, 1890, ibid., p. 401.

derived from previously cited writings. De Sainte Croix has further developed Marx's idea that the Roman Empire maintained itself through a pattern of exploitative relations that ultimately destroyed it. A surplus product was extracted from the non-Italian empire through the co-optation of local elites and indirect rule. The material demands of co-optation and the presence of unsubdued and warlike peoples at the border required constant efforts at expansion. The basis for these processes was the farming population of Italy, used to provide material and personal support for the core aristocracy, the working population itself (imports could not do the job alone), and the constantly expanding military effort. As the frontiers enlarged, the working people of Italy could not support all these demands. Given the process of co-optation and indirect rule, as against full integration, the supporting core could not be expanded. The economic structure collapsed under the burdens of empire it generated. Similarly, in Hilton's work, the evolution of power-relations yields structural change. The Black Death creates a labor shortage and a new level of domestic disorder. This gives rise to class struggles that ultimately destroy the classic form of feudalism and bring England to the point at which capitalist transformation is a realistic prospect. As a final example, consider Thurnwald's sketch of a means by which class divisions might arise. (Sahlins' Polynesian study is the most striking empirical argument for it.)[38] Through location or traditional prerogative, some families administer exchange among family groups for whom exchange is, initially, a marginal and sporadic enterprise. As the advantages of exchange (*not* dependent on new technology) lead to more specialization and interdependence, these families achieve material preeminence, and eventual class rule, based on control of a surplus extracted from the exchanged product.

If Marx was a technological determinist, more's the pity. The studies to which I have alluded in the last two paragraphs, the work of investigators sympathetic to Marx, constitute, as a whole, a case against technological determinism and in favor

[38] Marshall Sahlins, *Social Stratification in Polynesia* (Seattle, 1958).

266

of the broad mode of production theory. Indeed, they have an even more intimate relation to the hypothesis that Marx was a technological determinist in his own writings. Even if Marx himself accepted technological determinism, these subsequent developments would justify a revision, in retrospect, of the definition of "the Marxist theory of history."

De Sainte Croix's, Hilton's and Thurnwald's hypotheses are surely Marxist in some sense of the term. These and similar studies, together with such classical writings as Lenin's *Imperialism* and *The Development of Capitalism in Russia*, Engels' *The Peasant Wars in Germany* and Marx's *The Eighteenth Brumaire* are a case for some theory of history. And that theory might certainly be called Marxist. That, I suspect, is why debates over the meaning of the Preface seem so sterile to readers engaged in choosing among answers to real historians' questions.

Even if the texts did not make the mode of production theory Marx's own meaning, the normal process of defining a scientific theory would make the broad mode of production interpretation the Marxist theory of history. In characterizing the body of theory stemming from a great innovator's work, we commonly revise backward, importing subsequent successful adaptations of the innovator's ideas. In Darwinian evolution, natural selection is the sole mechanism for species change. This is true even though Darwin himself believed that natural selection was only the main mechanism, with Lamarckian inheritance of effects of adult use and disuse playing a real, though subsidiary role. In Newtonian mechanics, the force of gravity acts at a distance. This is true even though Newton himself thought that gravitational attraction must be due to some underlying cause that does not act at a distance. The more successful subsequent uses of Marx's ideas in writing history all fit the mode of production model. By the standard tactic of definition in light of subsequent successful development, these are cases of the Marxist theory of history.

Finally, suppose that my proposal is wrong and specific case studies will not confirm the mode of production theory. There turn out to be internal basic changes that are not to be explained in this way. Still, the case already made would support a cer-

267

tain positive judgment, that Marx discovered a causal mechanism that plays an important role in producing large-scale social change. Granted, political historians from Aristotle to Harrington to Guizot had recognized the impact of class struggle, as Marx would call it, on the political process. What one doesn't encounter until Marx and Engels is a systematic and empirically plausible explanation of how the array of classes itself might change. At worst, the mode of production theory does yield a useful account of one kind of causal mechanism governing a realm of phenomena, which is as much as most major discoveries yield. Of course, technological determinism also describes a mechanism for change, the pursuit of productive advances and frustration at rigid social structures inhibiting their further development. This is, however, no discovery but the common stuff of Enlightenment ideas about progress.

THE EXTERNAL, AGAIN

I have sketched a case for the mode of production theory, as explaining how basic internal change occurs when it does. Yet Marx, while acknowledging the existence of noninternal basic change, at least in the case of feudalism, offers the mode of production model as the fundamental explanation of basic change in history as a whole. Granting, for the sake of argument, that basic *internal* change fits the theory, why suppose the factors governing internal change have this general priority?

It is important to distinguish a number of claims that might be made for the primacy of those internal factors. So far as the features of a stable class-divided society are concerned, the previous argument that the economically dominant class will be the ruling class politically and ideologically implies that an internal factor, the economic structure, is primary in most cases. If Bloch is right in his account of feudalism, there have been cases to the contrary in which the main enduring features of a society are determined instead by repeated, severe external shocks from societies not integrated into a larger mode of production. But there is a reason for taking such cases to be very atypical. Societies subject to repeated, severe external shocks from forces beyond social control usually succumb.

In the second place, where basic change in class-divided societies is concerned, there is reason to give internal explanations a certain statistical primacy, in the broad sense of "internal" that I associated with Marx. Basic change will usually have an internal explanation. For noninternal change requires a very special circumstance, in which different societies interact, both have a substantial impact on the structure of social evolution, but they do not interact in the stable and systematic way that would integrate them into a single mode of production. For most of the history of class societies, societies have either been more isolated than that or more integrated, especially on account of integration through empire, with basic change due to the internal drives of the imperial society. As for such nonsocial processes as climatic change and epidemics, class-divided societies seem usually to withstand these blows with their basic structure intact.

Marx certainly thinks that the internal is primary in these first two ways. However, in his emphatic rejection of approaches emphasizing conquest as an ultimate explanatory factor, he goes a step further. Even when change is not internal, as in the origins of feudalism, it is supposed to be highly sensitive to the distinctive features of the interacting societies. This might be true in fact. But there is no reason to suppose that this is so.

Consider the explanatory strategies epitomized by Bloch's account of the rise of feudalism, in which basic change is governed by phenomena of interaction that are relatively insensitive to the internal structures of the interacting societies. Right or wrong, there is nothing inherently implausible in Bloch's particular explanation. And it is no more speculative than Marx's. Moreover, the dispute over feudalism to one side, the rationale for the mode of production theory of internal change does not extend to cases in which change is not even broadly internal. The class mainly extracting a surplus may be strong enough to prevent the effective mobilization of force

269

by subordinate classes. That is no reason why it can resist external groups. Of course, there will always be this much priority to the internal. The internal structures of each party prior to their interaction make a contribution to explaining the nature and outcome of the interaction, but not vice versa. If we ever find the book setting out a valid and complete explanation of the rise of feudalism, the first chapters should include an account of the societies of the Roman Empire and of the significant invading groups. What we don't know, as yet, is how important these chapters will be in the book as a whole. Marx's assumption that he knew the answers to such questions is, so far as I can see, a prejudice. Or perhaps it is better called an unreflective guess. His discussions of noninternal change are few, obscure, and uncharacteristically self-contradictory. The primacy of the internal in the first two ways was his main concern.

270

CHAPTER SEVEN

Replacing Positivism

THE OBSTACLE OF POSITIVISM

IF TECHNOLOGICAL determinism is so far from the theory and practice of Marx and most of his insightful followers, why is it the dominant interpretation? The most important causes are, I would suggest, political. There are great pressures on everyone, external and internal, not to adopt a theory that makes political revolutions instituting socialism a prerequisite for important change. In countries that are not fully industrialized, there are enormous attractions to the offers of nationalist businesspeople, technicians and bureaucrats to ally with Marxists to modernize productive forces, reducing dependence on the great powers and on technologically regressive landowners and import-export entrepreneurs. And such alliances are easier for Marxists to defend on the basis of technological determinism. The pressures, here, are by no means simply material. It was not unwillingness to avoid material hardships which led many Marxist rebels in Angola, Nicaragua, and El Salvador to ally with modernizing entrepreneurs and technocrats around a nationalist but nonsocialist program. Rather, living under capitalism, a political revolution establishing socialism has, even for most socialists, the character of an unlikely and risky leap into the dark. Since technological determinism gives much more room for argument that the leap is unnecessary, it will remain part of the climate of ideas among those sympathetic to Marx.

Technological determinism is also reassuring in quite another way. It purports to describe circumstances in which radical change has always occurred and is bound to occur in the future. If one believes, as nearly all socialists do, that socialism would now enhance material productive possibilities, then the general theory dictates that capitalism will end and socialism will replace it. The additional assurance that this highly general argument provides helps make the underlying interpretation of Marx popular, quite apart from its basis or lack of one in Marx's writings.

Paradoxically, the other main reason for the dominance of technological determinism is utterly abstract and methodological. The positivist conception of explanation and confirmation gives Marxist technological determinism the status of a scientific hypothesis, while denying such status to the mode of production theory.

The crucial methodological constraints are extremely general and widely shared. They have received their most specific and careful statement in the writings of Hempel and other twentieth-century philosophers of science. But they are also visible in Hume's and Mill's analyses of causation and experimental inference and in the highly influential writings of Mach, Kirchoff, Poincaré and other philosopher-scientists at the end of the nineteenth and the beginning of the twentieth centuries.

On this view of science, the basic methodological notions—for example, explanation, confirmation, simplicity, and the reduction of one realm of objects to another—are relations of logical form. There is a true analysis of each solely concerned with logical relations between propositions. This analysis is valid for all fields of knowledge at all times. It is justifiable a priori, without reliance on any further empirically controversial beliefs. I will refer to this set of ideas as "positivism," since it is the most influential and enduring legacy of the logical positivist movement between the two World Wars.[1]

---

[1] The emphasis on logical form is, in principle, independent of the emphasis on the general and the a priori. Recently, some philosophers of science have made use of this independence, developing general and apriorist accounts of confirmation based on probability theory, not solely on considerations of logical form. I will neglect these departures here, since the complications would be enormous. Someone attracted to these so-called "Bayesian" accounts of science may want to assimilate them to the anti-positivist alternative that I will subsequently sketch. In *Fact and Method: Explanation and Confirmation in the Social and the Natural Sciences* (forthcoming), I argue that the Bayesian approach fails, for essentially the same reasons as the earlier, positivist account of science.

The rest of this chapter and this book will be devoted to the conflict between positivism and Marx's social theory. For the sake of a detailed case study of this conflict, my explicit subject will be positivism and the mode of production theory, the theory of history that I have ascribed to Marx. But it should become clear that positivism conflicts with Marx's theory of the state, his theory of ideology and his theory of capitalist economics, indeed with virtually every aspect of Marx's approach to society, if the conflict with his account of history takes the forms I will describe.

For example, the absence of empirical laws of predictive import will turn out to deprive the mode of production theory of explanatory power, if positivist constraints are imposed. There are no predictive laws of history in this theory of history, because there is no general description of when the forces of change are strong enough to overcome the forces of stability. The theory of the state is limited in just the same way. Since there is no general description of when the bourgeois interest in coercive control overrides the bourgeois interest in acquiescence, the theory is not a source of empirical laws dictating political action. Similarly, Marx attributes the development of socially important ideas to a balance of truth-distorting social processes, truth-producing ones (for example, the increase in proletarian interdependence), and rational discovery, without any general formula for determining the balance of forces. In his economics, tendencies in capitalist competition that sometimes lead to instability or stagnation can be counterbalanced by other tendencies, which are also a part of the competitive process, with no rule by which an economist could predict when a business cycle or long-term stagnation would result, on balance.

The other main positivist worry about the mode of production theory is that it stretches too flexibly in accommodating recalcitrant facts: if it is admitted as a scientific hypothesis, the most obvious absurdities could be defended by similar after-the-fact defenses. The rest of Marx's social theory is flexible in the same ways. For example, Marxist political theorists can and have coped with empirical difficulties by res-

273

pecifying the social composition of a ruling class, identifying it as an alliance of classes or a cluster of factions of a single class, instead of a single unified class. What is ideology for one Marxist is a relic of earlier times for another, a mistake suggested by the real pattern of experience for a third. In explaining crises, Marxist economists can and have shifted from appeals to domestic pressures to appeals to external factors, and back again.

Granted, one version of Marx's theory of history will turn out to fit the positivist mold, technological determinism. But, as we have seen, this way of making his theory a testable explanatory hypothesis makes it an utterly false one.

Among those sympathetic to Marx, there is no consensus as to whether his social theory conflicts with positivism. Those who do see a conflict draw a variety of implications, usually claiming either that Marx follows a logic of social (or historical or human) science radically different from that of natural science, or that it is a mistake to portray Marx as a scientist, to begin with. In effect, I will be arguing that all the standard positions on Marx and positivism are partly right but deeply wrong. Marx and positivism are in conflict. But Marx does not follow a different logic from natural-scientific investigators. Rather, the positivists were wrong about the logic of the social *and* the natural sciences. There is sufficient diversity among the forms of explanation and justification in the natural sciences, that a natural-scientific analogue to a Marxist tactic can always be found. Whether the tactic will do its job in the case at hand is a matter for empirical debate, not philosophical legislation.

The two most important enterprises of positivism have been the attempts to answer these questions: "When does a set of propositions, if true, explain why something happened?" "When does a given body of data confirm a hypothesis?" Explanation is analyzed on a so-called "covering-law model," as a matter of deduction employing empirical general laws. Explanations provide true statements, including such laws, from which other statements can be deduced asserting that certain general properties were realized at a certain time or place or in a certain person or object. Perhaps the deduction of a high probability of occurrence should also be admitted. Perhaps it is enough that the deduction merely be sketched, provided that the complete, true deduction is known to exist and the explainer indicates how to find it. If a purported explanation departs any further from this covering-law model, it is a pseudo-explanation, unworthy of empirical investigation.[2]

Just as explanation is a logical relation connecting true premises and the phenomenon to be explained, confirmation and disconfirmation are seen as logical relations connecting a hypothesis with the data. The hypothesis is confirmed if it has an appropriate relation of entailment to the data. It is disconfirmed if what is entailed, in the appropriate way, is logically incompatible with the data. Not just any pattern of entailment will do. For example, if just any entailment of observed true consequences, given observed antecedents, were confirming, then the hypothesis, "The moon is made of Camembert and all ravens are black" would constantly be confirmed by bird-watchers. However, whatever the appropriate logical patterns are, they regulate testing in every science, regardless of subject matter. In Hempel's clear and powerful writings, this formalist assumption is quite explicit, and the absence of supporting argument correspondingly striking:

In fact, it seems reasonable to require that the criteria of empirical confirmation, besides being objective in character, should contain no reference to the specific subject matter of the hypothesis or of the evidence in question; it ought to be possible, one feels, to set up purely formal criteria of confirmation in a manner similar to that in which deductive logic provides purely formal criteria for the validity of deductive inference.[3]

On this conception of science, technological determinism is potentially a part of science. But the mode of production theory is not. A theory of history, all would agree, should be chosen

---

[2] I have omitted details and refinements that are essential in some contexts, but not, I hope, in the present one. The classical short exposition of this model of explanation is C. G. Hempel's "The Function of General Laws in History" (1940), reprinted in his *Aspects of Scientific Explanation* (New York, 1965).
[3] "Studies in the Logic of Confirmation" (1945), ibid., p. 10.

for its capacity to explain historical changes. In principle, Marxist technological determinism could do so, according to the positivist model. Its hypotheses can be construed as appropriate covering laws. For example, combined with the statement that the relations of production inhibited productivity at a particular time, technological determinism entails that a change to a different basic type of structure, optimal for production, will follow. The mode of production theory serves no such function. It only claims to describe mechanisms through which basic internal change occurs, in the cases in which it does occur. It does not yield even a sketch of the general circumstances in which the mechanisms of change are strong enough, as against the stabilizing mechanisms, to guarantee change. So it does not provide premises for a covering-law deduction of any episode of change from antecedent conditions.

It might seem that the mode of production theory at least provides material for covering-law deductions of a different format. If all internal basic changes are due to conflicts in the mode of production, then if an internal basic change occurs, it can be deduced that conflicts in the mode of production preceded it. In general, the mode of production theory entails a certain patterning of social change in which basic internal changes are preceded by mode of production conflicts.

One problem with this reconciliation is that it yields no explanation of why a certain property was realized at a certain time, the basic task of explanation in the positivists' view. Short of some implausible species of backward causation, the occurrence of a basic internal change does not explain why the preceding mode of production was conflicted. But even if this emphasis on event-explanation could be detached from the positivist approach, the reconciliation would fail. That basic internal change is preceded by some conflict in the mode of production is to be expected in virtually every theory of history. The distinctive principle of the mode of production theory is that such conflict explains why the change occurs. What does this general claim amount to? For a positivist, it must mean that certain general features of the mode of production are

276

followed by basic internal change as a matter of empirical law. When we try to formulate that law, however, our statements go tautological, as we saw at the beginning of Chapter Six. Squeezed into the format of covering laws, as against descriptions of causal mechanisms, these statements "tell" us that conflicts resulting from the mode of production lead to a change in basic type when they are severe enough to lead to a change in basic type.

Just as it fails to meet positivist standards for explanation, the mode of production theory is unscientific by the standards of the positivist account of confirmation. In the latter view, technological determinism is subject to test, as a scientific hypothesis should be, while the mode of production theory is not. In principle, we could discover a case in which an economic structure had come to inhibit production, ask whether basic economic change subsequently occurred, and regard technological determinism as clearly supported or undermined if the answer was a clear "yes" or "no". On the other hand, even allowing for vagueness, the mode of production theory does not have the right logical structure for generating test implications through generally acceptable kinds of derivations.

The problem is that the mode of production theory has built into its very structure devices by which the theorist can explain away recalcitrant data. These defensive tactics have the same logical form as those that can be used by partisans of the most absurd theories. And in the positivist program, what counts as disconfirmation must be specifiable by an utterly general description of logical relations. So for positivism, if the mode of production theory were allowed, everything would be permitted.

There are three major ways in which the mode of production theory provides special room for maneuver in the way of adjustments after the fact to reconcile theory and data.

1. *The balance of change and stability.* When an opponent points to a case in which the mode of production gave rise to capacities and desires directed against the status quo, but no change occurred, a mode of production theorist can argue that

the forces of change were not strong enough to counter the stabilizing power of ruling-class domination. There will be many cases in which this claim seems utterly plausible to non-Marxist investigators with no postivist bias. But the tactic seems no different in logical form from those that could be used to defend the heights of absurdity. ("Prussia won the Franco-Prussian War because this suited Germany's national destiny." — "Then why was Germany a collection of petty states when France and Britain were already unified?" — "The national destiny hadn't become strong enough.")

2. *The content of the economic structure.* What counts as part of the economic structure, and hence the mode of production, is not determined in general and in advance. In a particular case, a phenomenon that might be seen as outside of the mode and to be explained by it can be incorporated into the definition of the mode, as a means or consequence of control defining the dominant production relation. Thus, a Marxist disappointed by the failure of Wittfogel's hydraulic hypothesis to account for the political institutions of ancient China could incorporate those institutions into the definition of the ancient Chinese mode of production, in the *Grundrisse* style. Again, there will often be a consensus among investigators with no vested interest in a philosophy of science as to which revisions are scientific common sense, which legitimate, and which desperate last-ditch maneuvers. But these options for redefinition all have the same logical form as absurd defenses of the most outmoded theories. ("Chickens develop from hen's eggs because the latter contain the entelechies for chickens." — "What about evolutionary change, mutation, monstrous births produced by gross interventions during pregnancy?" — "In those special cases, an entelechy is a complex of internal and external factors.")

3. *Basic economic change.* One important type of objection to the mode of production theory argues that economic change in crucial periods has been too slight to account for the basic change of society as a whole that is supposed to result. For example, as against Marx's belief that classical Athenian society

278

was based on slavery, historians have pointed out that slaves were a minority of the Athenian population, in the Age of Pericles as well as in preclassical Athens. Criticizing his late date for the triumph of capitalism as the mode of production in England, historians have pointed to the widespread use of wage-earning hired hands by 1600. The best Marxist reply has been that the crucial economic changes are of a special kind, a new economic group's arising and coming to dominate the economic surplus. But what makes a group dominant in this respect? Quite apart from the problem of finding a common measure for incommensurable goods, a purely quantitative answer, "controlling most of the surplus," will not do. Most slave labor in classical Athens and most wage labor in Tudor England may have been controlled by relatively small-scale farmers and craftspeople whose interests did not mold the dominant institutions. In effect, the best historians who are receptive to Marx have treated dominance of surplus-extraction as a role with many dimensions, emphasizing the dimensions that yield the greatest overall social power in a given case. The relative amount of resources a class controls, the concentration of resources in the hands of typical members, the leisure afforded by the control over the results of others' labor, the pervasive or strategic geographic location of the control, the options for coordinating such control, and the ease of defending control over the kinds of productive resource in question—all of these factors can be important in assessing whether a certain class has become the main extractor of a surplus, in the way Marx has in mind. M. I. Finley takes advantage of this multidimensional quality in "Was Greek Civilization Based on Slave Labor?" to argue that slavery was a basic element in Greek society. The rise of a class of large-scale landowners controlling large numbers of slaves goes far beyond any simple change in the ratio of slaves to free citizens in its importance. For their leisure, coordination and concentration of resources gave these large landowners social power that small farmers could not command, while the kinds of resources that the former controlled were not as vulnerable to attack as the privileges on which great merchants' import-export fortunes were based.[4] Similarly, for Marx, the rise of capitalist yeoman farmers cannot yet be the triumph of capitalism in the economy when the landed magnates of the royal court, together with the merchants and guildmembers who ultimately depend on them, still shape the nation's economic life. Of course, there is no general, prior formula for ranking the different aspects of economic dominance. If only coordination counted, then Florence, not England, would be the first capitalist society. In defending the view that basic social change derives from basic economic change, Marxists rely on a flexible concept of the latter that they cannot reduce to a rule dictating particular usages. Again, a philosophically naive observer will often be untroubled. Finley can appeal to the generally shared view that control over the slave-based plantation economy produced a politics and culture based on slavery in the antebellum southern United States, while, as he reminds us, slaves were less than one-third of the slave-state population. But a positivist has to be troubled. For the shifting specifications of economic dominance resemble in logical form tactics by which obviously outmoded theories can be defended. ("If a significant trait is acquired in generation after generation, it comes to be inherited. Thus, proto-giraffes stretched their way to giraffe-hood." — "Then why aren't bulldogs born with short ears?" — "Necks have evolutionary significance. Ears do not.")

Throughout this book, I have been identifying the basic type of an economic structure by the nature of its ruling class, and identifying the ruling class as the group who "mainly control" the surplus, who "dominate" its extraction. Up until now, the complexities lurking behind these terms have not been important. No matter where an economic change in basic type is located, Marx's theory will explain it on the basis of the mode of production. Once a new economic structure is sta-

---

[4] M. I. Finley, "Was Greek Civilization Based on Slave Labor?" See pp. 100, 102, 111. While Finley's relation to Marx's social theory has been complex and changing, his framework is both very far from technological determinism and very close to the broad mode of production theory, with economic structures specified in the flexible and partly political way I have proposed.

bilized, the different aspects of dominance over the surplus will tend to single out the same group. For a ruling class consolidates its power by eliminating or incorporating rivals.[5] Still, the claim that political and ideological institutions adjust to the needs of a ruling class is crucial to Marx's theory. In disputes over this claim, transitional periods in which the question of economic dominance is complex are often central. The resulting flexibility for Marxists will seem a scandal to positivists.

The problem of testing posed by the mode of production theory is not just that adherents, faced with recalcitrant evidence, can try to explain the evidence away. This happens all the time in science, as reflective positivists came to acknowledge. There is always the possibility that a negative finding will be challenged on the ground that defective instruments were used, the sample was biased, or the observation reports reflected a mistaken belief about what was observed. This looks relatively innocent so long as the defense advances a further hypothesis, independent of the first, that can be matched against the total data available. Testing has not been rendered impossible, just prolonged by the need to match an additional hypothesis against the total data using entailment relations. In any case, this positivist account seems promising.[6] And the defensive strategy is too common to be ruled out as illegitimate.

What is troubling about the present cases is that they do not typically add an additional hypothesis, to be tested against the totality of data. Rather, an initial hypothesis based on the mode of production theory is modified in light of the facts of the case, so that it fits the announced data better. One says what

---

[5] The eventual outcome will be that most of the surplus resulting from control over productive forces, land, raw materials and people will be in the hands of one class. But this does not make the identification of a class as economically dominant a matter of routine statistics. For at least some judgment is needed as to what constitutes "control." Thus, small stockholders are not in the ruling class in the United States, even though they own most stock. For only a tiny minority of shareholders, those owning huge blocks of shares, have any impact on corporate policy.

[6] Eventually it fails, for reasons I will soon sketch. Entailment relations are not enough to describe the testing of any reasonably deep theory.

281

the general hypothesis implies in the particular case at hand, tailoring the implication to fit the facts. This possibility is built into the concepts used to frame the hypothesis itself, in the unspecified appeal to factors being strong enough, the tailoring of the political aspects of the economic structure to the needs of the explanatory model, and the freedom to appeal to different dimensions of economic dominance in identifying the dominant class. If such revisions and refinements are always permissible, the most absurd hypotheses cannot be falsified. For positivists, the line between what is permissible and what is not in the matter of confirmation must be drawn through an appeal to general considerations concerning the entailment relations between hypothesis and data. No such rule seems available to insulate the defense of the mode of production theory from the defense of chaos.

There is a problem in testing technological determinism, as well. Its principles of change often rely on two closely related, vague hedges, that fettering be "severe" and that the period of structural change begin "relatively soon" after severe fettering. Because of these hedges, technological determinism can only be tested within certain limits of precision. But within these limits, testing is possible. A hundred years may or may not be relatively soon, but five hundred years is not. In any case, these areas of vagueness, which the mode of production theory includes as well, are relatively few. One might reasonably take technological determinism to sketch more precise general laws, to be developed through further research. The more the mode of production theory is understood, the less it seems to be a sketch of such hypotheses.

Of course, Marx did not have to confront people who called themselves "logical positivists." But the same basic ideas had been presented by Hume, by the Mills, *père et fils*, and, in a crude but influential form, by the self-described "positivist" Comte in his physics-worshipping philosophy of science. It is no serious anachronism, then, to say that Marx declares himself against positivism in the following passage, where he emphasizes the two features of his theory of history that would rule it out as unscientific if the positivist account of science is right:

the failure to provide a basis for general empirical laws of predictive import and the need for genuine creativity in identifying the parts of a particular social process that fall under the
categories of his theory.

In several parts of *Capital* I allude to the fate which overtook the
plebeians of ancient Rome. They were originally free peasants, each
cultivating his own piece of land on his own account. In the course
of Roman history they were expropriated. The same movement which
divorced them from their means of production and subsistence involved the formation not only of big landed property but also of big
money capital. And so one fine morning there were to be found on
the one hand free men, stripped of everything except their labor
power, and on the other, in order to exploit this labor, those who
held all the acquired wealth in their possession. What happened? The
Roman proletarians became not wage laborers but a *mob* of do-noth-
ings more abject than the former "poor whites" in the South of the
United States, and alongside of them there developed a mode of production which was not capitalist but based on slavery. Thus events
strikingly analogous but taking place in different historical surround-
ings led to totally different results. By studying each of these forms
of evolution separately and then comparing them one can easily find
the clue to this phenomenon, but one will never arrive there by using
as one's master key a general historico-philosophical theory, the supreme virtue of which consists in being super-historical.[7]

An Alternative to Positivism: Explanation

There is an alternative conception of science which makes
the mode of production theory a genuine hypothesis, worthy
of empirical investigation. My sketch of this alternative will
be rough, and my advocacy a bit dogmatic.[8] But I think I can
show that this approach to explanation and confirmation is
much closer than positivism to the methodological common
sense of the best investigators, in the natural as well as the
social sciences. If so, the mode of production theory has broad
significance for people whose interest is not history as such,
but the sciences, both social and natural, or the general nature
of explanation and confirmation. For the mode of production

[7] Marx to *Otechestvenniye Zapiski*, in Feuer, *Writings*, p. 441.
[8] I develop this alternative in detail in *Fact and Method*.

theory is an explanatory framework developed over several generations by investigators who have had to resist the especially powerful influence of positivist constraints within the social sciences.

In positivism, the basic methodological relations are relations of logical form, the same for all fields at all times, identifiable without reliance on empirically controversial principles. In this alternative approach, any standard definite enough to tell us whether a methodological relation holds (the data confirm the hypothesis, say, or the hypothesis explains the phenomenon, if true), will be specific to certain fields at certain times, and the argument that it is appropriate will be empirically controversial. The two-person dramas in which a body of data confronts a hypothesis, or a hypothesis confronts a phenomenon to be explained, are replaced by dramas with many characters, a diversity of framework principles, rival hypotheses and alternative causal accounts.

Explanation, according to the alternative view, is the adequate description of underlying causes sufficient under the actual circumstances to bring about the phenomenon in question. Of course, many positivists also said that they were concerned with causal explanations and the rules for their adequacy. The main differences emerge in the ways in which "cause" and "adequate description" are analyzed, together with the different roles given to the causal depth that I indicated with the tag "underlying cause."

Causes. One important source of positivism is Hume's analysis of causation. Apart from the obvious claim that the one event happened and then the other did, the statement that one event caused another is taken to express a general expectation that events of the former kind are followed by events of the latter kind. So someone concerned to explain what makes things happen must ultimately be concerned to reveal covering laws. Such general definitions of "cause" have been specified, refined and revised in a variety of ways. More recently, many have tried to replace them with alternative definitions, just as general and a priori, relying on counterfactual conditionals ("this would not have happened if that had not preceded it") or conditional probabilities. All of these efforts have encountered basic and enduring problems. It is as close to a consensus as anything in present-day philosophy that these problems have not been solved in a satisfactory way.[9]

Why suppose that there is any definition of "cause", informative, noncircular and valid a priori? It seems much truer to the facts about causality to take the category as covering a variety of processes, whose title to causal status does not derive from a fit with such a definition. At the core of the family of causes are a variety of processes of making things happen, recognized as such by primordial common sense, processes as diverse as pushing's changing the position of an object, a desire's leading someone to pursue a goal, a blow's causing pain, or pain's making someone cry. As science develops, the repertoire of kinds of causes is revised. It may turn out that the old repertoire cannot account for phenomena that must have a cause, and on these grounds a new item is added. Thus, gravitational attraction was added when the old repertoire turned out to yield no cause for what, all agreed, must have one, regularities in celestial motion and free fall.

For positivists, the notion of cause, if scientifically respectable, must be analyzable in the style of textbook definitions of membership in a certain biological species, with noncircular, informative and general descriptions of necessary and sufficient conditions for membership. The Humean analyses are the means of filling this prescription. In the nonpositivist alter-

---

[9] Most of the counter-examples to the covering-law model that I will subsequently describe count against the Humean analysis as well. In the modern debate over the Humean analysis and the covering-law model, Michael Scriven's writings have been especially influential. See, for example, "Causes, Connections and Conditions in History" in William Dray, ed., *Philosophical Analysis and History* (New York, 1966). Some of the most recalcitrant problems for the counterfactual analysis derive from the cases David Lewis forthrightly discusses at the end of his paper first presenting that account. See "Causation," *Journal of Philosophy* 70 (1973). Nancy Cartwright, "Causal Laws and Effective Strategies," *Nous* 13 (1979) is a powerful and influential argument against all efforts to fully analyze causal notions in favor of probabilistic ones. For an array of problems for all three approaches, see Bas van Fraassen, *The Scientific Image* (Oxford, 1980), chap. 5.

native, a better model for the concept of cause is the concept of number. No one supposes that every given kind of number—for example, cardinals finite and infinite, rationals, reals, positive and negative numbers, infinitesimals, and imaginary numbers—is a number in virtue of its fit with a general definition. Rather, at the core of the concept are the (very different) numbers of primordial common sense, counting and measuring numbers. The repertoire has expanded as new kinds were found necessary to fulfill tasks appropriate to mathematics. To resolve the question of what could be a number by reflecting on the concept is to replace science with philosophical reflection, where only science can do the job. The same, I propose, can be said of positivist legislation about what can be counted as a cause.

This approach to causality already makes it easier to treat the mode of production theory as a scientific hypothesis worthy of the name. Even if it yields no covering laws, it might function as a source of genuine explanations if the phenomena it connects are linked by items in an acceptable repertoire of causal connections. And in fact, the connection between location in the mode of production, on the one hand, and resources and priorities, on the other, is a kind of link that everyone accepts as sometimes causally effective. In particular, that objective interests can influence someone's values and beliefs is a routine fact, as my banal story of the defensive nuclear engineer showed in Chapter Four. Marx emphasizes this banal side of his approach in *The German Ideology* when he contrasts standard ways of writing history with what "every shopkeeper knows" about the gap between self-portrayal and the real causes of action.[10] Marx is clearly on the side of the shopkeepers, here. His innovation is to argue that familiar kinds of causes (objective interests diverging from sincere reasons) play a surprisingly central role as the bases for the most important historical changes. The same mixture of the innovative and the banal occurs in many other fields. For example, Keynes, like every economic innovator, appealed to certain universally rec-

[10] *German Ideology* p. 67.

286

ognized economic motives—in his case, the preference for liquid assets in hard times and the reluctance to invest in productive capacity when the outlook for sales is grim—and showed that those motives had an unsuspected impact on economic processes. In the natural sciences, Darwin constantly relies on the banal fact that there is some cause of variation in the offspring of the same parents, operating before birth.

Adequate description. Even with the more liberal conception of causality, an effort to explain can only be admitted as scientific if the requirement that the description of causes be adequate is appropriately understood. As Hempel has insisted, the description of a cause of an event may be quite inadequate to explain, otherwise someone's winning the Irish Sweepstakes would be explained by her having bought a ticket. For positivists, there is one rule for such adequacy, valid in all fields, at all times and a priori: conformity to the covering-law model. Of course, attempts to explain may fall short and still be adequate for present purposes, just as impure water is sometimes pure enough for present purposes. But scientists do distinguish between an explanation that is adequate *simpliciter* and one that will do in a given context ("Why was there a staphylococcus colony in that petri dish?" — "It got dirty somehow."). The former concept of adequacy, not an invention of philosophers but implicit in scientists' practice, is the one to be explicated in the covering-law model.

When we look at adequate scientific explanations, the reality is very different. The patterns of causal adequacy imposed on explanations vary widely from field to field and time to time. In particular, there is great variability where positivism is most rigid, in the stopping rules that describe the point at which an adequate explanation can stop in its description of causes, without further specifying the general features of the circumstances at hand in virtue of which those causes were sufficient. In modern disease theory, for example, a description of causes of an outbreak of symptoms is adequate to explain if it describes an infectious agent that is the normal cause of those symptoms in the population in question. Thus, when your doctor takes

287

a throat culture, he or she may gain sufficient causal insight to explain why you have a sore throat. The total evidence may rule out all likely causes except a streptococcal infection. But, although in a position to explain that your throat is sore because of a strep infection, he or she cannot even sketch the general conditions in which strep infection always or almost always produces a sore throat. Usually, streptococci in the throat produce no symptoms. Now, and perhaps forever, immunology is not remotely ripe for empirical general laws of the form: In conditions C, when an infection of kind I occurs in the throat, a sore throat almost always results.

The relatively permissive stopping rule of modern disease theory is, in many ways, a loosening of the constraints on an adequate explanation of symptoms current in the Renaissance. In Renaissance disease theory, symptoms result from imbalances in certain bodily fluids, the humors. Theorists believed that they could sketch general circumstances in which pathological symptoms are bound to result, and required such determinacy of adequate explanations. Sometimes, on the other hand, progress involves increased rigor in stopping rules. In Aristotelian physics, motions governed by the inherent tendencies of matter are subject to interference "against the course of nature," as when a child bats to one side a clod falling toward the Earth. This physics offers no explanation of the resulting trajectory beyond the explanation of the course of nature and the identification of the interfering shock. For the new physics of the seventeenth century, this attempted explanation was a nonexplanation. To really explain, a description of the causes of a trajectory should make just that outcome inevitable.[11]

What should a standard of adequacy require beyond the obvious, namely, that the causes described should really exist and be causes of the phenomenon in question? There seems to be no super-standard of which the particular ones are instances. Rather, the appropriate standard for a given field at

---

[11] For more on this and other shifts in physicists' standards of explanatory adequacy, none motivated by philosophical analysis as opposed to scientific discovery, see Thomas Kuhn, "Concepts of Cause in the Development of Physics," in his *The Essential Tension* (Chicago, 1977).

a given time is the one that best facilitates the pursuit of explanations in that field at that time. Thus, in disease theory, science would be retarded if investigators were not required to identify the infectious agent producing symptoms, if there is one. Science would also be retarded if they were required to pursue their explanations until they could sketch the circumstances on account of which the infected organism was bound to develop the symptoms. To dismiss these strategic considerations as describing merely pragmatic, as opposed to true "logical" adequacy is to invent a standard of adequacy that is an artifact of a philosophical program, a standard of no interest to those concerned with explanation in any normal sense. There is no nonpragmatic concept of adequacy, if the nonpragmatic is the totally context-free.

This approach to adequacy has a surprising consequence for the assessment of Marx's theory of history. Marx is often criticized for mechanistic arrogance, the view that he had discovered physics-like laws making the course of history predictable, in principle. In fact, if the stopping laws appropriate to history required this, his mode of production theory would be inadequate. If it is adequate, this is because the standards of adequacy that dominated mechanics from Galileo to quantum theory are not appropriate to history.

Causal depth. It is true that Marx does not accept descriptions of people's reasons for believing and acting as adequate to explain the large-scale social changes that concern him. This is an intended implication of such mechanistic phrases as "the laws of motion" of capitalist society. But rather than reflecting what I have called "mechanistic arrogance," the concern with nonindividualist explanation is the outcome of the requirement that explanatory causes be underlying, the remaining element of the nonpositivist theory of explanation.

A cause is underlying if it is not undermined by a deeper one, so that "not underlain" would be the perfectly correct, but ugly phrase. A cause X of a phenomenon Z is undermined by a deeper cause Y just in case X is merely one of the ways in which Y brought about Z. More specifically, this under-

289

mining can fit one of two patterns. In the first, Z would have come about anyway, on account of Y. Thus, to start with a relatively uncontroversial example, that a policeman was reported to have beaten up a black taxi driver on a certain day does not explain why there was a ghetto rebellion in Detroit in the 1960s, even though it was a cause of the rebellion. At any rate, this is so if underlying tensions and frustrations made it inevitable that some incident would trigger a rebellion. Similarly, if Marx's account of the rise of capitalism in England is right, then the mistakes of Charles Stuart and the strategic brilliance of Oliver Cromwell do not explain why there was a successful revolution in the interests of the bourgeoisie, even if they were causes of the actual success. If Charles Stuart had been wilier, such a revolution would still have occurred, on account of the same social forces.

In the second pattern of undermining, Y is a cause of X and Z, just as immediately connected to Z as X is. That this deprives X of explanatory power helps to explain many otherwise paradoxical cases in which Marxist and non-Marxist historians see themselves as offering rival explanations when they agree on a great deal in the realm of causal description. In Marxist and non-Marxist descriptions of the Nazi seizure of power, the large-scale shift in middle-class opinion from traditional conservatives to the Nazis is an important cause. No one who believes in this shift claims that the Nazis would have come to power anyway without this basis of support. But Marxists think this shift reflected,in turn, bourgeois interests and bourgeois dominance of the media and the political process. If so, then the seizure of power, while having a "revolt of the middle classes" as a cause, is not explained by it. In much the same way, Engels and Weber could agree that the Reformation was an important cause of the triumph of capitalism, while regarding themselves correctly as offering rival explanations of that triumph. Engels' explanation does not just supplement Weber's.

Note that the criticism of causal superficiality is not just a charge of incompleteness: "Given the same causes, the effect would not have occurred in other circumstances." Once the

290

covering-law model is abandoned, many adequate explanations have this incomplete character. No standard of adequacy appropriate to history rules out such incompleteness. Rather, the requirement of causal depth shows that the covering-law model is, in one respect, too permissive, despite its excessive requirements of completeness. Suppose a superficial causal description fits the covering-law model. Suppose, for example, that enough is said about the incidents and rumors triggering the Detroit ghetto rebellion to enable one to predict it, given laws covering the beliefs and attitudes of people at the moment. Or suppose the abilities of each side in the English Civil War are described in such detail that general strategic principles dictate Puritan victory. Still, the phenomena entailed might not be explained if the causal factors are undermined by deeper ones.

Debates over Marx to one side, there are quite uncontroversial explanations that fit the whole causal model I have just sketched better than the covering-law model. I have already given one example from the vast number based on diagnostic sifting of likely causes, the physician's explanation of the sore throat. Psychological explanations also commonly display the tendency to go tautological at the level of general principles. A historian might be in a position to explain Lee's surrender at Appomattox as due to his despair at Sherman's march to the sea and at the fall of Richmond. To keep matters simple, suppose that her confidence is securely based on words to that effect in Lee's letters to his wife. Still, the historian cannot suppose that when military leaders are in despair over the prospects for their cause they always or almost always surrender. This has been untrue of many military leaders, and there is no reason to believe that these more stubborn ones have been a small minority. No one can even sketch a general empirical law of surrendering to suit Lee's case. There may be such a law in a psychology of the future. But the adequacy of the historian's explanation does not depend on the existence of such a law, much less her ability to sketch it.

Theories, as well as explanations of particular events, seem to conform more closely to the causal model of explanation.

In this model, general theories are best understood as descriptions of the causal mechanisms that bring about phenomena of the kind in question in the field in question. Thus, Darwinian evolutionary theory, with its account of how natural selection produces species change, is a real theory. It is not, on the positivist model, since definitions and measures of selective pressure are either too loose or too circular to yield empirical, general covering laws, for the reliable deduction of regularities or specific events. Similarly, the modern geological description of continental plates, their drift and their interactions as the basis for major geological formations is a real theory, here. But it is not general enough to fit the covering-law model. Geology refers to a single planet, the Earth, and knowledge of other planetary surfaces has made it less, not more plausible that geologists possess sketches of truly general laws governing surface features on all planets.

Just as Darwinian biology and plate tectonics are genuine theories in this account, sources of genuine explanations that depart from the covering-law model, *so too is the mode of production theory*. It describes general mechanisms by which changes of a certain kind are produced. It is not a source of empirical general laws figuring in covering-law deductions. But without providing covering laws, successful explanations of particular phenomena may identify them as the results of mechanisms of the kind the theory describes. If so, the mode of production theory works, as a successful theory of how change takes place.

An Alternative to Positivism: Confirmation

The relative liberality of this approach to explanation makes it all the more urgent to develop a corresponding anti-positivist account of how hypotheses are tested. The basic idea of the alternative conception is that testing is a process of fair causal comparison, in a framework of contingent background principles. A hypothesis is confirmed by the data at hand if its approximate truth and the basic falsehood of its current rivals are entailed by the best account of how those data emerged from the process of data gathering and theorizing. Thus, virtually every empirical study in every scientific journal can easily be put in the form: "These are the data. This is why they were to be expected on our hypothesis. You might think that they would have occurred anyway, as a result of this or this process, compatible with the falsehood of our hypothesis. These are the facts excluding those chains of events."

In the judgment of which account is best, substantive background principles inevitably play a role, for example, principles describing how observing instruments yield data. Despite the need for such a background, an argument for the superiority of a hypothesis is sound if it is fair, that is, if it relies only on principles that partisans of all the rivals have come to accept as part of the frameworks in which they apply their rival hypotheses. As for the inference, not just to the current superiority of a hypothesis but to its likely approximate truth, its availability depends on the actual history of the field in question. In some fields, but not others—physics since the seventeenth century, for example, but not astrology—there is a pattern of success that can only be explained on the hypothesis that the game of fair causal comparison is giving people an increasing grasp of reality, here, in which the approximate truth about most large-scale phenomena has been achieved.

Almost everyone agrees that the process of comparison, or something like it, is the actual practice of good investigators testing hypotheses. For positivists, however, this process reflects matters of convenience and practical limitations. If all premises in scientific inferences were made explicit, and if scientists never asserted more than they had really established, confirmation would be revealed as a certain deductive relation between hypothesis and data, detectable purely by logical analysis, the same in every field and at every time. The scandal for positivism was the difficulty of saying what this relation is, especially when theories must be matched against data. Positivists wanted to say that a hypothesis is only confirmed if it is indispensable to the deduction of data, given observed initial conditions. Otherwise, such inflated absurdities as "The moon is made of Camembert and all ravens are black" would be confirmed. But at any given time, vast stretches of perfectly respectable theories are accepted and applied to explanatory tasks, even though they are as dispensable in current empirical deductions as the Camembert conjunct. After all, Newton's *Principia* says much more than Kepler's laws, Galileo's law of free fall, and the table of tides. Yet these and a few other relatively observational principles cover all the data available to Newton. No positivist succeeded in describing a logical relation that gave theories their due without giving absurdities more than their due. There seems to be no formal and comprehensive measure of what distance from the data is near enough to confirm.[12]

Here are a few more details of the approach to confirmation that I have barely sketched. I hope they make it clearer how it differs from positivism by making confirmation more specific to particular fields at particular times and more dependent on background principles and the actual course of history. Also, these details should make it clearer how the characteristic flexibility of Marxist investigators can be admitted without opening the floodgates to obviously absurd or outmoded ideas.

If confirmation is the comparison of a hypothesis with its rivals, the two-body problem of positivism, in which hypothesis encounters data alone, is replaced by a many-body problem, in which confirmation is the question of which of several hypotheses fit the data best. For the contrast to be real, though, the relevant rivals must not be all possible ones. At least for relatively important hypotheses, there is no useful finite list of all possible rivals. Showing that the hypothesis fits the data better than all possible rivals would simply mean showing, in

---

[12] In *Theory and Evidence* (Princeton, 1980), Clark Glymour describes a strategy of deduction that is, he argues, adequate for the confirmation of theories. But this strategy, "bootstrapping", as he calls it, is not comprehensive, as he freely admits. For example, it does not cover Bohr's and Rutherford's confirmation of their model of the atom by the deduction of a few regularities such as the Balmer series in the hydrogen spectrum. The required double-checking was not available there. Similarly, it can, I think, be shown that Bayesian strategies are only appropriate in special cases, where the causal structure of the process studied is known to fit an appropriate statistical model. Otherwise, Bayesian theories are, at best, misleading statements of the process of fair causal comparison that really underlies confirmation.

294

positivist style, that it has the right logical fit with the data. Instead, in the theory of confirmation as causal comparison, the hypothesis is compared with actual current rivals, including of course, unformulated ones implicit in theoretical frameworks that are actually employed. This limitation fits our talk of confirmation very well. Newton's physics used to be confirmed. But it never fit the data better than all future rivals, much less all possible ones. Given limits of accuracy of which seventeenth-century astronomers were aware, general relativity fits the data at least as well. While permissive in one way, the requirement of comparison is more stringent than positivism in another, which also suits our usage. The fact that observed phenomena follow from a hypothesis, through normal sorts of derivations, does not confirm if the phenomena follow just as easily from the most likely rival hypotheses. Since all accounts of speciation that were current at the time entailed that there were likely to be many different species, Darwin could not confirm his theory by appealing to this consequence. It does not confirm even a little bit, as we all would say if not already drawn to positivism.

A hypothesis is confirmed if there is a good argument for an account of why the data are as they are that entails the approximate truth of the hypothesis as against the basic falsehood of its rivals. Such arguments need further premises that are not to be established a priori and that are not solely concerned with matters of logical form. The background principles usually include empirical beliefs concerning the reliability of instruments and procedures. For example, a standard type of alternative to a bacteriological claim is refuted by a principle that a certain laboratory procedure makes contamination unlikely. The usual background also includes established theories with which hypotheses are expected to cohere. ("It might be supposed that this effect was due to ordinary cosmic radiation. But, for the following reasons, that would violate the conservation of mass-energy.")

Although the background principles are not all valid a priori, it is essential that they be fair in the particular context of debate at hand. They should not presuppose the falsehood of background principles already employed by partisans of one of the rivals. Thus, it would have been unfair of Galileans to assume the superiority of telescopes to the naked eye in astronomic observations. Aristotelian theory included reasons for preferring naked eye observations, in case of conflict, even if telescopes were superior on the earth.[13] It would have been unfair of Dalton to assume, in his arguments, that the processes for which rival chemistries were more effective were not processes of true compounding. Fortunately, in these debates there was enough shared background for winning arguments to be developed. For example, in fair arguments against Aristotelians, the new science could rely on a common naked eye optics and a common belief that a periodic motion should have a uniform cause.

The restriction to current rivals and the requirement of shared background principles make the confirmation of a hypothesis by given data relative to a specific field at a specific point in history. It might seem that this relativity is so great that confirmation cannot be a sign of probable truth, just a sign of temporary superiority. Some fields really are this unfortunate. Sometimes when the history of a field is a story of sudden reversals, successive and unrelated fads, or diametrical rivals enduring for centuries, the best explanation of the total pattern is that investigators have so little grasp of the truth that superiority is just a sign of luck and cleverness in debate. (Perhaps we should not speak of confirmation in these fields. But probably scientific usage is not that determinate.) Other fields are luckier in their histories. When we look at the game of fair comparison in physics, say, since the seventeenth century, or in chemistry since the eighteenth, we see a pattern of mounting success in explanation, prediction or control (in these cases, all three), that can only be explained on the assumption that fair comparison is an increasingly reliable guide to the truth—fairly reliable, after a certain point in time, where the approximate causes of large-scale phenomena are concerned. More precisely, any account of how the apparent successes of

[13] Paul Feyerabend presents relevant texts in *Against Method* (London, 1975), pp. 109–11, 121–39.

296

modern chemistry, say, emerged in a world in which the atomic theory, the theory of valences and the regularities in the periodic table are not even approximately true must be based on the sort of hypothesis that only philosophical skeptics entertain. These hypotheses, of lifelong dreams, mind-controlling demons or causal mechanisms routinely disappearing for no reason at all, conflict with the background principles of ultimate common sense, for example, "One's immediate environment usually is, in its gross and medium-sized aspects, what it clearly and distinctly appears to be." "Things don't commonly disappear, for no reason." And, given the actual course of our experience, the common-sense principles are unequivocally superior to those rivals. They are better accounts of the course of our experience, in *every* dimension on which the explanations are fairly compared, fruitfulness, informativeness, accurate implications and the absence of explanatory loose ends (e.g., why does the all-powerful demon want the visual experience of walking into a table, but not that of seeing a table from afar, to be regularly followed by pain?).[14]

In short, the course of our experience together with the logic of explanation makes certain common-sense background principles unequivocally superior to all rivals. In light of these principles, certain enterprises of causal comparison are, objectively, a guide to the approximate truth, in fields whose careers have gone well. Substantive common sense and historical contingency do the job of defending scientific inference,

[14] In contrast, when we compare important scientific hypotheses, each has some failures where a rival succeeds. Often, failure along one dimension must be weighed against success in others. Thus, a theory of relatively deep mechanisms, the molecular theory of gases, for example, is apt to be less accurate observationally than some rival that just lists empirical regularities. Since the deeper factors are hard to investigate, their partisans are apt to make crucial mistakes about them, even if they do exist. There is no general or a priori rule for balancing competing virtues, say, depth and fruitfulness on the one hand, observational accuracy on the other. But sometimes, shared background principles, the common-sense core and the history of the field support a verdict in a particular case, as when we conclude that the best explanation of residual inaccuracies is the difficulty of measuring what the theory describes, not its nonexistence. Because an a priori list of explanatory virtues is less determinant at this level, we can say that the logic of confirmation is less a priori as we move from basic common sense to controversial science.

where positivists thought that a priori reflection on logical relations was enough.

If this is the nature of confirmation, it is perfectly possible for the mode of production theory to be confirmed. The question is whether the best accounts of the available data entail the approximate truth of the mode of production theory as against the falsehood of its rivals. Would the case for the theory that I sketched before survive fair arguments in favor of one or another rival? As before, the philosophy of science that makes this theory worth taking seriously also vindicates the perfectly respectable theories that are an embarrassment to positivism. We can also say, as we always wanted to, that Newton's physics and Dalton's chemistry were confirmed when their deductive connections to data were extremely sparse. They still did a better job than their rivals of explaining phenomena that everyone took to stand in need of explanation. Without the distinctive causal mechanisms, the force of gravity in one case, atoms and their valences in the other, there would be no causal mechanisms to do this explanatory work.

The main conflict between positivism and Marx's theory of history most directly concerned disconfirmation, much more than confirmation. It seemed that Marx's theory was so very flexible that it could not be disconfirmed. Indeed, if the mode of production theory was accepted as a scientific hypothesis, it seemed there would be no way to defeat hypotheses that are obviously absurd or outmoded. There is a piecemeal defense here appealing to the authority of generally respected theories. Darwinian evolutionary theory and the germ theory of disease are flexible in the same way. But the alternative account of confirmation takes us a step further, with a response that does justice to the important grain of truth in the positivist challenge.

Disconfirming the mode of production theory means showing that some rival is a superior basis for explanations of the data. The characteristic flexibility of the Marxist hypotheses neither makes such defeat impossible nor guarantees the ultimate defeat, relegation to the status of an untestable metaphysical article of faith. As I tried to show at the beginning of Chapter Six, Weber could be proven right, so that Marx is proven wrong. If this is so, the positivist challenge is met. But there is something right about the positivists' suspicion of reliance on tautologies and unpredictable applications of general categories to particular cases. All else being equal, a theory is a poorer source of explanations if defenders must construe it in these ways. These are defects, tending to make some rival superior. But this is only a tendency. The defects are not lethal, by themselves. They are certainly not infallible marks of pseudo-science.

A theory that says that certain phenomena emerge when a certain factor is strong enough to override countervailing factors is a less informative hypothesis than a rival lacking such tautological hedges. The less hedged rival is easier to falsify, if it is false. So, if the two hypotheses are subjected to prolonged and severe tests and still fit the facts equally well, the most likely explanation is that the less hedged rival is closer to the truth. Saying less, the hedged hypothesis, if true, should have fit the data more easily. Similarly, if a theory is defended by creative respecification, shifting the identification of "economic structure" (or "selective advantage" or "true compound") to fit new facts or to meet challenges, that creates a burden. It makes it more likely that the fit between theory and data results, not from the superior truth of the theory, but only from the ingenuity of the theorists. That is why Aristotelian astronomy stopped being of interest around the time of Newton. Epicycles could always be added to reconcile Aristotelian astronomy with celestial observations. Within the *Newtonian* synthesis, one would expect human ingenuity to produce such manipulations, given the data available. There was no corresponding Aristotelian explanation of why the differences between celestial and terrestrial forces did not block Newtonian efforts to refer planetary motion, lunar motion and terrestrial free fall to a single mechanism.

Now we can see why it was so absurd to try to revive such long-outmoded theories as vitalistic embryology or the theory of national destinies on the basis of tautologous hedges and creative respecifications. Of course, the theories can be defended in these ways. But we can account for the fit that is generated as a product of ingenuity and stubbornness, independent of any assumption that the theory is truer than its rivals. What could revive the old theory is a new instance of fit that cannot be readily explained on the assumption that the theory is basically false. This is the revival that does not take place.

In this treatment of appeals to entelechies and national destinies, they are not "pseudo-explanations," intrinsically absurd, as the positivists supposed. That is surely the more plausible approach, since highly intelligent people embraced these theories in the past when they seemed the best way of explaining the stability and resilience of the respective sorts of traits. Also, the distinction between effective and ineffective defense, here, depends heavily on timing. If a hedge that was always part of a theory copes with an unexpected challenge, the successful defense cannot be explained away so easily. If a hypothesis is not the product of respecification, its success is more likely to be a success for the theory, not just a tribute to the defender's guile. Thus, it is important to know whether a Lamarckian's hedge about relevant cases of use or disuse or a Marxist's concept of feudalism is just the latest *ad hoc* response to seventeen effective counter-examples, or emerges from the theorist's initial understanding. As the most conscientious positivists saw, their emphasis on logical relations between hypothesis and data made these questions about the history of testing irrelevant.

. . . [F]rom a logical point of view, the strength of the support that a hypothesis receives from a given body of data should only depend on what the hypothesis asserts and what the data are: the question of whether the hypothesis or the data were presented first, being a purely historical matter, should not count as affecting the confirmation of the hypothesis.[15]

Along with denials that the theory of evolution is a theory, the assumption that the timing of revisions is irrelevant and

[15] C. G. Hempel, *Philosophy of Natural Science* (Englewood Cliffs, 1966), p. 38.

the implication that thousands of intelligent investigators have actively advanced pseudo-explanations for want of basic logical acumen are the clearest superficial evidence that something must be wrong with the positivist account of science.[16]

A philosophy of science that makes it possible to test theories of history had better not make this testing easy. For, especially since Marx's time, rival approaches have persisted for generations.

To a large extent, the persistence of these disagreements in the social sciences has nonintellectual causes, based on social and psychological processes that a philosophy of science need not reveal. Everyone agrees that the persistence of both Marxist and non-Marxist approaches to history has this character. Marx's theory of ideology would be false if non-Marxist theories of history faded away under capitalism. For their part, anti-Marxist historians need to explain the Marxism of intelligent and learned colleagues, and they do so, by appealing to wishful thinking, social envy or the need for a secular faith. Those who think there is no basis for choice among the rival approaches take them to be due to different initial hunches of investigators, to be explained historically, socially or psychologically.

According to every approach, thousands, perhaps millions of intelligent, informed, scientifically minded people have been misguided for several generations. Whoever the misguided are, why is it so hard for them to see the error of their ways? A

---

[16] The denials that there is a genuine theory of biological evolution are especially vivid in Karl Popper's writings. "There exists no law of evolution, only the historical fact that plants and animals change, or, more precisely, that they have changed. The idea of a law that determines the direction and the character of evolution is a typical 19th-century mistake, arising out of a general tendency to ascribe to the 'Natural Law' the functions traditionally ascribed to God" ("Prediction and Prophecy in the Social Sciences," in Patrick Gardiner, ed., *Theories of History* [New York, 1959], p. 280). See also Karl Popper, *The Poverty of Historicism* (New York, 1960), pp. 106–9. Many people, I think, regard these statements as idiosyncratic. I have tried to show that they are a natural outgrowth of positivism. My examples of pseudo-explanations, "not amenable . . . to objective test or to significant explanatory . . . use,' are taken from Hempel, "The Function of General Laws in History," and from pp. 432f. of the title essay in *Aspects of Scientific Explanation* (where the quoted phrase occurs on p. 433).

philosophy of science *can* shed light on this question of degree, by showing how the structure of the disagreements makes consensus hard to find.

The intellectual barrier to consensus is the role of background beliefs in the testing of hypotheses. In framing and comparing answers to specific questions, investigators typically rely on a framework of fairly specific principles, concerning how phenomena are to be detected, what truths should not be violated, or what causes are most likely. Even in the simplest of the previous cases of explanation, the diagnosis of the sore throat, a rich framework had to be employed. For example, if Petri dish cultures were readily contaminated or if bacteria did not cause inflammation, the explanatory inference would be wrong.

The background principles can be justified in turn, up to the level at which the whole history of the field is surveyed from the perspective of essential common sense. But it is often unreasonable to construct these arguments, to see whether they withstand challenges or new evidence. It would be frivolous for an epidemiologist constantly to reassess whether infections really do sometimes cause symptoms. It is hard enough to describe or to test plausible hypotheses within the assumed framework, much harder than positivism suggested. Similar reasons of economy often justify social scientists in not examining their own frameworks, even if they tend to exaggerate the force of those reasons and postpone self-examination for too long. A Weberian sociologist investigating the tendency of movements in Islam to inhibit economic development has quite enough to do, applying Weberian principles about how people reveal the sources of their conduct and how they are likely to behave, without repeatedly subjecting those principles to testing-by-comparison.

This work within frameworks sounds like Kuhn's normal science, the practice of a "mature" scientific community that has transcended conflicts between schools of thought, functioning in between scientific revolutions. But such work can and does go on, and is, to some extent, desirable even when investigators are split between rival schools of thought, as in the social sciences. Consider these common splits in background principles. Some social scientists assume that people's reasons for acting and believing as they do are normally the real reasons for their conduct and belief; a contrary claim is unlikely and somewhat mysterious, requiring special argument. Others believe that it is normal and natural for objective interests to mold belief and conduct, even working at variance with people's honest self-portrayals. For some, it counts strongly in favor of a hypothesis if it explains the precise timing of events. For others, this is a frequent mark of superficiality. For some, religion, since it is concerned with the most important things, is bound to have a major impact on conduct. For others, religion, so malleable and so divorced from immediate things, readily adapts to nonreligious concerns. None of these assumptions is stupid. All regulate strenuous processes of hypothesis choice *and* hypothesis testing.

If diverse and contrary frameworks are current among informed investigators, they ought periodically to be compared in a fair way. I do not mean to absolve dogmatic Marxists or anti-Marxists of this duty, only to explain why it is natural for them to ignore it. The explanation is twofold. For one thing, having initially decided that a particular framework is best, it is a reasonable economy to persist in using it until anomalies accumulate, cases in which the evidence points to alternatives that are highly unlikely in one's framework. In the social sciences, a widely used framework for assessing evidence has usually survived because it rarely generates anomalies, even though its favored hypotheses would readily be disconfirmed if the evidence were read in a different framework. Great movements of religious enthusiasm that are proof of the social impact of religious psychology for Weberians are obvious distractions from ultimate explanatory factors for Marxists. The economic interests that lead to war for Marxists would require a bizarre extreme of bloodthirstiness in other frameworks, an implausible capacity for rational calculation in yet others. Because social scientific frameworks tend to be self-supporting, a hasty choice of a framework tends to be self-maintaining. Also, agility in developing and testing empirical hypotheses within a framework does not necessarily produce skill in comparing the higher-level hypotheses defining frameworks. Philosophers, rather good at the latter, are rather bad at the former task. Conversely, learned practitioners within a framework in social science can be extremely clumsy at defending the framework through fair comparisons. The unfairness to Marx's political theory described in Chapter Four is one case in point.

There is comfort for philosophy here. Whatever their limitations in gathering data, philosophers are good at showing that an inference is hasty, or that a question has been begged. They have the means to reduce vehement and unjustified differences, even if they cannot end them.

POSITIVISM AND POLITICS

Before, I noted that there is something odd, even paradoxical about my description of resistance to the mode of production theory. Extremely abstract methodological constraints seem to combine here with influences of quite a different kind, emotionally compelling political factors. I will conclude with a guess as to a real connection underlying this diversity.

On my very broad understanding of the positivist conception of explanation and confirmation, it characterizes trends as diverse as these: the empiricism of Hume (in his constructive moments), Mill and Comte; the effort of Mach, Kirchoff, Poincaré and allied philosopher-scientists to show that scientific theories were simply instruments for summarizing data; and the twentieth-century positions stemming from logical-positivist groups in central Europe between the World Wars. These writers all share the assumption that causation, explanation and confirmation have a general analysis, the same for all fields of inquiry, relying on relations of logical form. They all take such an analysis to be useful in excluding certain claims and arguments as unworthy of investigation. Often, one is struck by how little examination these formalist assumptions receive from otherwise resourceful writers in these trends. In the words of the previously quoted passage by Hempel, these assumptions "seem reasonable;" "it ought to be possible, one feels" to develop a philosophy of science respecting these constraints. (Ironically, Hempel's expressions of feeling are immediately preceded by a warning that "a 'sense of evidence' or a feeling of plausibility" does not decide whether a hypothesis is acceptable.)[17]

Almost all of the writers to whom I have alluded also share a similar general view of the social and political conflicts of their time. They are appalled by the violence and repression to which extremists are prone. They typically regard such extremism as based on people's ill-founded confidence in their knowledge of causes, confidence that is not just founded on inadequate evidence, but based on fundamental conceptual confusions concerning the nature and limits of evidence, causes or explanation. Simply to argue on empirical grounds that such extremists have false beliefs might be a never-ending task and, in any case, would give their controversies added importance and vigor. It is more productive to show that the whole style of thought of extremists on all sides is based on confusions. The positivist assumptions have been tools for accomplishing this task. My speculation is that this function has been a main source of their attractiveness. This is not wholly speculation. It fits the political situation of most leading figures in these trends, and accords with some of their statements of the practical point of their methodological inquiries.

Almost all of the first generation of logical positivists were beleaguered Social Democrats in central European universities.[18] In some seminal positivist writings, the practical point of the methodology is explicit. For example, in Hempel's "The Function of General Laws in History," the urgent appeal is to exclude pseudo-explanations from the social sciences, and the ones explicitly excluded, because they violate positivist constraints, are almost all either appeals to the destiny of a race,

---

[17] Hempel "Studies in the Logic of Confirmation," p. 9.

[18] For a concise and vivid sketch of the logical positivists' attitudes and personalities, see Carnap's autobiography in P. Schlipp, ed., *The Philosophy of Rudolf Carnap* (LaSalle, Ill., 1963). The one notable exception to the Social-Democratic rule was Otto Neurath, a Communist whose materialism and criticisms of any sharp division between theory and observation tended to undermine the whole positivist program.

nation or individual leader characteristic of right-wing nationalism or the appeals to underlying economic structures characteristic of Marxism.[19]

Even where the commitment to exclude extremes is not explicit, its influence on a logical positivist's work sometimes turns out to have been strong. Popper's *The Logic of Scientific Discovery* (1934) is concerned with the most abstract questions of epistemology, probability and the structure of the physical sciences. Yet according to his autobiography, it reflects commitments formed in political turmoil fifteen years earlier. During a very brief period as a communist, Popper was part of a socialist demonstration that was fired on by the police. ". . . I felt that as a Marxist I bore part of the responsibility for the tragedy . . . [Marxist theory's] thesis is that although the revolution may claim some victims, capitalism is claiming more victims than the whole socialist revolution. . . . I now asked myself whether such a calculation could ever be supported by 'science.'" Due to this "revulsion," and a contrasting observation of Einstein's reflectiveness soon afterward, "[t]hus, I arrived, by the end of 1919, at the conclusion that the scientific attitude was the critical attitude, which did not look for verifications but for crucial tests; tests which could *refute* the theory tested though they could never establish it." In short, the commitment to undermine extremes would have motivated Popper's distinctive methodology, even if this commitment had not become explicit in such later works as *The Open Society and its Enemies* and *The Poverty of Historicism*.[20]

My final example from positivism between the World Wars, Rudolf Carnap, is fairly representative of logical positivists who did not write about political, moral or social scientific

[19] See pp. 234, 237, 238, 239, 242.

[20] Karl Popper, "Autobiography," in P. Schilpp, ed., *The Philosophy of Karl Popper* (LaSalle, Ill., 1974), pp. 25, 29. Responding to Popper's conception of the scientific attitude, Hilary Putnam once wrote, "Consider men striking against sweatshop conditions. Should they say 'it is only a provisional conjecture that the boss is a bastard. Let us call off the strike and appeal to his better nature.' The distinction between *knowledge* and *conjecture* does real work in our lives" ("The 'Corroboration' of Theories" [originally in *The Philosophy of Karl Popper*], in Hilary Putnam, *Mathematics, Matter and Method* [Cambridge, 1975] p. 252).

issues. Yet his autobiography makes clear that there was an important relation between his philosophical inclinations and his situation in a time of turmoil. The thread running through his account of his intellectual development is the use of methodology as a basis for tolerance, describing the strict limits within which people can reasonably lay claim to factual beliefs. Apparent differences in principle that seem subject to rational argument are to be revealed as nonsubstantive choices of different languages or frameworks. This impulse for tolerance first emerged, Carnap writes, as he adapted to the radically different outlooks of his friends in conversations "about general problems in science and in practical life."[21] No reader of his autobiography would want to discount the role of Carnap's genial disposition in this process. But when he describes the shared personal tenets of the Vienna Circle, it is clear that they added a powerful reason for making precise and general principles of tolerance part of a philosophy of science, especially in the 1930s: "[A]ll deliberate action presupposes knowledge of the world . . . and the scientific method is the best method of acquiring knowledge. . . ."[22]

A generation or two earlier, turn-of-the-century positivism is dominated by German-speaking academics whose political situation is also extremely poignant. They are cosmopolitan liberals (in the twentieth-century American sense), teaching in state-run universities where right-wing nationalist sentiment is powerful and state intervention routine, while the leading socialist parties in the world are growing in influence outside the universities. In Germany, the pressures of politics are especially intense. For decades, the Anti-Socialist Laws made it illegal for Marxists to teach in universities. The more humane academics seem to have been both disturbed by this intervention and appalled by the revolutionary and anti-patriotic program of the socialist party. Even in the physical sciences, the Wilhelmine establishment, including the all-powerful Ministry of Education, attempted, with some success, to politicize physics and biology. They attacked mechanism and atomism as

[21] Carnap, "Autobiography," p. 17.
[22] Ibid., p. 83.

reflections of crass English individualism, or, worse yet, Marxist materialism, incompatible with the German organic state.[23] An ethical consensus of the twentieth-century American sort that politics should not have an impact on science was simply nonexistent. An epistemological argument that the characteristic beliefs of the right and the left were, by their nature, nonscientific was an important means of self-defense.

Among social scientists of this period, Weber is the magisterial advocate of a positivist approach to explanation and testing. In effect, his discussions of empathic understanding, ideal types and the role of values are efforts to show that positivist principles can meet the demands of social scientists, even though those principles had most recently emerged in analyses of the physical sciences. Empathic understanding of actions is essential to social science, as nearly all of Weber's German-speaking contemporaries supposed. But it is essential as a way of marking off the scope of social science and of originating hypotheses, *not* as a means of confirming them.[24] In all science, confirmation proceeds by the deduction of consequences from general laws and initial conditions, and their comparison with the data. The special values of cultural phenomena are, nonetheless, important, as all insist, but not as explanations of those phenomena. Rather, investigators choose what questions to ask and what results to use and appreciate in accordance with their values, values that cannot themselves be established by scientific means.[25] Once explanatory questions are chosen, causal explanation seeks to subsume phenomena under empirical covering laws.[26] Given the complexity of social reality, this covering-law model might seem to condemn social science to si-

---

[23] See Norton Wise, "Entropy, Atomism and German Socio-Intellectual History" (Department of History, U.C.L.A.; unpublished manuscript).

[24] See Max Weber, *The Theory of Social and Economic Organization* (New York, 1949), pp. 96f., 99f.

[25] See Max Weber, ";'Objectivity' in Social Science and Social Policy," in *The Methodology of the Social Sciences* (New York, 1949), pp. 76–82; "The Meaning of 'Ethical Neutrality' in Sociology and Economics," in ibid., p. 11; "The Logic of the Cultural Sciences," in ibid., p. 123; "Science as a Vocation," *From Max Weber* (New York, 1958), p. 146.

[26] See Weber, "'Objectivity' in Social Science and Social Policy," pp. 79f., *Theory of Social and Economic Organization*, pp. 99f.

lence or banality. The method of ideal types avoids this dilemma, by taking advantage of the "if-then" character of most covering laws. One constructs precise concepts that can be grasped empathically and connected to one's values. General laws are formulated using these concepts and compared with the course of the data. Though the fit is never precise, if it is approximate one can conclude that the ideal type captures part of the explanation of the actual course of history.[27] In effect, ideal types are materials for covering-law "explanation sketches," by which the positivist model is reconciled to the special needs of social scientists.[28]

Weber takes this methodology to be justifiable through accurate conceptual analysis. But in his hundreds of pages of methodological writings, it is very hard to find much positive argument, as students often complain. The positivist conceptions of causal explanation and scientific confirmation are assumed without argument. The warnings about excessive intrusions of values are defended by quick assertions that no "ought" statement describes what is the case, and other quick assertions that every value judgment is harder to establish in the face of differences in outlook than any scientific judgment.[29] What *is* present in these methodological writings, in substantial and convincing detail, is a case for the practical urgency of conducting social explanation and testing through the value-free comparison of data with the deductive consequences of precise and general laws. Unless views that are not testable or explanatory by Weber's standards are excluded or rigidly segregated in academic discourse, efficient social scientific work will be impossible in the setting of German universities. Radical differences will make cooperation impossible. State intervention will insure that many useful investigators are excluded. By confusing verbal or evaluative disagreements

[27] Weber, "'Objectivity' in Social Science and Social Policy," pp. 89–99; *Theory of Social and Economic Organization*, pp. 96–100.
[28] Cf. C. G. Hempel, "Typological Methods in the Natural and the Social Sciences," in *Aspects of Scientific Explanation*.
[29] I discuss Weber's arguments and others concerning value-freedom in "Reason and Commitment in the Social Sciences," *Philosophy and Public Affairs* 8 (1979).

with factual ones, investigators will constantly talk past each other, failing to reconcile science and value-relevance with the help of ideal types. In short, Weber's positivism is intended as a response to "the fact that for the younger generation the objective situation has changed" in the direction of a plurality of passionate commitments.[30]

It is a standard surprise in the history of philosophy that the best nineteenth-century German philosophy changed in a few decades from the construction of metaphysical systems to insistence on tight constraints on the scope of knowledge. Indeed, this change is a source of the most popular joke about the history of philosophy, the one about new philosophies being born in Germany, dying of old age in Britain, and being resurrected to everlasting life in the United States. This sketch of the social circumstances that emerged in German-speaking universities suggests one factor in this change. A methodology excluding both right-wing and left-wing extremes from the scope of scientific debate came to answer a deeply felt need of many German-speaking academics in the late nineteenth and early twentieth centuries.

Finally, founding fathers such as Hume and Mill explicitly seek to overcome extremism through methodology in their writings. For Hume, for example, even the most negative results of the "accurate and abtruse" kind of philosophy, that is, the kind he writes, have an important practical point. They undermine sources of fanaticism in religious and, hence, political life.

But this obscurity, in the profound and abstract philosophy, is objected to, not only as painful and fatiguing, but as the inevitable source of uncertainty and error. Here, indeed, lies the justest and most plausible objection against a considerable part of metaphysics, that they are not properly a science, but arise either from the fruitless efforts of human vanity, which would penetrate into subjects utterly inaccessible to the understanding, or from the craft of popular su-

---

[30] Max Weber, "The Meaning of 'Ethical Neutrality' in Sociology and Economics," p. 3. See also "'Objectivity' in Social Science and Social Policy," pp. 61f., and Weber's contribution to "Die Produktivitaet der Volkswirtschaft," *Archiv fuer Sozialwissenschaft und Sozialpolitik*, 1909.

perstitions, which, being unable to defend themselves on fair ground, raise these entangling brambles to cover and protect their weakness. Chased from the open country, these robbers fly into the forest and lie in wait to break in upon every unguarded avenue of the mind, and overwhelm it with religious fears and prejudices. The stoutest antagonist, if he remit his watch a moment, is oppressed, and many, through cowardice and folly, open the gates to the enemies and willingly receive them with reverence and submission as their legal sovereigns.

But is this a sufficient reason why philosophers should desist from such researches and leave superstition still in possession of her retreat? Is it not proper to draw an opposite conclusion and perceive the necessity of carrying the war into the most secret recesses of the enemy?[31]

Hume's political essays, such as "Of the Original Contract," and his history of Great Britain, the basis of his contemporary fame, make even more explicit his intense commitment to moderation. The enthusiasts reminiscent of the previous century and its bloodshed, old-style Whigs and Tories, Jacobites, and clergy who base political appeals on religious doctrines are the main threat to peace, prosperity and culture. They must be exposed as unreasonable, in part by showing that they pretend to knowledge that the human understanding cannot, in principle, attain. Not surprisingly, in his formative years, Hume found his friends and allies among the academics and moderate clergy working to free Scotland from Jacobite passions and from the deadening hand of the old guard in the Church of Scotland.[32]

My speculation, then, is that the recurring attractiveness of positivism has had, among other sources, a political one: the desire to dismiss as unworthy of empirical investigation claims about underlying causes that have a disturbing political and cultural effect. In this aspect, positivism is a means of dismissing views that are too far left or too far right without engaging in detailed empirical criticism of them. This is just

---

[31] David Hume, *An Enquiry Concerning Human Understanding*, sec. 1, ed. E. Steinberg (Indianapolis, 1977), pp. 5f.

[32] This is a recurrent theme in E. C. Mossner's standard biography, *The Life of David Hume* (Oxford, 1970).

a speculation, a stimulus for further research. Even if it is wholly valid, it does not imply that positivists have practiced any deception, tailoring methodological views to suit political predispositions. Rather, this is an explanation of why positivism, in a very broad sense, has been genuinely attractive to a great many people, despite the inherent defects which I previously described. This speculation would also help explain why the assumptions defining positivism have been accepted without examination by investigators who are otherwise so critical and resourceful. Of course, other forces have been at work as well, both traditions internal to philosophy and scientific trends originating outside it. Schlick's interest in quantum mechanics, Reichenbach's in relativity theory and Hume's attempt to reorganize philosophy on what he took to be a Newtonian model are three important examples of the latter influence. But the political hypothesis helps to explain why, of the many philosophical traditions available and the many interpretations to which relevant scientific revolutions have been liable, only some have come to influence the most creative philosophers at certain times.

Even the most preliminary research would show, I think, that the wish to use methodology to rule out extremes has been a much more powerful influence than the alleged desire to manipulate human beings, emphasized in the most popular social analysis of positivism, that of Habermas, Adorno and other members of the Frankfurt School. The pursuit of empirical general laws and deductive test-implications is at least as likely to support the passive collection and explanation of unalterable facts (witness astronomy) as it is to further manipulations. If manipulation of others is described, less tendentiously, as the effort to change society for the better, it is neither a distinctive goal of positivism, nor a covert one that needs to be unmasked. More so than most other philosophies, positivism has been the premise of tolerant, moderate people, suspicious of radical political intervention. Such a role has not always been beneficent. The moderation of the German Social Democratic Party may well have crippled it as a force against the Nazis. Hume's archenemy, the zealous Reverend Warburton, was a zealous opponent of racism and the slave trade, while Hume combined mild disapproval of slavery as inefficient with speculations, unusual in his time, about the biological inferiority of blacks.[33] Still, it is significant and disappointing that when the Frankfurt School names names, such intellectually trivial figures as Carl Schmitt are indicted as the positivist manipulators.

At best, an interpretation of Marx should be, not just accurate, but useful. It should describe a framework for current research, debate and refinement. Before, I tried to show that the mode of production interpretation has such life in economic history and anthropology, while technological determinism does not. By shedding light on the role of positivism in the assessment of Marxism, the argument for the mode of production theory may also give life to a project that promises so much and has produced so little, the social history of philosophy.

[33] See the essay, "On National Characters," in Hume's *Essays, Moral, Political and Literary*. Wylie Sypher, in *Guinea's Captive Kings* (Chapel Hill, 1942), establishes the distinctiveness,at the time, of Hume's thesis of racial inferiority.

Index

Acton, H., 202f.
Adorno, T., 312
Allen, D., 35–41, 73
Allen, W. S., 135n
Almond, G., 103, 160
Althusser, L., 129
anarchism, 20f., 219
Aristotle, 18, 75, 76f., 81, 101, 268, 288
Arkhangelski, S., 188, 262
Arrow, K., 34
Asiatic mode of production, 198, 201f., 210, 253, 265
Avineri, S., 8n, 116–21

Bachrach, P., 142, 143n, 150–52
Bakunin, M., 20, 21
Baratz, M., 142, 143n, 150–52
Bayesian theories of confirmation, 272, 294
Bentham, J., 33, 34, 35, 38, 76
Bernstein, E., 182n
big business. *See* bourgeoisie
Bloch, M., 252f., 268–70
Bonaparte, Louis Napoleon, 109, 110, 123, 125, 260
bourgeoisie, 103n, 105f., 110, 115, 144f., 164, 208; in United States, 111, 127, 138–40
Bowles, S., 137, 139n
breakdown theories, 182f.
Brenkert, G., 56–58
Buchanan, A., 8n, 65–73

Capital, 11, 188–90, 194, 216f., 259f.
capitalism, origins of, 188–90, 192f., 215f., 224f., 237–41
Carnap, R., 305n, 306f.
Cartwright, N., 285n

causal comparison, 292f., 295–98, 302–4. *See also* confirmation
causal depth, 289–91. *See also* individualism, methodological
causation, 284–87, 289–91
character, 64, 74–76
Cherry, R., 137, 264n
Chile, 110, 125, 160
Civil War in France, 122f.
class, 9, 177, 195, 268
class interest, 67, 132–34, 146f., 149
class struggle, 9, 126, 171, 268
Cohen, G., 8n, 175, 176, 180f., 183, 186, 190, 212, 232
colonialism. *See* imperialism
Commune, Paris, 15, 64, 67, 94, 125
communist society, 22, 34, 38f., 57
Comte, A., 282, 304
confirmation, 49f., 126–28, 203f., 255f., 258f., 272, 273f., 275, 277, 281f., 292–302. *See also* causal comparison; falsification; scientific theories
conquest, 191, 192, 206n, 214, 230, 241f., 245–49, 269
conspiracy theories, 105, 106, 109f., 139, 163
Contribution to the Critique of Political Economy, Preface, 174–80, 211–13
Council on Foreign Relations, 108n, 132f., 140
Croce, B., 27

Dahl, R., 102, 143, 146n, 150, 152–56, 161f., 166
Darwin, C., 180, 185, 187, 233–35, 236, 255f., 258, 267, 287, 292, 300n

315

INDEX

Poincaré, H., 272, 304
political activity, 9, 30f., 35, 39f.,
    42, 84f., 88–90, 113, 150, 257f.;
    Marx's, 121, 124, 219. *See also*
    revolution; workers' movement
political power, 104f., 136f., 142,
    150–52
political science, 102–4, 160f., 165f.
politicians, 106, 110f., 113, 134,
    139, 145, 151, 153–55, 164
Polsby, N., 166
Popper, K., 301n, 306
positivism, 4, 43, 196, 198, 204,
    233, 272–74, 277, 284–86, 287,
    294f., 299, 300f., 304–8, 311f.
    (and Chapter Seven, passim)
Poulantzas, N., 129, 130n
power-structures, 102f., 157–60
prediction, 196, 232–35, 255f., 273,
    283, 289, 291
productive forces, 83, 175f., 194f.;
    alleged primacy of, 180, 183,
    188–95, 209f., 212f.
productivity, 53f., 86, 184, 189–91,
    192n, 209f., 220, 253
Protestant Reformation, 238, 240,
    290
Proudhon, P. J., 20, 21, 81n, 85,
    178, 212, 219
pseudo-explanations, 300f., 305f.
Putnam, H., 306n

racism, 166, 263f.
rationality, 15, 35, 44f., 51, 56,
    59f., 61–63, 65, 71, 90
Rawls, J., 17, 18, 24–26, 43n, 94
reciprocity, 19, 31, 58f., 67
reform, 62, 106, 108, 112, 140, 166.
    See also elections; revolution
Reich, M., 137, 264n
Reichenbach, H., 312
relations of production, 83, 171,
    176f., 195–202, 258
religion, 229, 238–40, 262, 303

revolution, 39f., 62f., 65f., 68, 72,
    85, 114–26, 185f.
Ricardo, D., 261
rights, 19, 22–30, 47. *See also*
    freedom
Rome, 214f., 220, 244, 247f., 250f.,
    253, 266, 283
Roosevelt, F. D., 109, 127f., 140
Rousseau, J.-J., 76, 94
ruling class: political, 105–12, 114,
    129, 136–38, 142, 144, 161; in
    United States, 138–40, 159; in
    economic structure, 206, 226,
    256f., 270, 279–81.

Sahlins, M., 266
Schlick, M., 312
Schoenbaum, D., 134n
scientific theories, nature of, 43,
    198, 232–36, 286f., 291f.; terms
    in, 82, 203f.; interpretation of,
    187, 219, 267
Scriven, M., 285n
self-interest, 61, 63, 65–73, 93f.
Shaw, W., 8n, 181
slavery, 41, 112, 191f., 201, 209f.,
    214, 278–80
socialism, 22, 34, 38f., 55, 58f., 95,
    271
solidarity, 68–73. *See also* character;
    class interest; free-rider problem;
    reciprocity
spontaneity, 95
state, 107–8n, 112. *See also*
    elections; political power;
    politicians; ruling class
stopping rules, 287–89
structural functionalism, 103, 160f.
structuralism, 129–36
superstructure, 197f., 229f., 258
surplus, social, 179, 206, 256, 279–
    81
surplus value, 11, 28f., 91
Sweezy, P., 182n
Sypher, W., 313n

318

LIBRARY OF CONGRESS CATALOGING IN PUBLICATION DATA

Miller, Richard W., 1945–
  Analyzing Marx.

  Includes bibliographical references and index.
  1. Marx, Karl, 1818–1883. 2. Ethics, Modern—19th century. 3. Elite
(Social sciences)—History—19th century. 4. Power (Social sciences)—
History—19th century. 5. History—Philosophy—History—19th century.
6. Economic history—1750–1918. 7. Positivism—History—19th century.
  B3305.M74M55 1984   193   84-42571
  ISBN 0-691-06613-2 (alk. paper)   ISBN 0-691-01413-2 (pbk.)

Richard W. Miller is Associate Professor of Philosophy
at Cornell University